"This book is an important invitation to join the work, from men with a unique mix of historical perspective, vast experie~ lical insight, and innovative methodologie~ ere else."

—**Dr. Randy White,** national coc r-Varsity Christian Fellowship, and c *God in the City.*

"This book is wonderfully dangerous. You can't read it and stay disconnected from God's love for cities. It will break down your immune system against urban pain and will shock you with the enormity of opportunities lurking in the neighborhoods of your city."

—**Dr. Jan Hettinga,** senior pastor, Northshore Baptist Church, author of *Follow Me: Experience the Loving Leadership of Jesu*s

"Ray Bakke and Jon Sharpe are special partners for ministry to the city in the 21st century. Best of all, knowing Ray and Jon as well as I do, I can assure readers that they walk the talk."

—**Dr. David L. McKenna,** president emeritus, Asbury Theological Seminary

"Based on 30 years of lessons learned in over 200 cities, *Street Signs* is the must-have pocket guide for kingdom-minded leaders. The beginning of hope for our cities is in the emerging leaders and stakeholders from cross sectors of the city who convene around consultations to learn what the city has to teach them!"

—**Eric Swanson,** Leadership Network, coauthor of *The Externally Focused Church* and *Living a Life on Loan*

"*Street Signs* is both challenging and pleasurable reading for anyone called to urban ministry and for Christians fascinated by their city. Read this book and be delighted, instructed, and blessed!"

—**Dr. Robert C. Linthicum,** Partners In Urban Transformation

"Ray Bakke has ignited the imagination of countless people around the globe. Now, he and his colleague and ministry partner Jon Sharpe have given us *Street Signs,* a remarkable weaving of rich personal histories and insights that point us to a new paradigm of cutting-edge urban ministry."
—**Dr. Bob Lupton,** president, FCS Urban Ministries

"This book is a unique confessional in a blended format of autobiography alongside consultations. Anyone serving Christ in the city needs to read *Street Signs.*"
—**Dr. Bill O'Brien,** BellMitra Associates

"Bakke and Sharpe provide a personal guide service into the city and give us eyes to see God at work in ways never noticed before. These two men are outstanding leaders, proven guides, and generous almost to a fault when it comes to sharing their experience and insight."
—**Jim Henderson,** executive director, Off The Map and author of *A.K.A. Lost*

"The intimidating realities of urban life often detour the church from its calling to bring transformation to the slums and neighborhoods of our world. I heartily recommend this book to anyone hearing God's heart and call to the streets."
—**Dr. Jim Hayford Sr.,** senior pastor, Eastside Foursquare Church, Seattle, Washington

Street Signs

A New Direction in Urban Ministry

Ray Bakke
Jon Sharpe

A Bakke Graduate University publication

new
hope
PUBLISHERS

Birmingham, Alabama

New Hope® Publishers
P. O. Box 12065
Birmingham, AL 35202-2065
www.newhopepublishers.com

Library of Congress Cataloging-in-Publication Data

Bakke, Raymond J., 1938-
  Street signs : a new direction in urban ministry / by Ray Bakke and
Jon Sharpe.
     p. cm.
  Includes index.
  ISBN 1-59669-004-6 (softcover)
  1. City clergy. 2. Church work. 3. City churches. 4. City missions.
I. Sharpe, Jon, 1950- II. Title.
  BV637.5.B35 2006
  253.09173'2—dc22
                              2006008217

ISBN: 1-59669-004-6

N064131 • 0806 • 3M1

DEDICATION

To Corean, my partner in the journey.
Ray Bakke

To my wife Laila, who releases me to the Kingdom.
Jon Sharpe

Table of Contents

Part Two: By Jon Sharpe

Amid all the word-making, it also is great fun for two friends and colleagues to collaborate on a book together. While the preface comes first in the book, we wrote it last—after all the thinking, reflecting, word generating, rethinking, restating, editing, discussions, rethinking, and more reflecting is finished. When one writes a preface, the book is nearing its destination.

Street Signs points toward a destination. For Jon and me, the signs pointed from our rural origins through hundreds of the largest cities in the world, and finally to Seattle, Washington, where we ended up together. We followed different paths, confronted by different street signs along the way, but arrived at the same destination, as colleagues in ministry that extends from Seattle to cities on six continents. As we write this, we are still on the journey looking for more street signs to provide us direction.

The book you are about to read is full of journey, theological reflection, and praxis. Its flow is straightforward. The first seven chapters were produced by me (Ray) and the last six chapters were produced by Jon. Each section contains journey chapters and theological reflection chapters. Chapters 1 and 2 allow you inside my journey as I moved from Acme, Washington, to Chicago, Illinois, and back to Acme. Chapter 3 takes you on a tour of the five street signs that influenced my life and ministry—that literally changed the route of my journey. In chapter 4 I discuss the concept of the world as urban and the need to alter our worldview in light of this. I point out that the urban population of the world in 2004 was larger than the entire world population in 1938, the year of my birth. In chapter 5, I recommend that we learn to embrace the city as a parish. Chapter 6 challenges us to begin thinking about the "signs of hope" all cities possess. Cities are large and varied, and the majority of citizens never see many of the ongoing ministries within a city. Finally, in chapter 7, I discuss the kinds of programs that have been used to try to evangelize cities, noting that outsiders usually bring an outside agenda into a city.

I (Jon) wrote the remaining chapters. In chapters 8 and 9 I share my journey from rural America to the city, including some of the street signs along the way that brought me to my present destination. While Ray introduces the idea of consultation in chapter 7, in chapter 10 I explore the spirit and nature of a consultation facilitator using the biblical character Barnabas as a model. Chapter 11 takes you on a deeper journey of what happens in a city consultation. Then in chapter 12 I discuss the concept of how all consultations are the same—only different—and the many ways they can be designed. Finally, in chapter 13, I discuss the assumptions, objectives, outcomes, and all Ray and I have learned from providing consultations in world-class cities.

We are sure you've had street signs in your own journey and we offer this book as a way of suggesting other street signs you may wish to evaluate and possibly follow.

We would be remiss if we did not thank some of the many people who have influenced and helped us on the journey that culminated in the writing of this book.

I (Ray) would like to thank Andrea Mullins, who came to study with us at Bakke Graduate University. When she became head of New Hope Publishers, she repeatedly challenged us to write this book, and she revised her publishing calendar to fit our schedules. While Andrea made me want to write, Carol Quinlan and Winn Griffin came into our lives this year and made it possible. Carol organized my office and Winn organized this book and kept us focused. They also conspired together to keep us on task. Jon Sharpe is a special friend and colleague who had a vision of and for Northwest Graduate School when I and many others did not. He brought me together with other Northwest leaders who shared the vision for this school in 2001. Together, and with the help of many others, we created a leadership team. How ironic, or even unfair, that later the trustees chose to call it Bakke Graduate University when, in my mind, it might not even exist today were it not for Jon Sharpe. Doing a book with Jon is one way of saying thanks for all the ways he continues to impact my life.

I (Jon) would like to thank the staff at Bakke Graduate University for allowing us the time to plunge into this writing process. I would also like to thank Winn Griffin, who stepped in and helped us bring this book to closure with his edits, his constant time-lining for us, and his patience. He helped us develop coherence throughout the book. I also want to thank Kelly Pearson and Cal Uomoto of World Relief in Seattle for their tireless servant hearts for all who come their way. I realize our work would not be possible without the incredible work of God's people like Cal and Kelly within their cities, working tirelessly for transformation. I want to thank my wife Laila for her support through the years. I would not be involved in this project if she was not a constant encouragement to me. My children have all played a significant part, too, as Jonathan did some writing and editing for me and Katrina provided expertise with anything computer or high tech. Christopher, my youngest, continually encourages me to keep moving forward, and his life of young leadership is my inspiration.

Finally, I want to thank Ray Bakke, my mentor and friend, who continually encourages me and countless others to be transformational leaders in our cities, and who encouraged me to write the book with him. Ray is a visionary with limitless enthusiasm for the possible. He sees potential where others see despair.

Ray Bakke
Jon Sharpe
Seattle, Washington

Chapter 1

From Acme to Chicago to Seattle

What has Athens to do with Jerusalem?" So asked Tertullian in the second century. Consider another interesting question: "What has Acme to do with Index?"

We're sure you know the cities in the first question, but what about the second question? Both Acme and Index are found in the great Northwest of the USA. Both are in the state of Washington, about a hundred miles apart, as the proverbial crow flies. Both are rural cities, the places Jon and I grew up and then left, later to meet in the world-class city of Seattle many years later. I, Ray, was raised in Acme; Jon was raised in Index.

Acme is a small rural town located in a valley in Whatcom County, Washington, with a total population of 263 as of the 2000 census. When I grew up it was a farming town about the same size it is today. The Nooksack Valley lies between two small mountains some might call foothills. Early in the mornings, when the day's light begins, you can see small patches of fog in the lower ground, sometimes reaching up into the hills, providing a soft white contrast to the green valley floor. Acme is crisp and cold most mornings. Some of the old-timers gather daily at the hundred-year-old general store a few steps away from the Burlington railroad tracks, which used to be the entry and exit point for people working in the logging industry. In the days of my youth, valley folks would talk about Montana being "out east," even though it borders Washington.

This pristine valley was a little pocket of Norwegian culture, and it was anything but a city. My grandparents on my father's side were immigrants from the Sirdal Valley in central Norway—mountain people. My mother's family came from an island off the coast of Norway—fisher folk. They came from different environments and had different Norwegian dialects. My father and mother were both born into what I call *sturdy* Lutheran homes. Their heritage, and mine, was Lutheran pietism, a sort of warmhearted pietism versus the more intellectual German Lutheran heritage. These folks cared about missions and people. They were not hung up on listing things one could not do as a Christian believer. A mug of beer was as cherished as a warm glass of milk. Some, like my great-grandfather, made and drank their own berry wines. I could describe my early home culture as "thousands of hours of conversation greased with thousands of gallons of coffee," built around the warmhearted pietism of my parents.

> They were not hung up on listing things one could not do as a Christian believer.

My community was almost indistinguishable from the local Lutheran church group up on Saxon Hill Road. Most folks who lived in Acme were part of this community of prayer. While the church was Lutheran, it was not narrow in its practice. For example, the Sunday school superintendent was Episcopalian, and some members had a Covenant background, yet they worshiped alongside Presbyterians and others. Some in my family were Pentecostal, so when we had a family gathering it was somewhat ecumenical. Yet we were family, and our family themes were *love God*, *follow Jesus*, and *serve the world*. Religious labels were simply not that important.

I grew up milking cows and logging, like all the other kids in the community. During the '40s and '50s our family scrambled to make a living from our little farm, where we grew mostly grain. Often Dad went to work in Alaska for five or six months a year to supplement the income from the family farm. So in many ways my mom raised my brothers and me. She gave me what I like to call the "gift of space." When I was in high school she allowed me unfettered opportunity to walk in the mountains or drive my tractor to just think about things, to wonder about the big world outside our cozy little valley, to wonder where I would end up. These many hours of reflection due to her "gift of space" helped me develop a discipline of reflection that is still vibrant in my life today. I lived in a contemplative world, not a media- or commercially-driven world. Life was good and natural.

In 1947, when I was nine years old, after milking the cows one night on my grandfather's farm, I was reading the *Bellingham Herald* newspaper, which came to us a day late in the mail. That evening about dusk, I read that the Brooklyn Dodgers had signed a black baseball player by the name of Jackie Robinson. To that point in life, I had never seen a baseball game or a black person. As I read that story that night, something happened to me. I remember thinking, *You mean white people won't let black people play baseball?* That possibility was so contrary to what I had grown up to believe. As young children in Sunday school we sang, "Red and yellow, black and white, they are precious in His sight." That night, right there in my grandfather's house, I had a baseball conversion. I became a Brooklyn Dodger fan for life because they had signed a black man to play baseball. Jackie Robinson became my hero; he had broken the color barrier. To this day I can still quote the entire baseball team from 1947—guys like Roy Campanella, Don Newcombe, Pee Wee Reese, Duke Snider, and Gil Hodges were some of my favorites. This was one of the first conscious windows I found to the outside world.

While the Dodgers were some 3000 miles away from Acme, they became my team. So there I was, a third grader, being awakened to the larger world where deliberate black discrimination persisted on a daily basis. It was so foreign to the all-white Scandinavian community in which I lived. Little did I know that, later in life, seven of my eight grandchildren would be black, and also one of our closest family friends—my wife's college roommate.

As I reflect on that time, I realize something important happened to me in 1947 when the Dodgers signed Jackie Robinson. God surely uses everyday, common things to shape our lives for what He calls us to do. I don't think anyone else in this valley had the same experience I had. It did not become a local topic of conversation at the general store or within my family, school, or church. But it laid a foundation for the course of my life.

HABITS OF LIFE: READING

Another result of the "Jackie Robinson" experience, one that would serve me well over the years, was that it set me on a lifelong habit of reading. Every night after milking, I would go into my grandfather's house and read the *Bellingham Herald* from front page to back, including all the ads. Reading the daily newspaper was my window on the great big world lying just outside of that pristine little valley.

Two examples of my hunger for reading come to mind. First, in the fourth grade I asked the elementary school in Acme for all the discarded history books I saw in their book room. When I finally got permission to take them home between the fourth and fifth grades, I completely memorized the world-history timeline from Alexander the Great (333 BC) to that present time (about 1949). You could ask me what happened in any year between those two dates and I could tell you what occurred. For me those history books were like a telephone directory of the past.

Second, a friend of mine throughout our Acme school years was Norm Maleng. Norm, as of this writing, is the prosecutor for King County, Washington. He prosecuted the Green River serial killer, the biggest mass murder case in United States history. Norm may be the most popular politician in Washington State. He and I grew up together. His family's farm is just down the hill from where I presently live. His brother, Henry, still lives on the old farm site. Norm and I grew up together, talking almost every day about politics, sports, and religion on the school bus. In the ninth grade we had a reading contest. Together Norm and I set school records for reading the most books within a school year. I read 267 books and reported on all of them.

I don't know how a couple of farm kids became so interested in such things and ended up as Norm and I have. It's one of the great mysteries of life. We both still have ties to the Acme community. We both have daughters buried in the little country cemetery. His daughter died in a sledding accident when she was twelve; my daughter died at birth. Now they lie not many feet apart. We reflect often how two boys from this valley left the farm community of Acme—one to law school, the other to seminary—and traveled to the ends of the earth only to be back together again. Norm is now the chairman of the board for Bakke Graduate University in Seattle. All of this gives me a profound sense of awe about the leading of God.

NO PROFESSIONAL PASTORAL MODEL

Our farm valley was special to me in another way. Our little, white, country Lutheran church never had a full-time pastor. We had a circuit-riding pastor, and on occasion, missionaries would come and show us slides of the outside world. In that little country church, I went to Sunday school with the same group of guys I went to school with, played football with (in high school), and worked with in the fields and logging camps. While we had a two-room public school, we had a one-room Sunday school with the same teacher for many years. As this little crowd of boys advanced in school grades, our teacher, Roy Johnson, stayed with us in our graded Sunday school program. Roy still lives in Acme, Washington, and is a member of a Covenant church in Bellingham.

Roy poured his life into us. He prayed for us, cared for us, and often let us teach the Sunday lesson to each other. When our little church closed down, we just moved our Sunday school to his home. We even worked for him. Roy had four D7 logging cats (Caterpillar tractors); we would follow behind the machinery and go up into the mountains with him on Saturdays to work hauling logs. It was the best of times.

My early days in the valley that houses Acme taught me to love Jesus and work hard. I learned about life interacting with family and friends, and never missed my daily appointment with the *Bellingham Herald.*

To Chicago—The First Time

I grew up playing in the cemetery across the road from our little church. Often my dad would take me on tours through the cemetery and introduce me to my family and the church family that I never met in person—the great cloud of witnesses that lived a life of faith before my time. He would stop by gravestones and tell me their stories. To this day I consider myself a "historical charismatic." The church has 2000 years of family history, and to neglect any decade of history in the church is to blaspheme the Holy Spirit and deny the gift of teaching in the church. My dad made sure I knew that on those historical tours through the cemetery.

I loved growing up in Acme. I never felt it was a handicap. I had parents who loved me, a community that cared for me, and was encouraged and affirmed by both.

All along the way my desire to be a history teacher was fed. In those early days, I thought I wanted to be a high-school history teacher and a football coach. My love of history was spurred on by all those books I retrieved from the elementary school. I knew I didn't want to be a logger or farmer. Loggers often lived relatively short lives because of accidents.

During my teenage years I began asking different members of my community where I should continue my education after I graduated from high school. Finally Roy Johnson's friend, who lived in Seattle and had seen a bigger part of the world, suggested I attend Moody Bible Institute in Chicago, Illinois, for at least one year. I had never heard of Moody Bible Institute, but I had heard of Chicago. In my junior year I had been as far south as Olympia, Washington, about 150 miles away. I had never been east of Wenatchee, Washington, about 180 miles away. I saw Moody Bible Institute as a way out of my valley. Needless to say, my parents were not terribly excited to have their oldest son leave home for a big city halfway across the US.

Still, it was time for me to go, so in 1956 I bought a Greyhound bus ticket from Bellingham to Chicago for $48 and took a three-day, two-night journey to the big city. I thought I would never arrive. We must have stopped at every little town on that two-lane road to pick up others on their way to somewhere else. Mom had fixed a box of fried chicken and sandwiches so I wouldn't have to spend money eating along the way. Now out of the valley and on my own, eating that chicken kept me attached to my family roots and values.

When I finally arrived in Chicago, I had a *wow* moment. My eyes must have bulged out of my head. The buildings were so big and there were so many of them. I instantly fell in love with Chicago. The city life was exhilarating for me. In those days I could get on a subway train for 25 cents and ride for 30 miles, all the time listening to the cacophony of languages of the people that lived in the city. I saw a variety of colors, smelled a multitude of aromas, and touched the diversity of the human fabric of life that made up the city. It was like being in a human zoo. Little did I know that I would spend the rest of my life being in or traveling to big cities all over the world.

The next three years of my life were focused on being a student at Moody Bible Institute. Moody began as the Chicago Evangelization Society in 1889 and later changed its name to Moody Bible Institute, after the famed Chicago evangelist Dwight L. Moody.

As a first-year student at Moody, I was given my first ministry assignment in Chicago. I was excited because I was earmarked to lead a gospel team to the Pacific Garden Mission every Tuesday evening. Pacific Garden Mission is a homeless shelter in Chicago, founded in 1877 by Colonel George Clarke and his wife, Sarah. It still operates today and has been nicknamed the Old Lighthouse. On these Tuesday excursions our team testified, preached, and prayed with many of those gathered for the service. These early memories of rescue are etched in my mind to this day.

At Moody I met a young lady, Corean, who eventually became my wife. She arrived at Moody from the Ozark Mountains in Arkansas. Like me she was from a rural area. What immediately intrigued me about Corean was her request for a black roommate. This was certainly uncommon from a teenager who lived in the segregationist South. As the pianist who accompanied a gospel choir at Moody in which I sang, she noticed that a young black girl about her age was not going on tour with the rest of the choir and assumed it was because no one wanted to be her roommate. This decision by Corean brought Anita into our life, and she became our first window into the African American world. All of this came about in 1956, just about a year after Rosa Parks refused to give up her seat to a white man on a bus in Montgomery, Alabama. I was intrigued that I had a girlfriend with a black roommate, and I couldn't help but tie this experience to my Jackie Robinson experience, noting how horrific it was that whites regarded blacks as inferior people.

The Moody choir traveled all over the United States and Europe, quite a stretch for a lad who grew up on a rural farm in Washington. At Moody I studied in what was called the pastor's course, and also sang in the Moody Chorale and played my trumpet in the accompanying brass group. We spent the summer of 1958 traveling and singing through eight countries in Europe.

In 1957 our United States choir tour took me to Little Rock, Arkansas, where just a few weeks before, Elizabeth Eckford and eight other black American teenagers were turned away from Central High School. While the choir was in Little Rock, President Eisenhower sent military troops into the city. For the first time in my life I saw the behavior of evangelical Baptist churches as they screamed, yelled, and taunted black people. I was shocked that Christians would do such a thing. These were turbulent times.

CROSSING TRADITIONAL BOUNDARIES

At that moment in time, Moody Bible Institute was an island in a sea of color in Chicago, but not quite yet a bastion of white protectedness in that sea of color. Moody was not yet walled in or fenced. I was aware that at Moody the students were all given a party line about what we were to believe, but coming from my Lutheran roots, I never got used to being dictated the boundaries of belief. Being told what we should believe and what we should not believe only caused grains of mistrust for people who taught a narrow way of thinking and then labeled those who believed differently. For instance, I never really bought into Moody's dispensational theological way of looking at the world. By dispensational theology, I mean that there are two distinct peoples of God—the Jews and the church. Neither did I buy into Moody's brand of evangelism, which taught that the world was going to hell in a handbasket, so we should pluck as many from their sin as possible, saving them from eternal fire, because after the rapture of the church, during the tribulation, somehow the Jews would evangelize the world. That was contrary to Scripture and sounded far-fetched to me.

Still, I graduated from Moody with a profound appreciation of many things, chief among them a love for Chicago. I simply took a different street sign when it came to their understanding of the church. Moody's benefit to me was that it was in the middle of Chicago and served as a bridge to the world that became my life. Moody was a conservative theological school, but in a way an open door to the urban world of Chicago. I also give thanks to God for three professors at Moody who profoundly impacted my life and work to this day: Joseph McCauley in theology, Howard Vos in history and historical theology, and Donald Hustad in music. Each brought a global perspective to their life and work, and I remain in touch with two of them, Professors Vos and Hustad, to this day.

As one example of how my curiosity led me to cross traditional boundaries, I decided to explore and see what I could learn from

Catholics, by far the most dominant church in Chicago. On May 27, 1958, His Eminence Samuel Cardinal Stritch, the Roman Catholic cardinal of the Archdiocese of Chicago, died. I decided to go to his funeral, though I had never been in a Catholic church before. After his funeral I determined to learn as much as I could about Roman Catholicism because Chicago was a Roman Catholic city. While taking one of my many train rides, I saw an ad above the car's windows for a free correspondence course on the Roman Catholic Church. I enrolled. So while attending Moody, I also took a correspondence course with Father Fitzgerald, a Paulist priest. I craved dialog with Catholics while studying at Moody—a theological conundrum!

In 1959 I finished my three years of study, receiving a certificate in the pastor's course from Moody. I left Corean in Chicago and moved to Seattle, where I became a youth pastor and music director in a church. My theological journey continued. Raised as a Lutheran I had now become a member of the Baptist General Conference, a Swedish Baptist church. The Baptist General Conference developed from a revival in the nineteenth century, but its roots were in Swedish pietism. In 1852 Gustaf Palmquist emigrated from Sweden to the United States. Only 47 days after his arrival, Palmquist and three others organized a Swedish Baptist church in Rock Island, Illinois. Today the Baptist General Conference operates the Bethel Theological Seminary and Bethel University near St. Paul, Minnesota, and offices in Arlington Heights, Illinois.

> **I decided to see what I could learn from Catholics.**

For me it was a fairly short step from Lutheran pietism to Swedish Baptist pietism. The fundamental difference was the doctrine of believer's baptism. Beginning in high school I had studied the concept and continued to do so at Moody. I needed to be sure I wanted to make this change. For my family, changing from Lutheran to Baptist could be mistaken as becoming apostate, but as it turned out, no one was hostile to me when I made the switch.

My study affirmed that every believer is a priest. If true, then the church is comprised of ministers. Everyone who is baptized is a minister. My studies led me to the belief that when a person is baptized he or she is being ordained into their ministry, in the marketplace or in the church. Baptism is ordination. Luther had already taught me that every believer was a priest, so this was a logical next step.

Yet because I was already an ordained minister after baptism, was I to pastor a church? If so, I would have to be an assistant minister in the church, because a pastor worked under the body of ministers in the church as their helper in their ministry. The pastor did not work *over* the church but *under* the church. When the issue of women in the ministry arrived on my doorstep, I did not have what I consider the present dysfunctional belief about women in the ministry. Why? Because when a woman was baptized she became a minister. Since she was a minister, she surely could exercise her ministry gifts. The only way to stop a woman from being a minister was not to baptize her. I formed a belief that I was ordained to *task* not to *position*. I am fully aware this still is a controversial subject, though it's hard to believe it's still so in the twenty-first century.

My belief system came as a result of studying Roger Williams, a writer and thinker from the 1600s. Today the church is often run by management theory, where somebody must be in charge. This, in my theological opinion, has turned the paradigm of Roger Williams upside down, making male hierarchical leadership an article of faith. According to Williams, the church has the authority; there is no higher authority than the members of the church.

Embracing my belief system was the beginning of my commitment to seeing baptized congregational members of the church as ministers of the church, and the pastors as *assistant* ministers, who work under the authority of the congregation. My theological take on this is that it is no different than the call of Israel, who was called as a chosen people with the task of pointing others toward God. The more I studied Old Testament theology, the more I shaped my view of the church as the people of God. Switching to the Swedish Baptists allowed me to keep most of my Lutheran theology.

ON TO SEATTLE

It was my great fortune on my move to Seattle in 1959 to rent a room in Ron and Jan Thompson's house. Ron was director of InterVarsity Christian Fellowship on the campus of the University of Washington, with duties on other campuses in Washington and Oregon. His was a stimulating ministry. I participated in a number of international Bible studies, and it was awesome to watch students take the Bible into their academic disciplines. This exposure whetted my appetite for the academic world. I wanted to study Darwin, Marx, and Freud and their impact on Christianity.

During this first year back home in the Northwest, I entered Seattle Pacific College (now Seattle Pacific University), a Free Methodist Christian school that began in 1891 as a local seminary and college. I wanted to work on a bachelor of arts degree, having only a three-year certificate from Moody. Because I majored in history and minored in philosophy, less than one year of my Moody studies transferred, and because I worked in ministry all those years, and paid for school as I went, it took me nine years, from 1956 to 1965, to complete my BA degree. A couple of master's degrees and a doctorate took another twelve years, because I alternated studies with Corean, who also finally received two master's degrees and a doctorate.

During my second year after Moody, Corean came to Washington and we were married. I was just 22, and three months into our marriage, we decided to begin a family while I worked at the church and continued studies at Seattle Pacific College. We barely survived financially on my salary of $212.50 a month. The $12.50 was my gas allowance for hauling dozens of kids everywhere in our church's youth programs. Our college Sunday school class had more than 75 regularly attending. Two years later, at age 25, I became the interim pastor of the church where I had been youth and music director. The majority of our church congregation worked at Boeing, a large aerospace company in Seattle. The church grew steadily.

An important change happened to me during this time in Seattle. My friend Ron gave me a copy of *Charles Simeon* by H. C. G. Moule. Reading this book was like standing at a street sign and deciding to follow the direction the sign pointed toward. I was 23 when I read *Simeon*, and Moule was 23 when he began his ministry in England. As I read, something in me clicked. My ministry was changed forever by that book. I will share more about that in chapter 3. From 1963 to 1965, I began to emulate Simeon. I visited folks in my church neighborhood, greeting them with, "Hello, my name is Ray Bakke. I am the new pastor of Elim Baptist Church. I'm here to inquire about your welfare. Are you happy?"

OUR FAMILY BEGINS

I was still working hard to finish my bachelor's degree at Seattle Pacific College in 1965. During our years in Seattle, Corean and I had two sons, Woody and Brian, born in 1961 and 1963. Elim Baptist Church decided not to call me as pastor in 1963, so I took a two-year call to another Baptist church on the south side of Seattle, as assistant pastor and youth minister. A few months later, my senior pastor resigned, and I took on another interim preaching situation at Dunlap Baptist Church. Corean and I had no intention of having a third child, but Corean became pregnant in late 1964.

During the early months of this pregnancy, Corean was exposed to German measles (rubella). She had taken our boys to a birthday party for the two-year-old child of a friend who was a public health doctor. This marvelous couple, Dr. David and Mickey Templin, led our college group, which they once took on a summer mission trip to Alaska, where they later moved. Without question, the Templins were our closest friends and colleagues in ministry.

During her prenatal visits Corean was told that the baby in the womb would most likely have serious heart trouble, be blind, and have severe brain damage, all because of the rubella. It was a trying time. We had no insurance, as I only worked for the church part-time and neared the finish line of my college career at Seattle Pacific College.

Our local doctor encouraged Corean and me to consider an abortion. Roe v. Wade (the abortion case decided in the United States Supreme Court in 1973) had not yet occurred and abortions were not illegal in Washington State. The doctor suggested this because his own wife had delivered a stillborn child and she never got over the emotional difficulty of that experience.

In addition to the rubella exposure to the baby in her womb, Corean and our unborn child also had a blood incompatibility. Corean's blood type was Rh-negative, and if our unborn child's blood and Corean's blood were somehow mixed, there would be a serious war in the womb.

As a Lutheran I had studied Luther's theology of "just war" and had concluded that in a sinful world, evil happens. And in an evil world, if I were presented with a choice of the death of my wife or the death of my unborn child, I would choose the death of my daughter over that of my wife. However, in my mind such a decision was like choosing to stop Hitler like Dietrich Bonhoeffer during WWII. I also studied Exodus 20–24, the covenant section in Exodus, where the text says that if a fetus is injured in a fight, you have to pay damages, but if you take a life you pay with your life. So I was convinced that if there were a war in Corean's womb and, according to the best advice of our specialist, someone was to lose her life by medical intervention, we had to make a choice.

I read as widely as I could, going back first to my old systematic theology notes on the origin of the soul, as interpreted through history. At that time, the basic Catholic position was *traducian*, which means "to draw across"—the idea that the soul of the child derives from the mother. In Catholic hospitals, as I understood it, there was a bias to choose the baby over the mother if both were in danger. On the other hand, the Reformed position was called *creationist*—the idea that the soul of a person begins when that baby becomes a living, breathing person. Given the medical and theological data, I decided to choose Corean in our case, for reasons similar to any just war. War is sin, because it causes death in this world. That doesn't mean that I don't believe in the sanctity of all life. But, in some cases, not to intervene, for instance, not to stop a Hitler, given the opportunity, might mean we are culpable in his continued killing. So Corean and I applied for the abortion. I understand that this can come as a shock to many readers—that a Baptist pastor would do such a

> **War is sin, because it causes death in this world.**

thing. I must affirm that I believe that the origin of life begins at conception when a human being is being created in the womb. But I decided, and have believed since 1964, that in our own case of a diseased fetus, or in the cases of incest or rape, that the government must find a way to write a *just law* that permits, not requires, abortions in these three areas.

Our hospital of choice was Swedish Hospital in Seattle. They had a medical board and a moral board to make decisions on these kinds of requests. We applied for the abortion. The medical board said *yes* while the moral board said *no*. So the pregnancy went full-term. If our daughter had lived, we would have had an institutionalized child. I would have had to go to work to care for her for the rest of my life, and we would have stayed in Seattle. But she gave her life for us.

When we buried our daughter, whom we named Robin, in the country cemetery in Acme, Washington, I announced that Corean and I were moving to Chicago. I told the small crowd of about 50 family members and friends that leaving my daughter there would be a reminder of my roots, where I came from—my Ebenezer's stone, my monument to God's faithfulness, my "thus far the Lord has helped us." I reaffirmed my call to the city and that I was going to Chicago to study and to serve, and I didn't know if I would ever return. Corean and I moved to Chicago in the fall of 1965.

REFLECTIONS

Before we turn to the next part of my story, reflect on some of the aspects of my journey that might resonate with your own. Here are a couple of thoughts to help you begin that process.

1. What are your own roots, and how have those roots formed who you are and how you minister today?
2. What experiences can you recall that served as one of God's street signs pointing you in a different direction? What was the result of your choice?
3. What tragedies in your life caused you to take a theological look at how you would respond?

Chapter 2

From Chicago to Acme to Seattle

I arrived in Chicago in August 1965 to attend seminary at Trinity International University. My family and I settled into a church apartment at Edgewater Baptist Church, about a half mile from Lake Michigan, in a one-square-mile area with a population of about 60,000. I had attended Edgewater while a student at Moody. It was a Swedish Baptist church like the one I served in Seattle. On my return to Chicago, the pastor hired me as assistant pastor.

By the time I returned to Chicago, a lot of water had passed under my bridge. I had changed. One of my priorities in ministry was now a commitment to racial justice, but at Edgewater I found that the pastor, who was my friend, was a racist. He had a paranoid worldview about blacks and would not allow them to become members of his all-white church. I never noticed this when I attended the church during my Moody days. To my surprise, over the ensuing months, I discovered his mind-set was fairly typical of most of the pastors in the area, regardless of their denomination. This created a paradox for me: I was expected to work with the good white kids in this traditional church, but my experiences had led me to different conclusions. I was not a safe person to lead an all-white youth group.

TWO LIFE-ALTERING EPISODES

A couple of things happened early that first fall in Chicago. First, I was introduced to Jim Queen, a Chicago Bears football player. Jim

31

was drafted by the military after college in the Vietnam War era, so he arrived three years late for his Bears tryout under legendary coach George Hallas. He was led to Christ by quarterback Bill Wade and given an assignment on the Bears' taxi squad, where several other reserves spent their weeks, mostly in practice, running the plays of the next opponents. It did not help Jim that the Bears had signed Gayle Sayers and Brian Piccolo at his position. As Jim and I met together during that first fall, we decided to start an athletic program for the street kids in my neighborhood. It really was Jim's idea. He asked me to organize the board, create the official organization, and raise $100 a month, and he would work the streets full-time. We called it the Inner City Athletic Mission. That allowed me the opportunity to work in the city in addition to my all-white church.

Inner City Athletic Mission's plan was to place volunteers, mostly high school and college athletes, in the neighborhood playgrounds to play basketball with the kids and get to know them. Erwin Mueller, then with the newly organized Chicago Bulls, actually hung around and volunteered, as did some of Jim's other professional athlete friends. We put together an ad hoc "playground league" where the playground team competed against each other. This led to organized basketball camps for the players. Eventually Jim became involved full-time with Inner City Athletic Mission. This was the first organization I started during my ministry, but not the last.

The second milestone event during that fall in Chicago began late night and early morning October 16–17, 1965. It begins to get cold in Chicago this time of the year. According to Midway airport data, from 1928 to 2003, Chicago's average cold autumn temperature was in the 30s around October 5, freezing (32 degrees) on October 23, and in the 20s around November 2. Late on the evening of October 16, after Corean and the kids were tucked into bed, I studied and practiced reading aloud my biblical Hebrew for my seminary class at Trinity Evangelical Divinity School, where I was in the master of divinity program. Before midnight I went downstairs into the church's youth room to turn down the thermostat, which controlled both floors of the two-story flat. When I entered the room, I smelled something and realized that gas was escaping from the stove, but didn't realize gas also was hovering on the floor level. I opened the back door to let the room air out a bit, and when I lit a match to start the pilot, the room literally blew up. The old curtains in the room were extremely flammable and burned in the blink of an eye. I yelled for Corean to get the kids out of the building. The blast blew out 45 windows. In that instant all the skin on my face, arms, and hands burned off, but I was able to escape through the back door that I had opened, hobbling on one foot over the broken glass.

My volunteer secretary, Sandy, who had been working late on a project for me, heard the explosion and came to my rescue in the alley behind the building, and took me to an inner city hospital nearby. There in the emergency room, now around midnight, two doctors began working on me, removing burnt skin and inserting IVs in my feet because of the severity of

> **I yelled for Corean to get the kids out of the building.**

the burns. One doctor was a Chinese woman who had come to Chicago from China through North Korea with several others, burying their dead in the snow along their journey from South Korea. After making it to America she settled in Chicago. The other doctor was a Cuban man who had owned two hospitals in Cuba and traded them to Castro for five plane tickets so his family could leave Cuba and come to America. He too ended up living in Chicago.

To keep me from going into shock, these two international doctors talked to me and to each other about their journeys to Chicago as refugees from other countries. As they worked on me and talked to each other and me, I began to understand how both of these doctors saw Chicago as their promised land. There I was, flat on my back being ministered to by the very folks I had come to Chicago to serve. Our roles were reversed, and I am eternally grateful for what they did for me. I experienced some sobering moments during the excruciating pain of that early October morning.

Today it's hard to tell that I had mostly second-degree burns on my face, arms, and hands. These doctors did an amazing job on me. Corean arrived at the hospital around midnight after she found some folks to take care of our kids. By that time I was beginning to look like an ancient mummy. I was so focused on what I had come to Chicago to do that I was bound and determined not to let the accident or my pain detour me from my education goals. So I asked Corean to drive to Trinity to attend class and take notes. Later that morning, and for several weeks afterward, she drove our little red VW bug the 26 miles to Trinity to attend all my seminary classes (except Hebrew), and take notes for me. Such commitment!

My saga continued when the church's insurance denied our claim. The insurance company said that turning down the thermostat in the youth room was not on my job description. The pastor had assured me that all my medical needs would be taken care of, so the insurance company's denial came as a shock. The agent, a Christian man, showed up to interview me and asked me for a copy of my job description, which, of course, did not include working with thermostats. Here's the irony: if I had been the church's custodian or an ordinary church member, I would have been covered, but because I was a youth pastor and it was not part of my job description, I was denied. Fortunately I also was covered by Blue Cross as a seminary student, and that company took care of all my medical bills. I learned that companies people do business with often have no loyalty to their customers.

During my recovery, Uncle Louis came to Chicago to rescue our kids and take them to my sister's house in San Jose, California. He worked in the airline industry and had contacted the founder of United Airlines and told him my story. Pat Paterson, the founder, sent him tickets to gather my kids and take them out of the city. Years later, while flying abroad on a United flight, I wrote the chairman of the board of United and told him this story. He responded with a warm letter. Why is this important? Loyalty. I have a loyalty to people who step up to the plate during trying times, as Corean and I experienced in our early days in Chicago. It's just the right thing to do.

After my release from the hospital, I dropped out of Trinity for a year while Corean finished her bachelor's degree. I became a house-husband, along with my duties as part-time youth pastor and my work with the Inner City Athletic Mission.

WHITE FLIGHT

The events of the mid-1960s took me further into my city ministry. The time was ripe for unrest. Every major city was having riots; Chicago was no exception. You could cut the racial tension with a knife. During my time at Seattle Pacific College, I took some seminars from the University of Washington, including one on Darwin, Marx, and Freud. This was a stiff breeze for my mind, but even that did not hold a candle to what I witnessed during and after the Chicago riots.

The failure of the white churches was overwhelming. They simply picked up and moved into the suburbs—"white flight." These folks believed the Bible, but in a moment of panic they grabbed their Bibles and literally ran from the city. Good folks who believed and sponsored foreign missions ran from the city as foreigners moved into their neighborhoods. The Baptists took their evangelism and ran. The Pentecostals and charismatics took the Spirit and ran. The Reformed churches took their justification by faith and ran. The city became a religious ghost town. Even staff members from Moody, Trinity, and Wheaton fled the city.

It struck me that people seemed to think missionaries are expected to go into some pretty tough places to share the gospel, but those who support the missionaries are not expected to be in some of these tough places themselves. Instead they left to hide in safe, all-white neighbor-hoods. This made no sense to me.

A DIFFERENT KIND OF EDUCATION

During this time I read an article in the *Community Renewal Society Journal* by Stephen Rose, a sociologist. His thesis was that conservative Christians could not survive in the city. Why? Because they take the Bible literally. God used the reading of this article as another street sign pointing me in a direction I never anticipated. After reading that essay, I made a vow in January 1966 to discover a theology of the city. I will share more about this in chapter 3.

At this point, just a few months into my life in Chicago, I realized I didn't really understand the city I lived in. My vow to understand a theology for the city, primarily for Chicago, took its focus from Isaiah 40:11. In our many talks about the city, Corean and I realized that social needs alone would not keep us in Chicago. I needed to know if God had an agenda for the city. If "white flight" was any indication, it appeared he did not. So I set out to learn as much as I could from Scripture about "city."

The second part of my vow was to study Chicago and its 77 communities, 228 square miles of space, and 5,200 miles of roads and streets. I planned to discover what made

> **The word *city* is mentioned 1,250 times in the Bible.**

Chicago tick. The city's politics were Irish; its architecture, German; its ambience, Polish; its music and jazz culture, black, but including many black cultures, like cotton culture and coal culture.

I also set out to visit all of the 440 Roman Catholic parishes and Protestant churches I listed from the yellow pages. With list in hand, I began to knock on all their doors. The magic questions I used were inspired by questions from Evangelism Explosion, including, "If God were to ask you, 'Why should I let you into My heaven,' what would you say?" When I arrived at a parish, I would say, "Hello, my name is Ray Bakke. I'm a new pastor in the city and I need your help. Can you tell me the most important lesson you have learned about being a pastor in this city?" It was a neutral question, designed to put no one on the defense. Rather, it made me the learner, and the parish priests, nuns, pastors, and so on, the teachers. Sometimes I amplified the question and asked, "What's the best book I can read about this city?" or "Where do you go for help?" Nobody turned me down. Once accepted, I asked for an appointment with them to drive me or walk me around their parish so I could see it through their eyes. Having dropped out of Trinity for a year, I entered the local parish (or informal) seminary in order to study Chicago.

To truly get my arms around Chicago, I had to understand the Polish community. During that year of study, I discovered that Chicago had more Polish people than Warsaw. Only recently has Warsaw caught up with Chicago. Chicago had 100,000 more Polish people than San Francisco had people. To understand Chicago, I also needed to learn about the Germans who came from the Rhine, Danube, Oder, Elbe and the Weser Rivers to understand the German people of this city. Irish politics shaped Chicago, so I needed to understand the Irish. I needed to understand Chicago culturally and architecturally. My love for history and my college studies were indispensable during this year.

Next I made a list of all the cities mentioned in the Bible. To my amazement I found some 160 occurrences of the word *city* in the New Testament (*polis* in Greek) and 1,090 occurrences (*ir* in Hebrew) in the Old Testament. The word *city* is mentioned 1,250 times in the Bible.

The virgin birth is mentioned in Scripture only a couple of times, yet a lot of ink has been spilled about the subject, and rightly so. In contrast, the word *city* and its 1,250 occurrences in scriptural text are *largely overlooked* by Bible specialists and readers. So I decided to study them.

The result of my study was mind-boggling. Of the total number of references to *city*, 51 relate to the city of Sodom, the one city God blew up. That bit of information caused me to want to know why God rained down fire and brimstone. I held a popular belief, but did it match what the Bible says? These 1,250 occurrences of the word *city* in the Bible mention a total of 142 different cities, some mentioned only once, others many times. In addition I discovered 1,100 years of history of the city of Jerusalem. That small amount of information caused me to want to understand how many methods God used to reach Jerusalem, including prophets, priests, kings, and poets. I discovered how many cities Paul visited in the Mediterranean world. I developed a healthy curiosity to learn what Paul did on his missionary journeys. What did he do in all those cities to which he traveled?

In my search I found people—including scholarly rabbis such as Robert Gordis and Joel Finkelstein—to teach me what to learn about the cities to help me understand the Old Testament, and also some New Testament specialists to help me understand *city* from that perspective. While the whole Scripture is flavored with a Jewish mind-set, its language is part Hebrew and part Greek. The Old Testament helps us understand the uniqueness of *community,* while the New Testament helps us understand the uniqueness of *persons.*

I was one of those New Testament believers who carried a Bible around with me everywhere, but had no real clue about the story of God in the Old Testament. I woke up to the reasons why we have such an overbite about individuality, while community sits in the background. I realized why we focus as a church on reaching folks one by one. I realized that the church was practicing *reductionism.* We had truncated the significance of the two-thirds of the Bible from which we get a formidable look at community—the great gift of the Jewish culture. It dawned on me during my studies that I needed to bring these two themes of *community* and *persons* together instead of leaving them divided.

My study led to a meeting in 1988 with Pete Hammond of Inter-Varsity Christian Fellowship. We met in the small backyard of our Chicago home and shared our vision for a new kind of Bible. Pete wanted a marketplace Bible and I wanted an urban version.

We discovered that all, or at least most of, the study Bibles we had seen had taken the text and applied it personally to the life and work of individuals. Of course, nothing is wrong with a personal application study Bible. Yet we felt the need for at least one Bible that applied the text to public sectors as well. We wanted to highlight the family texts; the urban texts; the vocational texts; the arts, politics, governments, culture, and society texts of the whole Bible. We had learned that 85 percent of the characters of the Bible are not clergy but laity, and we wanted Bible readers to be aware of this information.

We knew that to disciple the powerful, one must demonstrate the possibility of incorporating personal faith into public national or international vocations. We wanted to list every occupation mentioned in the Bible in an occupational index, still the only one we have ever seen. So we joined forces, and with a team Pete built, produced with Thomas Nelson Publishers the *Word and Life Study Bible*. I was responsible for the nearly 1,200 articles on cities in Scripture, and I worked on it with Pete, Bill Hendricks, and the rest of the team for the next eight years.

After I had completed my part of the study Bible, I decided to write *A Theology as Big as the City* to show mostly young pastors that it is possible to read the Bible from a city perspective. Clearly most pastors wax eloquent on the sheep and shepherd texts. Yet the Bible is not silent on cities or city ministries. Its story begins in a garden and ends in the city, where we will live forever.

I graduated from this "parish seminary" after one year, having learned some amazing things about Chicago and what the Bible says about cities. Part of my self-education came through writing and lecturing about the city every opportunity I had.

I also developed church tours where I took people around Chicago as a model for a way to think about a city, a model that hopefully helped them in their own journey of understanding their own cities. I provided church tours, ethnic tours, gangster tours, political tours, and sports tours. By the end of that year I had fully adopted Chicago as my city. My conversion from rural to city was complete.

RETURNING TO SEMINARY

The next year when I returned to Trinity an amazing thing happened. The faculty allowed me to take independent studies in this area and skip some of the required courses. I am eternally grateful to Trinity for this educational opportunity, which formed me in those early years in Chicago and has served me well during my ministry to Chicago and many other world-class cities.

When I graduated from Trinity, I'd planned to move on to study at Yale in early church history. But first I went to McCormick Theological Seminary, which was established in 1839 and moved to Chicago in 1859. McCormick is an urban seminary that was swept over by the swirling currents in the '60s and '70s related to the civil rights struggle, the polarizing of the country over the Vietnam war, the call for more open political processes, and the rising awareness of poverty in America.

I went to McCormick for the S.T.M. post–master of divinity program in church and community, which was the equivalent of a doctorate of ministry in those days. McCormick's library had important urban research materials I needed, and the faculty included a couple of professors I wanted to know. I finished this degree in 1970, one year after Trinity. I taught part-time at McCormick in church history from 1969 to 1977 while also pastoring. I also taught Bible classes part-time at Trinity College from 1970 to 1973. Then in 1974 I went in search of a doctoral program. While chatting with the dean at McCormick about going to Yale for a PhD, he said, "You don't need a PhD. We have a new doctoral degree here at McCormick. What would you like to study?" He told me the degree was called a doctor of ministry. I had never heard of such.

When I arrived home that day, I told Corean and the kids I had been accepted at McCormick to a new doctoral program and also been asked to continue to teach some church history courses for them. The courses I agreed to teach for them sponsored my doctor of ministry degree. It was like my situation at Trinity, for I got to write my own curriculum and study areas that would prepare me for my continuing desire to work in the city of Chicago as well as the other world-class cities to which God would send me.

THE LAUSANNE CONFERENCE

This going out to other cities began several years later when out of the clear blue I received a call from David Howard, director of the Billy Graham Center at Wheaton College. He told me that the Lausanne Committee Billy Graham had started, and with which David also served, needed an urban coordinator for the Lausanne conference in Thailand for 1980. He told me he had seen my name in a file that came across his desk, with comments about my ministry in urban Chicago.

I told him I might be too radical for this assignment. I was not in lockstep with the church growth department at Fuller Seminary, which had a large presence in the new church growth movement. They believed in homogeneous churches, which for me meant resegregating the church in an apartheid form. Yet suddenly I found myself with an opportunity to work with Donald McGavran and Pete Wagner, who were the leaders of the church growth movement.

I suggested to David that I take him on a tour of Chicago to let him get to know me, with a request that after the tour he tell me if he still thought I fit the Lausanne position. He agreed to the tour and afterward told me I had to accept his request because no one in the Lausanne council talked about urban ministry the way I did. He explained that I made the culture come alive, and he compared church growth leaders to former tribal missionaries coming at mission work from an anthropological point of view, while I came at missions from a sociological, pastoral point of view.

I recently had been appointed to the faculty at Northern Baptist Seminary—a "protest" school against theological liberalism, which began in 1913 out of Second Baptist Church of Chicago—because I was now an American Baptist, of which the Swedish Baptists had been a part when it was the Northern Baptist Convention. American Baptists had two poles—liberals on one end and fundamentalists on the other—with a very strong conservative middle. Northern Baptist Seminary wanted me to take the Lausanne assignment and come back and teach the seminary students what I learned. Like me, Northern Baptist Seminary was committed to a strong center and building of ministry bridges to the whole church of Jesus Christ.

So I became Lausanne coordinator and traveled every summer to world-class cities, visits which World Vision helped set up. As a part of my research for the Thailand conference in 1980, I set up more than 100 study groups in major cities all over the world, and asked them to develop reports highlighting the most effective evangelization strategies in their city, both historically and presently. I generated more than several huge notebooks of reports, which fed into the urban track in the Thailand conference. Summaries of those studies were published in a 435-page book for which I was designated "special consultant": *Unreached Peoples '82: The Challenge of the Church's Unfinished Business: Focus on Urban Peoples*. For the next ten years, I traveled to some 200 cities to help them implement strategies for reaching their cities.

OUR CHILDREN IN INNER-CITY SCHOOLS

As I was finishing school, teaching, and traveling the world, Corean and I chose to send our kids to inner-city schools. This decision was a great gift to them. On God's green earth, white people only comprise 13 percent of the population. In Chicago the white population in public schools was only 11 percent. I believe that if you are a white parent with white kids and you haven't taught them to live as a minority within the earth's population, you have done them a disservice. You haven't prepared your children for a world reality.

We discovered that the inner city was the safest place to raise our kids spiritually in America. We found not a shred of secular humanism in the inner-city public schools. In those days my kids and I were always asked to pray at sporting events and banquets. As a help to our kids' schools, Corean and I worked as volunteer teachers. Our belief was, if you put your kids in an inner-city school, you should go in with them as volunteers. We followed this pattern for years as our kids moved through the inner-city school system. One year our son Woody was the only white kid on the basketball team. Our two sons dated girls of every race. Race was simply not an issue within our family.

One day Woody brought home a black kid named Brian. We fed Brian for six months, finally realizing he was homeless. It took me a month to find his mother and get her to allow us to legally adopt Brian. This gave us two Brians in our family, a black one and a white one. On one occasion when our three boys were getting physicals from a doctor to play ball, the receptionist was rather startled that I had a black son. Woody spoke out to help her in her dilemma and said, "Don't worry about Brian; he's Dad's son from a former marriage." The tension was broken as we all had a good laugh. At family gatherings today, the kids still talk about growing up in the inner city.

In one sense, our adoption of Brian brought me full circle on the "Jackie Robinson" event of so many years before. I moved from being put off by how whites were treating blacks in baseball to adopting a black basketball player into my family. Presently, as of this writing, Brian's son, Jordan, is in his second year in college. He is among our eight grandchildren, of which seven are black. It's quite amazing.

My natural son Brian was recruited to Harvard but declined. He is an artist and was recruited to play professional football, but chose not to do so, though for a time he played semiprofessional football in Japan. He attended Wake Forest University and majored in theater and art. He is currently the only white student at Howard Divinity School studying the black church and black theology. He and his wife, Lisa, are members of a black church in Washington DC and he works in the inner city with the homeless, as well as working for our family foundation as the director for "the Americas," providing grants for worthy causes.

Woody is a public school teacher and coach in Oak Harbor, Washington. He and his wife, Andrea, have two young children, both adopted. Amber is 11 and white, while Elijah Ray is 5 and black. An African American mom in Arkansas saw Woody and Andrea's pictures on an adoption Web site and personally chose them to parent her baby. Woody graduated from Judson College in Illinois, a sister college of Northern Baptist Seminary, and after some years as a paramedic, changed his career to special education. He was a great medic, especially with the special needs elderly, so we were not surprised when he eventually chose special education, finishing the master's program at Pacific Lutheran University in Tacoma, Washington.

Because of her black son, Andrea has developed a special concern for black people, evidenced dramatically in at least two ways. First, she serves on the Africa committee for the Mustard Seed Foundation of Arlington, Virginia. (The Mustard Seed Foundation is our family foundation, where we all come together as families to help steward my younger brother Dennis's money. The foundation has provided a little more than $60 million in grants to more than 80 countries to date.) Second, Andrea and Corean wrote the book *Time to Talk in Church about HIV/AIDS*, and created a small publishing company called Bakken Books, (www.bakkenbooks.com) to publish this and other books of special interest they think may be overlooked by larger publishers.

Brian Davis, our adopted son, lives in Chicago with his wife, Ednarine, and their family of six, including three adopted out of the children's program where Brian was a caseworker. Currently Brian is a caseworker with special needs adults at the more than 100-year-old African American social agency, the Abraham Lincoln Centre in Chicago. They love him very much, and find it a bit difficult to comprehend that Brian has a white dad. I love watching him in that setting. Brian's oldest, Jordan, now 20, is a second-year student at Bethune-Cookman College in Daytona Beach, Florida, on a full-ride basketball scholarship. Jordan is a special joy. For several years he served on the junior board of Mustard Seed Foundation, where he learned to read and vote on grant requests, as we have taught our children to do in our family.

Corean and I reflect with amazement on our multiracial sons and grandchildren. It's a miracle! There's no way we could have done that. It's taken all of them a long time to get their master's degrees because they worked the whole time they were in school, and they all shifted careers along the way. From the educational side, perhaps they graduated two to four years behind in English, math, and science from their inner-city schools, but two to ten years ahead in social skills with other nationalities and worldviews. This trade-off we can accept. However, Corean and I have been good models for them to continue to seek education. Both of us have two master's degrees and doctorates, Corean finishing finally at age 51. Our children and grandchildren watched us, and now we watch them.

Over the years of our children's inner-city education, people told us we were masochistic, hurting our kids by putting them in inner-city schools. My answer was and still is a short story. My cousin was a missionary in Africa and raised his kids in the bush where they had pythons in their gardens. We raised our kids where there were pythons (gangs) in our neighborhood. Why was he a hero and Corean and I masochistic? Why such a radical dichotomy between urban missions and missions in a foreign land?

CHANGES ON THE HORIZON

Several years ago Corean told me I'd been on center stage long enough. It was time to partner with people and give them access to places where I had been visible for decades. She also suggested I model partnerships with and accountability to women in my ministry. She was right, of course. For 28 years I had been part of a small support group called the Chicago Network. That group began as white males, but it was not long before we began to add women and people of color. That group had a huge impact on me over many years.

When Eastern Baptist Seminary asked me to help them design a doctoral program in 1994, they hoped I might consider directing the program. Shortly before that I had team-taught a course on urban ministry in Philadelphia with Dr. Leah Gaskin Fitchue. We met for sessions in city hall, where she worked with Mayor Wilson Goode, and from group sessions in city hall, we went out into the city to experience models of ministry for reflection and learning. I had never seen anyone hug her way around a city hall like Leah. When Eastern asked me to assume the directorship, I instead proposed they make Leah the director, and me her assistant. I enjoyed several years of traveling the world, and acquainting people with my accountability to this brilliant African American woman, my friend and my director.

For 40 years Corean assisted me in ministry. It is now her turn. Our home is her world, and from this base she has branched out with major assignments in her church, a regular Taizé-style vesper service in our home, her piano recitals, her writing, and even the creation of a small publishing company. It feels as if I now am her assistant, and that feels good.

Bakke Graduate University became the unplanned surprise in my life since leaving Chicago in 2000. I began the Pacific Rim Think Tank in the 1980s, which morphed into the Transpacific Alliance for Urban Theological Education (TPA), which served as a strategic alliance of church, seminary, and mission leaders focused on the evangelization of large cities in Asia by the late 1990s. When I returned to Seattle in 2000, I thought TPA would be the vehicle to move from an ad hoc relationship to Asian cities to something more concrete. One of the seminaries that showed interest was Northwest Graduate School (NWGS), located in a suburb on Seattle's northeast side, which had joined the network.

Then in the fall of 2001, the provost of NWGS, Rick Kingham, pastor of Overlake Christian Church, asked Jon Sharpe and me to take over the school. I was skeptical, but Jon, who knew the school better, helped me convene some key pastors and educators in the area, who told us they would support us if we took over NWGS. They really felt it was important for the Seattle area to have this school, and their pledges of help pushed us over the top. I asked the leaders of First Presbyterian Church in downtown Seattle if we could move the school onto their historic church campus. They agreed. In January 2002 we relocated. The transition was difficult; this was a suburban, all-white, male student body of around 80 who were in master's and doctoral programs designed to replicate pastors for megachurches such as Overlake, which had been the founding church and host since 1990.

We asked a branding team, and got one that contracts at Microsoft, to study us and give us a recommended name change. They proposed the name change to Bakke Graduate University (BGU) in 2004, over my protest. They had many pages of possible names, but reminded us that Harvard, Yale, Stanford, Fuller, and many other great schools were named for families. But usually they were dead families, I thought, until someone reminded me I would be dead soon enough, so I should get over it. BGU has what some consider a paradoxical brand, in that we are committed to the powerful, who steward resources on behalf of the powerless. The term *university* is equally

> **We are committed to the powerful, who steward resources on behalf of the powerless.**

daunting because we are so small today, but we are setting up partnerships with schools in large cities on several continents. Our goal is to joint venture our research and training from certificate to doctorate. In January 2006 the fourth anniversary celebration acknowledged more than 260 students in more than 30 countries, with growing commitments especially in Asia and Africa.

When it became clear to Corean and me that we would move back to the Northwest after 35 years in Chicago's inner city, it also occurred to us that the Native American communities around us might become an increasingly defining reality in our new location. We were right about that. We have begun to explore the reservations, buy books, and listen to those communities. It turns out that one of our doctoral students is the acting dean of students at Northwest Indian College on the Lummi Reservation near Bellingham, Washington. I have gotten to know the NWIC president, Cheryl Crazy Bull, who is also now the president of the association of tribal college presidents, a network of 36 college presidents in the US. A group of us is exploring with her ways to participate in creative campus developments for the future. It is critical that we dialogue with "first nations" and indigenous leaders around the world. The problems of black people are now recognized also to be the problems of Native Americans.

How Does One Learn?

I now am aware that my students at BGU seem less interested in what I know than how I learn. This awareness is shaping my approach to graduate theological education, where my teaching approach is a bro-kering of resources in a consultative style emerging from intentional relationships. At BGU, where we are trying to turn cities into labora-tories and ministry practitioners into the next generation of professors, we are intentional about pluralizing the design of every class syllabus, so multiple voices are heard in every course, usually in dialogue but sometimes in sharp disagreement. We are committed to contextual integrity and cultural sensitivity, so designing courses becomes a group process.

Part of my own awareness on these issues came because I lived in Chicago's inner city and commuted 26 miles to my seminary in a totally different suburban context. When we studied biblical texts, we always exegeted the cultural and literary background of the texts. In church history courses, we always studied the social, cultural, and geographical locations of persons, events, and movements. But when we took the so-called "practical courses," the professors usually began with a "here is how you do it" introduction to the model of ministry presented. On my way home from these classes, I remember often thinking how impractical these so-called practical courses were. I finally realized that most of the seminary practical theologians had not reflected on their own social or contextual locations in the white, middle-class, county-seat towns of America. They lectured prescriptively. But the biblical and historical faculty lectured diagnostically. The difference was huge for me. Because I lived far off the white, middle-class American map, the way we approached Bible and history was the way I also needed to approach and understand ministry, and that is what we are trying to do now at BGU. We design entry strategies and discover learning approaches, rather than assuming we come with answers or programs. It is most disorienting to white males, but affirmed by almost everyone else.

In chapters 8 and 9 you will read about Jon's journey to the city: from Index to Seattle. But now we turn our attention to five important street signs in my life that caused me to think and reflect about the urban world the way I do. As I have just pointed out, I have found in my later years that folks are much more interested in *how* I think rather than *what* I think. To that end, we offer the following five street signs.

REFLECTIONS

1. Reflect on at least one life-altering circumstance you have encountered and the resulting direction toward which the experience moved you.

2. What do you think about the education of children? Is academic excellence the only lens through which one can be successful?

3. Why do you think the model of education we propose at Bakke Graduate University would be "disorienting to white males"?

Chapter 3

Five Street Signs that Changed My Ministry

Y ou need a map when you go on a journey. The map gives you directions and points you to street signs. The street signs show you where you are and point you toward your destination. If you are headed toward 1234 First Street, Any City, USA, but you turn down Second Street to the 1234 address, you've taken a turn that gets you to a destination, but it's the wrong destination.

Think about this for a moment: a street sign always provides you with a choice. When faced with a choice at a junction, the choice of one street sign will get you one place, while following another street sign will get you somewhere else. You may not be able to get where you want to go if you stay on the same street all your life.

Some street signs lead us to choices that take us in a completely different destination than we ever imagined. Such has been my journey for six decades (as of this writing). I want to share with you some of the street signs I took along the way, in hopes they help you understand why I ended up thinking and ministering to cities the way I do. Hop on board for this whirlwind tour.

Often I am asked about the ways I do ministry to cities. No one is a product of isolated study and meditation. We all are a collection of experiences that form who we are and how we minister. The following five experiences worked out to be street signs God set in my path, and with His help, I was wise enough to follow.

STREET SIGN #1: THE SIMEON STORY

As a young pastor in Seattle, I was introduced to Charles Simeon by my roommate Ron Thompson, who was the director of InterVarsity for Washington State, located at the University of Washington in Seattle. Ron gave me a book by H. C. G. Moule, who was ordained in 1867 and was a curate and the first principal of Ridley Hall Theological College in Cambridge in 1882. B. F. Westcott succeeded him as bishop of Durham, a post now held by New Testament specialist N. T. Wright. The book was a biography titled *Charles Simeon.*

Charles Simeon was born into the home of a barrister (attorney) who had no faith in God. His father sent him to schools in England, first Eton College and then Cambridge. Charles was intelligent and athletic, but somewhat ostentatious. Fellow students disliked him because of his braggadocio attitude, his short fuse, and his homely appearance.

During Simeon's life, England's working class was in spiritual decline, and conditions of the Industrial Revolution took their toll. Simeon spent his late teens and early twenties in academia, untouched by the troubles of his countrymen. When he arrived at Cambridge, he discovered that the dean required every student to take communion. This dictum often resulted in students going through the motions with no apparent change in their lives.

Simeon was different. He was uncomfortable about taking communion like many of his classmates. He did not feel worthy of such an encounter. He spent months working on his worth, to no avail. On Easter Sunday 1779, he had an experience he later explained as "the sweetest access to God through my blessed Savior." The tragic reality of his situation was that he seemed to be the only believer on campus.

One day while walking through town, he noticed Holy Trinity Church in Cambridge and thought to himself that he would like to pastor that church and teach in the university at the same time. When graduation day came, he took a lecture post at Cambridge and became the curate in charge of Holy Trinity Church.

He was 23 years old at that time. He knew no one at Holy Trinity, no one at Cambridge, and no one in the city with the same belief system he had developed. As he began his ministry at Holy Trinity and Cambridge, he became the beneficiary of many cruel acts and pranks.

When he started calling on the slum people, they began flocking to his church. The old-timers at Holy Trinity were appalled that these scruffy slum folks came into their Sunday morning service and ruined it for the regular members. On his arrival to the church building one Sunday, Simeon discovered that the elite in the church had locked their paid pews, thus disallowing the rabble from sitting in them. They even hired a guest lecturer to preach to them in the afternoon in the accustomed manner of the Church of England.

In those days Simeon was salaried at 49 pounds a year. As the pew owners locked their pews, Simeon responded in an intriguing way. He took his own personal money and had portable benches made and set up in the aisle, foyer, and platform area of the church. Every Sunday he found the benches in a heap outside the church, where the warden (usually the top layperson in the church) threw the benches during the week. Simeon, with the help of others, brought them back into the church, dusted them off, and set them up again. This cycle continued for 11 years. His philosophy was, if half the people received a double blessing, he would be satisfied. In the twelfth year of this standoff, there was a revival, and the two congregations reconciled.

Those whom Simeon taught at the university did not like him either. They often disrupted his service by throwing bricks through the windows of the church building while he was preaching. Students who were converted under his ministry were nicknamed "Sims" because they adopted his theology. The folks in town did not treat him any better than his church people or his students. They often threw garbage out their windows as he passed by on his way to and from Holy Trinity.

Things slowly changed, but it took about 20 years. A few students began to join the poor folks to hear Simeon preach. This was the beginning of hundreds of students who were influenced over the next 34 years of his ministry at Holy Trinity and Cambridge. He remained pastor of this church for 54 years until his death in 1836.

From this ministry of Simeon's longevity came a ministry to China, the ministry of Henry Martyn, who served as Simeon's curate, and the Cambridge Seven: C. T. Studd, M. Beauchamp, S. P. Smith, A. T. Polhill-Turner, D. E. Hoste, C. H. Polhill-Turner, and W. W. Cassels. These seven young aristocrats abandoned the comforts of England to work together in the backcountry of China. They were the founding fathers of InterVarsity Christian Fellowship. In addition, Simeon appointed chaplains to the slave ships delivering slaves to Australia. These finely tuned chaplains had eight short weeks to convert the slaves on their trip.

On a trip to Australia, because of my interest in Simeon, I met with the bishop of Sydney, John Reid. He told me that the Archdiocese of Sydney was one of the most evangelical in the world because of Simeon. How could that be? I thought. Simeon never saw an ocean. He never visited Australia, but he had a vision of appointing chaplains to the slave ships.

If that weren't enough, Simeon worked with William Wilberforce and William Pitt to ban slavery in the British Empire. Abolition of the slave trade by the British Parliament was achieved in 1807 for those in the UK, but it took 30 more years of strategic planning and work to get Parliament to pass the second bill, to ban slavery from the British Empire, which occurred one year after Simeon's death in 1836.

As I read this book on Simeon by Moule, I realized what a pastor was like. A pastor pastors the poor, brings them into the church, hassles the elite, holds possible different congregations together, stays through years of trouble, and finally stays for a lifetime. During that lifetime he or she helps found organizations such as Intervarsity, produces ministers such as Henry Martyn and the Cambridge Seven with missions to China, appoints chaplains to work in social justice, and teaches at the university during the week.

Reading this odyssey was a life-changing experience and the first of many street signs that led me toward my ministry to the city. In Simeon I discovered a model for pastoring, in which a pastor could be an academic working in the seminary, serve as a pastor to the poor in a given community, have a global mission, work for social justice, and train curates in his church to become missionaries. In Simeon I discovered that a pastor could work with legislation; work in the slums; teach academics in the university; be the friend of government officials, helping them work for social change; and do all this for 54 years in the same church.

Although Simeon had been dead for more than 100 years, he became my hero and mentor. I adopted him as a pastoral model to use in the last part of the twentieth century and even into the twenty-first century. The vision of a city pastor who was an academic during the week, took care of the poor, worked in evangelism and justice, and even changed systemic evil in a governmental system was an enthralling possibility. This was gold! If that is what pastors do, then I wanted to be one. Simeon, an Anglican, had given me, a former Lutheran and now a Baptist, a picture of what the church could be and what I could be.

WHAT DOES A PASTOR LOOK LIKE?

I had never really had a pastor growing up in Acme, so I didn't have a firm idea of what one should be or do. The Simeon book gave me an openness to see in Simeon something to be emulated that might have slipped by me if I had taken another street sign during my previous ministry years.

On top of a small hill in Acme, away from the main road, sat the little white church where my family attended on Sundays. Across the dirt road that led up Schoolhouse Hill, which was covered with tall evergreen trees, stood the old cemetery. It is still there today, though the little church building is gone. It was a serene place until all us kids showed up on Sunday for our weekly lessons. Mrs. Alura Galbraith, all four foot ten inches of her, was the Sunday school superintendent of the little Episcopal church in this rural area where I grew up. She taught us that we controlled time. She waited until the last member of the class arrived and then with great pomp and circumstance walked over to the upright piano in the room and turned the hands of the clock back to the start of the hour so we would get one full hour of lessons. Often on Sunday afternoon, the Sunday school class would go to a neighbor's farm and help them in their fields harvesting crops. We grew up loving God and helping each other. That was my concept of church: a community that helped each other, had women leaders, and where time went backward in order to go forward. My view of the church was certainly shaped by growing up in a church in Acme, Washington, without a pastor. I came to believe that the church *is* the minister.

Let me digress for a moment on the subject of women leaders. In the days when I was growing up in rural Washington, women were the executives of the farms. The men were the brawn. We milked cows and gathered hay together, but the women were the bookkeepers and arranged for the farm supplies. Growing up, it never occurred to us that women could not be leaders. My grade-school teacher was a woman. My school bus driver was a woman. My band director was a woman. My Sunday school superintendent was a woman. My Aunt Alice was the executive of the family farm.

Contrary to my experience, most of the students with me during my college days, both at Moody and then at Seattle Pacific, already had some idea of what a pastor looked like. They knew what would be expected of them as they entered church ministry after graduation and they understood the boundaries within those churches. I watched students leave school and go to pastor churches as *hired hands* to run the programs of the church efficiently. They were church-program focused. They may from time to time have ventured out to do some community events or ministry, but not often enough and not as a lifestyle. One might say that this form of pastoring was not proactive outside the local body of members. They typically did not get involved in anything global, in local social concerns, or in ongoing academics. So when I saw how Simeon put all these eggs into his basket, so to speak, and stayed in one place to effect change for 54 years, I knew I needed to take that street sign to wherever it led.

I still have the copy of the Simeon book I read all those years ago. It was extremely influential in my life. It was truly a street sign pointing me in a new direction I needed to go. Taking the path this street sign pointed toward was the first of several shifts that shaped how I think about the church and its ministry in the city.

STREET SIGN #2: THE BIBLE AS A RURAL BOOK

Fresh out of the hospital burn ward in Chicago, I read an article by sociologist Stephen J. Rose, which served as a second street sign in my ministry journey. His argument was that conservative Christians cannot survive in cities. Why? Because the God of the Bible is a rural God. The controlling images in the Bible are shepherds, camels, tents, deserts, tribes, sandals, and gardens. God made gardens. Evil men like Cain made cities. Rose had a sociological hierarchy for this rural Bible idea. God's favorite people were shepherds, his second-favorite were vineyard keepers, and least of all, he liked city dwellers. His example of the shepherd was David. He posited that as long as David stayed on the farm and cared for the sheep, he was okay. But when he left the farm and went to the city, he found himself in trouble with politics and women. His whole point was that Christians should stay away from the city because, as David did, they would only find trouble dealing with the political structures. Rose went on to say that memorizing Scripture in fact produced an antiurban bias in Christians because the Bible's worldview is rural.

When I read this article, I was watching Christians flee urban Chicago. "White flight" was the new Christian theology. Baptists and charismatics, along with others, were running to the safety of the suburbs. New churches where they landed promoted foreign missions, but they never made the connection that the city they were fleeing from was a foreign mission field because the nations had come to their neighborhoods. Still they fled, largely because they did not want to live with foreigners.

After reading Rose's essay, I made a vow in January 1966 to discover a theology of the city. I had graduated from Moody and Seattle Pacific College, and was a student at Trinity Seminary. I knew Greek and Hebrew, but I had never been taught a theology for the city.

Corean and I had many conversations about our observations and what I was reading. We concluded that if an exodus from the city and flight to the suburbs was what God was doing, then I didn't want to stay in the city to salvage something God was not doing. Did Scripture offer a theology of the city, or was it really a rural book as Rose had argued? Had I missed something in Scripture? Were my fellow brothers and sisters fleeing back toward a rural life because God really is a rural God? I was living proof that you could graduate from a Bible school and leave without knowing what God thinks about cities. This same deficiency is still prominent in Bible colleges and seminaries today.

When I returned to Chicago and was attending Trinity, I remember sitting in a Pentateuch course and listening to a lecture on Moses.

Is God really a rural God?

I was amazed at how different the professor's reading of Moses was from my own. My urban glasses colored Moses differently than the professor colored him. For me, an inner-city pastor in Chicago, Moses's mom was a classic public aid case. Moses was fatherless in the story. His mom floated him down the river so he could be saved from the tyranny of the government, only to be retrieved by the government. Then she received government pay to help her raise her own child. She had beaten the system. I was pastoring people just like her.

Another aspect of the life of Moses I viewed through my urban glasses was that he became a learned person in the city, and then God sent him to work with sheep in a rural neighborhood before he could work with people in the bad neighborhoods of the city.

Reading Rose caused me to look for and discover a different way to approach Scripture. I began to read the Old Testament with the glasses of a migrant worker. Of course, this was the kind of people that made up my congregation. Moses had to work with brick makers in the city. I worked with migrant workers with similar physical jobs. I remember taking up the habit of reading Luther, who worked in academia during the day and preached to the peasants on Sunday. I wanted to know how I could take the sacred text and make it come alive to the people I pastored.

I dropped out of seminary for a year to begin this fascinating journey. I began to see as I studied Scripture that cities were important, especially in the Old Testament. This was an amazing discovery for me. Using a concordance, I made a list of all the texts about cities. I discovered 1,250. I also used Jewish commentaries, which helped me begin to see the doctrine of community within a larger framework than simply a rural one.

One cannot study just the cities without studying the people who inhabit the cities mentioned in Scripture. The story of Joseph grabbed my attention. His story is told in Genesis 37–50, minus the Tamar story in Genesis 38. He grew up in a rural community. He was favored by his father, which drove his brothers to a plot to rid the family of him. He was sold and worked as a slave in Potiphar's house, where a run-in with Potiphar's wife got him thrown in prison. Many years later, when he was released from prison, he rose in the national government to second chair under Pharaoh. He was reunited with his family, and his wisdom led him to move them and others into a pagan city. This action saved the family God had chosen to reverse the rebellion of the Garden of Eden. As a governmental official, he used a blend of capitalism and socialism to keep famine from wiping out Egypt.

In consultations, which we will discuss later, I often ask pastors in emerging nations whether Joseph was a capitalist or a socialist. Most of these pastors, who are trained in local Bible schools, are only exposed to Joseph as a type of Christ. For them the high point of the Joseph story is his moral integrity when he refused the sexual advances of Potiphar's wife. During our conversations about Joseph as capitalist or socialist, I have the opportunity to help them understand that these 13 chapters of the sacred text in Genesis might offer more than ideas about inappropriate sexual involvement. They might have something to say about living in a hungry world.

I soon came to the conclusion that while God may have a rural address, He also has an urban address. While God's story began in a garden, it ends in a city. Rose's proposition was simply not correct! Still, the reading of that article was a street sign God used to help me concentrate on discovering a theology of the city in the sacred text.

Sometimes, because of my so-called cavalier approach to reading and interpreting Scripture, I have been accused of reading into the text of Scripture things that are not really there, a practice called *eisegesis*. This is simply not true, for the following reasons:

1.   I accept the original context of Scripture, i.e., that it must be interpreted in the light of its historical, cultural, and linguistic context. It was written *to* people, centuries ago, but *for* me today. I believe in the integrity of the written text, as we have it.

2.   When the plain text makes common sense, I seek no other sense. I have seen how both conservatives and liberals use hermeneutical *a priori* to screen out the most obvious meanings of Scripture for today.

3.   I think what I often do is take the "stained glass" off the text, by which I mean that once I think I know what it meant to the original audience centuries ago, and have some idea of how that text has functioned in the life of the church for 2000 years, I must try to explain it in ways normal people can understand it today.

4. I accept the plurality of the Gospels, and the diversity of the text. I think of the Bible, in the words of Rabbi Robert Gordis, as a "divine library," with multiple spiritualities and multiple images of the church. I don't try to harmonize everything. Cities are pluralistic, and as I read the text, I see that Jesus is the way or the door, but that there are many ways to that door. I see a plurality of ministry in the Old Testament with prophets, priests, and kings, and assume that God blesses many kinds and styles of ministry today as well. I have found up to 25 types of urban ministry in the historical books of the Old Testament alone. Obviously, in the more than 1,100 years of biblical history we have about Jerusalem in the Bible (from 1000 BC to AD 100), we find a huge variety of ways God approached that city.

Today, when I have conversations with evangelicals, I don't use sociological arguments to argue a point, I simply try to "out-Bible them."

Lots of folks all over the world live and minister in cities yet don't understand what Scripture teaches about the city. They don't understand their ministries within this paradigm. They usually don't see the prophets and priests of the Old Testament within the city paradigm. As I mentioned, there are 25 kinds of urban ministry in the historical books alone. Here are a few. A priest in the Old Testament was not allowed to work outside the city. Priests worked with housing. They had to inspect houses to make sure they were safe. Priests

> **When the plain text makes common sense, I seek no other sense.**

were also involved in education. They ran cities of refuge. Sacramental priests worked within the theology of *place*.

Prophets, on the other hand, were like a modern parachurch organization. They were single-issue messengers. They could come and go in the city, while priests were required to be among the people in the city. Kings were the rulers of the people living in the city. All three of these Old Testament categories were called ministers, and they surely were. Shepherd was sometimes a metaphor for a king. So when the text suggests that shepherds were feeding themselves and not the sheep (Ezekiel 34:2), it may be talking about the kings of the day.

During this hiatus year from Trinity, I was in my own personal seminary program. This street sign helped me begin to form a process of reading Scripture that led me later to write a book devoted to those findings. It would be about 30 years before I published my findings in *A Theology as Big as the City*. I knew something was missing in evangelical theology. We certainly were great producers of *programs*. By the 1960s we also were developing a theology of *persons*, helped by such writers as Paul Tournier and his work *The Whole Person in a Broken World*. What was missing for me was some rationale for the theology of *place*.

In the first half of the twentieth century, H. Wheeler Robinson and H. H. Rowley, along with other Old Testament specialists, had identified corporate solidarity and corporate personality doctrines in Old Testament studies. I drank at those wells. In Scripture, Deuteronomy is a profoundly urban book. I began to see that two-thirds of my Bible was a gift from the Jews, to whom God had given insights on community reality. People were hyphenated to families and communities. Paul of Tarsus is a clue. In Israel, everyone was somebody from someplace, without exception.

But in America, places were like paper cups to be discarded after use or abuse. We threw away neighborhoods and church buildings where the prayers of faithful people had gone up, often for generations. We bought into the Greek idea that persons are all that matters. We individualized the gospel and its application. Whereas Catholics had their parishes (we will talk about this later as well) and stayed anchored in communities, evangelicals threw them away when their communities no longer worked in the manner their culture or class prescribed. In America, we live as if our sense of place and our sense of community are broken.

STREET SIGN #3: REFUGEE

I realized one day that the one square mile of Chicago in which I lived was home to people from 63 nations, represented in the high school my sons attended. This led me to begin a study on the concept of refugees, folks who transplanted from other regions of the world to live in Chicago and other major cities.

So my third street sign was the discovery that the city is made up of nations from all over the world. God had been bringing the nations to the cities for many years; I just was not aware of this phenomenon. I discovered this when my sons went to an inner-city school in Chicago and brought home friends of all races and colors. Two of my sons ran against each other for homecoming king in their senior year. When my natural-born son defeated his adopted brother for the honor, I asked Woody how he had defeated his brother Brian, quarterback and the best basketball player in the school. Woody told me it was simple: he got the Arab, black, and Chinese vote. That whole experience, of watching my sons attend school with kids from 63 nations, where classes were taught in 11 different languages, was an enlightening education. Of the 200 nations in the world, in the Atlanta Summer Olympics a decade ago (1996), 197 nations competed. Sixty-three of these lived right in my own neighborhood.

I began studying in the area of immigration and discovered that between 1963 and 1965, the US Congress passed three significant laws: the immigration law, the Civil Rights Act, and the Voting Rights Act. The whole country was caught up in the Voting and Civil Right Acts, but few paid any attention to the change in the immigration law, which abolished racial quotas. Until 1965, Africans and Asians couldn't really migrate with ease to the United States. After 1965 a flood of African and Asian immigrants came to America, and now about a million per year migrate to the United States.

The world was in motion, and I wanted to know if God knew about it. The world's greatest migration has happened in the last 40 years, from east to west and south to north. *Time* magazine, in its

April 9, 1990, issue, called this migration "the browning of America." *Time* said, "During the 21st century, racial and ethnic minorities will collectively outnumber whites for the first time. The "browning of America" will affect every aspect of society." You can see this in New York, which is the Jewish capital; Chicago, the Polish capital; LA, the Latin capital; and San Francisco, the Chinese capital.

The first time I went public with the data from my studies was at the SCUPE Congress in 1980. SCUPE is the Seminary Consortium for Urban Pastoral Education, which I helped found in 1976. It was an effort to take the middle year of seminary education to teach students urban ministry. SCUPE provided an educational opportunity to join the theoretical and experiential together. Interns in the program were involved in the meaningful life of a city neighborhood and learned the necessary systems to work effectively in an urban context. Today some 11 schools are members of SCUPE.

This program was developed to help seminaries train pastors who were going into urban ministry with their denominations. Seminary graduates in urban ministries were getting beat up and giving up their ministries. We suggested to seminaries that because they would not send a missionary into a jungle without some training, why not offer training for those called into an urban ministry? Every two years from its inception, SCUPE has held a Congress on Urban Ministry.

At the 1980 SCUPE Congress, I received an angry response from an African American pastor. He said, "There you go again, telling me that my experience is not unique." I had come to a new way of thinking about the city based on the migrations I had discovered in my study. The old definitions were that cities were understood as a place of poverty, while suburbs were seen as wealthy. Cities were seen as black, while suburbs were understood as white. I discovered that these old definitions were no longer valid, especially outside the United States, where all the big cities are "black, brown, or yellow."

I believe that the reason the African American pastor responded the way he did was that blacks still wanted to be understood as "the" minority. It is a fact, however, that blacks have become the second minority in the United States, following the Hispanic ethnic groups.

In my studies, I discovered Psalm 107:1–7:

> O give thanks to the LORD, for he is good;
>   for his steadfast love endures for ever!
> Let the redeemed of the LORD say so,
>   whom he has redeemed from trouble
> and gathered in from the lands,
>   from the east and from the west,
>   from the north and from the south.
>
> Some wandered in desert wastes,
>   finding no way to a city to dwell in;
> hungry and thirsty,
>   their soul fainted within them.
> Then they cried to the LORD in their trouble,
>   and he delivered them from their distress;
> he led them by a straight way,
>   till they reached a city to dwell in.

While it is true that this text was prophetic for the exiles, it also pictures a world crying out to God from all directions and being led by Him to the city. In addition, when one reads other migrant texts, such as Jeremiah 29:4, where God says that He sent His people into exile, one begins to see that exiles were not victims but were sent on a mission. The hermeneutic of my world shifted from seeing migrants to the United States as victims. God was bringing them to the city to incubate and in many ways to leverage their capacity to do mission in their own language.

I began to refigure my missiological thought pattern. I thought, instead of sending missionaries to foreign countries at great expense, let's begin to work with the migrants who can return as missionaries to their tribal peoples in many different situations. I began to see cities not as white/black or rich/poor but as nations to be evangelized so they in turn can evangelize their own people.

I asked myself, "Why are there a million Japanese in Sao Paolo, Brazil?" Missionary efforts have been working in Japan since 1552, yet there is only .29 percent Protestant converts after 500 years of ministry. Was there another way? As an example, in the late 1990s one Baptist Church in Huntsville, Alabama, baptized four Japanese PhDs who were working on a space project and would eventually return to Japan and become missionaries to their people. Think of all the Japanese car makers in the South who regularly bring Japanese citizens to the United States and then send them back home. While they are here by the providence of God, they become prime candidates for evangelism and training, so on their return they can share the gospel of Jesus to their family and neighbors.

These migrants who have come to the city return to their homeland in a variety of ways. As one example, they return for weddings. When I pastored in Chicago, 37 members of one family went back to their homeland for a wedding and shared what God had done in their lives.

God is urbanizing the world and internationalizing the cities. The nations are in the neighborhoods. In 2004 I spoke at two Bellevue, Washington, churches, Westminster Chapel and First Presbyterian Church. About that time the *Seattle Times* ran a story on changes in Bellevue. I actually read the article at First Presbyterian to the adult Sunday school class. Whereas Bellevue was developed by people who fled the Seattle public schools and the racial issues resulting from the busing culture 30 years before, by 2004, more than 30 percent, or nearly one-third, of all children in that suburban school system were going home at night to bilingual families. The nodding of heads by the professionals in that class confirmed the news reports. I've witnessed the same phenomenon all over the US. Several years ago I preached in Decatur, Georgia, a suburb of Atlanta. They had 55 flags hanging in their sanctuary, because they had 55 nations represented in the membership of their church.

The planet is being rewired around this move to the city. I have been "blowing the clarion call" since 1980 at the SCUPE Congress. Folks were not ready for that message then, and some people today still find it troubling.

This street sign helped me refocus my understanding of how to do missions in a new and emerging world where nations live in our own backyard.

STREET SIGN #4: ALL THE BILLYS OF THE WORLD

It dawned on me one day as I sat in a recruiting meeting for a Billy Graham crusade that all the outsiders who came to our city came bearing the same message: "We have an agenda that will reach your city." Regardless of the focus—Billy Graham and Bill Bright on evangelism, Bill McCartney on men's fellowship, or Bill Gothard on discipleship—the message was the same: God has sent us here to help you and your churches.

So as I sat in one of those meetings where all the Billys of the world came to Chicago with specific agendas for how to reach our city, I began to ask, "Could there be another way?" I just wanted the Billys to understand that we were in the belly of the city during a turbulent time, and we had some thoughts and something to say about how to reach our own city. I wanted a humble group of Billys who might ask how they could learn from those of us on the inside of our particular city.

Many churches in the city of Chicago were impacting the city and connecting with the nations in their neighborhoods. One of those was Holy Angels Church, led by George Clements, a black priest. He was the first black priest of Holy Angels Church. I took my seminary students to visit his church for a live model of what ministry in the inner city looked like. Father Clements had six Sunday services—different services for different people—from traditional, to conservative, to family, to rock, to what he called the "Alka-Seltzer" service. The latter was where all the ex-cons and street people attended and served as ushers, readers, and witnesses. He preached the same homily for each service, but preached it with each particular audience in mind.

During those visits I began to see the opposite of the "church growth movement," imprimatur of homogeneity. The pastor was not adapting the church to himself and his personality; rather he was adapting to the audience made up of the nations within his church.

Father Clements introduced me to semiotics. He had painted the colors of the African flag (black, red, and green) around the top of his 100-year-old Irish Catholic church building. By painting the flag colors of the black people, he told them this was their church. I never realized that sentient families needed a model within their sense perception that would help them feel accepted. I always thought the only important thing was the information being delivered.

Here's what I began to learn. One church could meet the needs of a diverse community. The prevalent church-growth theory of the day was autobiographical: the church was designed in the image of the pastor (a current illustration of this would be Bill Hybels and Willow Creek Community Church in Chicago). The church-growth gurus of Pasadena taught the homogeneous theory of church growth, i.e., that everyone in the church should be of a like group, but here in the bowels of Chicago was a booming church made in the image of its people, all different kinds of people. Holy Family Church had a membership of 73,000 people. Willow Creek would not make the top ten of big churches in Chicago. One must remember that *bigness* was not invented by white Protestants.

> **One church could meet the needs of a diverse community.**

Everywhere I traveled for the Lausanne group, I tried to reach my destination early in order to observe what was happening in that church community. I learned from the local pastors and ministers what worked in their communities. In tough neighborhoods all over the world, churches and ministries were making shifts as the culture shifted around them. These churches were truly the Michael Jordans in what they accomplished.

I wanted to ask all the Billys of the world, "When will you recognize that God is already doing something within the city and come bring these people together to teach each other what is working within their specific locations?" Then encourage them to get together and work in their neighborhoods to bring the gospel of God's kingdom into their communities. This is how the whole consultation idea began to take shape.

There is an expectation of city ministers around the world that when a Western white minister comes to town to deliver his expert advice about how to work in their cities, they should honor him and give him the keys to the "religious" city. These pastors and leaders have been impregnated with the belief that Western white ministers have the answers for the problems of their cities. So far this plan has not worked well, but we still move into cities with that predominant model. I was and still am repulsed by the whole idea of a white minister coming to tell a Nairobi pastor what to do in his city. I think that is totally inappropriate and somewhat arrogant of Westerners.

I watched how this worked in large cities by observing the overseas travel habits of the Western white religious celebrity coming to town. The traveling Western guru would fly in on Sunday and begin the pastor's conference on Monday, telling the attendees how much of a privilege it was to be with them and what a busy schedule he had. This was done so he could leave immediately after the conference. A hard look at that model nauseated me. By arriving on Sunday instead of Saturday, the gurus sent a loud ringing message: the churches were not interesting enough for them to see or participate.

When I worked for Lausanne and made trips to world-class cities, I made a shift in travel plans. I flew into a city on Friday and informed the steering committee that on Saturday I wanted a sociological tour of their city. I requested they reserve a van big enough for them to join me on this tour from dawn to dark. To accomplish this, they needed to find the best local sociologist in the city so she or he could explain, in our presence, what was happening in the city. In addition the sociologist should take questions and provide beginning answers.

The committee members with whom I worked had lived in their city most of their lives and had never asked questions of someone who knew the city. I attempted to help the committee understand that I was not coming into town as the Western white savior with an outside agenda for what should be done in their city. Another change for them was that I didn't want to preach in their churches on the Sunday I was there. I did want to visit their churches, beginning early so we could get in as many visits as possible. I explained that I wanted to observe and get a visual feel for the churches in their city. I also requested that someone who represented the church be available to answer a few questions for me. I wanted to know: "Do the cars in the parking lot match the cars in the neighborhood?" "Are their services monocultural?" "Is the church old or young?"

This request was contrary to current religious culture. Normally if a Western white guru with any visibility in the larger religious community came to their city, the guru was expected to go to the most prestigious church and speak. Instead of following that Western tradition, which by this time had impregnated other cultures, I visited all kinds of churches.

When Monday rolled around, I began the consultation by telling the attendees about my special privilege of having a sociologist show me around their city, which provided me with the opportunity to ask some pointed questions. Then I presented the attendees with some of the things I had learned about their city. I told them about how I had enjoyed the incredible privilege of visiting their various churches. I told them about all I learned during those visits. I wanted to see what God was doing in the variety of churches within their city. Then during the week I was with them, I frequently used illustrations of things I had witnessed within their city, not just some transported illustration from another place. This experience was totally different from that of watching an outsider come in with an agenda for their city, one which often took a great deal of getting used to by the steering committees and attendees.

STREET SIGN #5: THE CITY WAS NOT THE PROBLEM, THE CHURCH WAS

Until 1983 I thought the city was the problem for urban ministries. I thought I had to be the most knowledgeable urban person in the world. Before I visited a city, I read scores of books on that city. I thought I only needed to walk in and tell them what should happen in their city.

Once, before traveling to Pittsburgh, Pennsylvania, I called their historical society and asked for their recommendations on the best books about Pittsburgh demographics, religious studies, and history. They were delighted to provide such research for me. When I called the next day, they gave me a list and where I could purchase the recommended resources. I received the material and showed up to speak in Pittsburgh with these books in tow.

As I spoke I frequently held up a book and told them what I discovered about their city. I showed them what was true of a lot of major cities, namely that the freeway systems within the city were created to divide ethnic groups. The freeways were the new railroad tracks of the day. Originally freeways ran to the edge of the city as they did in Europe, but the mayors of cities discovered they could get federal funding to put the freeways through their cities, and at the same time used freeways to keep ethnic groups separated.

After traveling to 50 cities, I was in Cairo in May 1982 when I discovered for the first time that all the major barriers to effective urban ministry were within the church, not the city. For the next two years I did quick surveys to see if I could substantiate that the church was the problem instead of the city. In 1984 I announced my findings—85 to 90 percent of the problems for effective urban ministry were in the church. Such findings as "We've never done it that way before," or "competition," or "tradition," or "name calling with labels like liberal" all came to the fore during this time period.

This was a major shift for me, from being an expert on the city to helping pastors understand how the conflict within their churches was causing their urban ministry to fail. Two things reinforced my taking the direction of a new street sign.

The first reinforcement came when I was invited to speak at Andover Newton Theological Seminary in Boston. My hosts, a pastoral care couple, essentially told me I didn't have a clue about the people to whom I was talking. They told me I thought the people to whom I was speaking could do the same things I did if armed with the same information and motivation. They suggested that my self-worth had been fully developed when I was a kid down on the farm in Acme, and that it was easy for me to take a risk in the city. I didn't have to succeed to understand my worth. They insisted that most of the students to whom I would speak had not grown up with that advantage. The ministry of this pastoral care couple was to help their students have a better understanding of their self-worth. If they didn't understand their own self-worth, they would need a safe church, a safe environment, and success to know they were called and were okay. This was an eye-opener for me. I had never considered how growing up in a rural area had developed my self-worth so that when I got involved in ministry in an urban area, I was sustained by that self-worth, rather than being driven to succeed to accomplish it.

The second reinforcement was an invitation to the place outside Richmond, Virginia, where Southern Baptists train their missionaries. A friend of mine had gathered several urban gurus together—Harvey Conn, Roger Greenway, David Barrett, and a few others. As each one talked to this small group, I listened and learned. I had just written a chapter for Harvey Conn, which was a high-water mark for me as an academic. In one of our sessions, David Barrett asked me how I accumulate my data. I told him about my time-intensive way of gathering the data I used. He told me he compiled his data by using a computer.

This was a brand-new concept for me. I also realized that everyone in that small group was different from me. They had all lived abroad as missionaries. When it came to cities, they all viewed cities through an anthropological framework, so when they taught about the city, they did so from their anthropological point of view. None of them had come through the structural, sociological, and historical grids I had experienced.

Right then and there, I decided that they were the scholars and specialists and I wasn't. I decided to use their scholarly material to teach pastors how to use that information to overcome the barriers inside the church, so their ministries would be more fruitful. I realized we needed a new kind of pastor.

I began to test these new ideas in a series of lectures at Oxford. The notes from that set of lectures ultimately became a book. Within a year I had written a different kind of book than I could have imagined, called *The Urban Christian*. It was a story of my journey. *The Urban Christian* would never have been written the way it was if not for the Cairo exchange, the Andover exchange, and the conversation

> **I was helping pastors deal with the internal conditions of the church.**

with the urban gurus. Collectively these experiences helped me form a theology to help pastors break up the barriers within their churches so their urban ministries could flourish.

Ministry had taken another shift. I was helping pastors deal with the internal conditions of the church. Today we teach this form of ministry at Bakke Graduate University in Seattle—a different way of training pastors. Often when asked to explain what is so different about Bakke from other seminaries, I use the metaphor of a county hospital. Like doctors serving these kinds of hospitals all over the United States, we take students and instructors to the origination of disease, letting them get their hands bloody in the same operation. A doctor ties the suture, the student ties the next one, and together they analyze what they did. We use that model in our seminary courses. We call it an action-reflection model. We have classroom time and then we take students to ministries where we observe or sometimes help out. When we return to the classroom, we reflect on what we saw and learned. We seek to teach students that the models of ministry they see in a city has a theology attached, explicit or implicit, and then help them begin to learn how to read that theology.

In educational circles, this is a move from pedagogy to andragogy, which is adult learning. We do not lecture to people, offering a prescriptive method, i.e., how to do church, but instead offer them a discovery mode, where we use the city and explore it to learn about it. It is exhilarating and exhausting at the same time.

So here was another direction change caused by a street sign pointing me on my way. I let the gurus be the scholars, and I, the user of their scholarship, bringing it to pastors to help make sense of it in their context. In shorthand, one might say that my method moved from a "here's how" to a "show and tell" model. Of course, this is a biblical concept. Jesus showed his disciples by doing, then he would explain it to them and send them out to do the same thing.

I can hear the question now: How did you help break the logjam of barriers in the congregation, where the problem was, by helping pastors? What a fine question! In order to get the pastors to help their congregations, I often told stories about three hypothetical city dwellers.

> **I told stories about three hypothetical city dwellers.**

First, I told them about a pastor in metro Manila. The Philippines are made up of 7,100 islands. When missionaries first came to the Philippines, they dispersed to many different islands. Baptists went to some islands, Methodists to other islands, and other religious groups to yet others. So a Filipino person could grow up on a Baptist or a Methodist island. The missionaries on these islands raised up Bible schools within the different language dialects of the Philippines to train leaders to become pastors. The gospel was spread to different tribes on different islands. No one foresaw what might happen when all those island people began pouring into Manila.

Pastors, trained by these small Bible schools, often followed the migration of their saints to the city. When they arrived, they saw a mass of churches they didn't recognize. Every church used a different Bible and a different hymnal. Each pastor believed he had the right Bible and the right hymnal and knew very little about the rest of the churches in the city. Therefore he concluded they must be wrong. The pastors held many nightly meetings to help his flock not become contaminated by all the other expressions of religion around their city. Because the pastor held so many meetings to help control the contamination, there was no lay ministry or lay theology available to those in the pews, and no theology of the kingdom that was bigger than the one they huddled in.

A second set of hypothetical dwellers was Jaime and Rosa, who lived in the jungle in Brazil. They decided they needed to get to the city they saw on TV to raise their kids in the best schools and be able to get the best health care. So they moved to a barrio outside Sao Paolo in a slum where the arriving people from the jungle came to live. Every morning Jaime would go off to work at a construction site. He worked and spoke *peasant* all day long. When he came home at night, he was still the peasant husband. Rosa, however, took a bus to the subway and went downtown to a high-rise building, where she was a cleaning lady in an office with lots of clerical people working in little cubicles. To do her job, she had to dress differently than she did as a jungle wife. She noticed that if she used her lunch break to learn how to type, she could upgrade her job and make more money. So she began to learn data entry. When she returned home at night, she was no longer the village wife; she had become bicultural. In their home the marriage took on a different flavor. Jaime realized his wife was not the same as she was in the village. When Rosa tried to tell Jamie about her newfound world, the tension between them grew. Jamie began to frequent the local tavern at night so he could shrink the world down to his size. The stress in the marriage finally drove them to the local Pentecostal pastor for help. This young pastor welcomed them, but immediately began to work on Rosa to become more submissive because the tension in the marriage was caused by her not submitting. Nobody in this story, including the pastor, understood what the city was doing to this couple.

What happened to Jamie and Rosa also happened to black people in the US during the slavery period in the South. There were house blacks and field blacks. The field hands were monocultural. They worked all day with other blacks. They lived, ate, and worshiped together with other field blacks. On the other hand, the house blacks were bicultural. They dressed differently. They were the cooks, the seamstresses, the butlers, the bakers, and even the candlestick makers.

After the Civil War, the first migrants who came to Chicago from the South were house blacks. They settled in on the south side, and served the elite of Chicago. About 100 years later, when the cotton picker was invented, which put the field blacks out of work, they also migrated to Chicago. However, they were not allowed to live on the south side. They had to live on the west side. They were monocultural. The house blacks on the south side were prejudiced against the field blacks on the west side.

One of my African American seminary students came to me one day and asked, "Do you know anything about the 'blue vein clubs' in Chicago?" I admitted I didn't. She said, "Make a fist." So I did. "See the blue vein in your hand? Blue vein clubs were set up by black people with a light skin color to keep people like me out. I'm so black you can't see the vein in my hands," she said. Ironically, in this racially discriminatory society, the light black discriminated against the dark black. My student informed me that there were five categories of color in black churches.

The third hypothetical dweller story is set in the Middle East. When I made my second visit to Evangelical Theological Seminary, the Presbyterian seminary in Cairo, I realized that evangelical people were considered third class. The *first-class* people were Muslims; the *second-class* were the historic orthodox, Catholic or Coptic; and the *third-class* were evangelicals.

When a child is born to a Presbyterian or evangelical, the parents begin to connive to get the child into the best medical school, the best law school, the best business school, the best pharmacy school, or the best educational school to compensate for what an evangelical cannot become in Middle Eastern culture. This is not much different from pre-Hitler Germany, when Jews lived in ghettos from which came great artists and musicians, because they hypercompensated against what they could not become.

In Cairo, evangelical parents push their children to take the compensation options. Failing to do so, they can go to Cairo Seminary and get a bachelor of theology degree, graduate, and become a pastor of a local congregation where the congregants are all lawyers, doctors, educators, or business people. The pastors of these churches are terrified in these situations. It's a social position somewhat akin to caste.

What I emphasized in all these illustrations is that pastors retreated to an authoritarian way of handling the sheep. They were not university trained but trained in the Western seminary box.

Using my own journey and insecurities, I started telling stories about these hypothetical dwellers and talked about how we needed to overcome this obstacle. As an example, my brother Dennis went to Harvard. I went to Moody Bible Institute. It took me nine years to get a bachelor's degree. It took Dennis about as many years to become a millionaire.

Telling these stories began to help me see the need for lifelong learning, to continually ask questions and seek answers. The realization was clear that my thinking was not finished and never would be.

I tried to help folks unpack what it meant to live and minister in the city. I wanted to help pastors overcome the fear or their lack of ego strength or educational strength. I wanted to teach them coping skills and spirituality that was more realistic than the traditional Western take on such subjects. I wanted to show them texts they might not have understood before as they related to the city.

Now, when I speak to an audience, I try not to say anything about my own material for at least an hour. If I speak for two hours, the first hour I ask the audience two series of questions. First, if you are to stay alive spiritually in the city, what texts speak to you these days and help you along? On your journey, what text would you show me to support what you are doing as ministers in the city? Second, if you had to prove God were alive in your city, where would you take me? What ministries should I see in action? Attendees always have places they want to take me. These small exercises help attendees receive clarity about God being alive in their city. Instead of bringing the product of my study right away, I allow the attendees to get involved. From that involvement I often suggest the pastors form an orientation tour of their city and begin to get together for other reasons as well.

The assumption I have when I enter a city now is that God is already there working and I am on holy ground. I need to take off my shoes and hear and see what the Holy Spirit is doing there. When I ask folks to show us what God is doing in their city and they show us, I endeavor to help them see "signs of hope." There are many "signs" around the city.

So the barriers within the church that cause urban ministry to fail can be changed, in my opinion, by giving pastors a new paradigm of the city in which they minister. The problems within the church are caused by the isolation of the pastors of the churches within a city. Getting them together begins to break down the internal barriers.

These are the five street signs that radically shifted my ministry. They led me to think and reflect differently about how to be involved in urban ministry.

We now turn our discussion to the urban world and our need to inspect our worldview to determine what needs to be changed as we encounter ministry in world-class cities.

REFLECTIONS

1. Reflect on your own journey and discover the street signs that have led you to your present destination in your ministry.
2. What specific street signs were the most important radical changes of direction in your ministry?

Chapter 4

Rural to Urban: The Greatest Migration in Human History

As you can see from the previous chapters of my journey, and will see from the chapters about Jon's journey, we are microcosms of what is happening in the world. Jon and I are mirror images of the great move in the world from rural to urban. I believe that many pastors and leaders, as well as many of you who may not think of yourselves as church leaders but are reading this book, have not been made aware of the urbanization and urbanism going on around us.

Michael Todd created a film in 1956 from Jules Verne's book *Around the World in 80 Days*. But things have sped up since then. FOX News now has a segment on one of its daily news programs called "Around the World in 80 Seconds." As the world turns, it seems things speed up. So fasten your seat belt for a quick tour of the world turned urban.

Imagine, if you can, a world in motion—the south coming north; east coming west—as everyone streams into cities on six of the seven continents of our world. This rural-to-urban migration is nothing short of the greatest migration in human history. Cities are growing at an unprecedented rate. Cities have become the catch basins of migrating humanity. The nations have been and continue to be moving into our neighborhoods.

THE URBANIZATION OF CHINA

Let's take China as a representative of how fast the world is becoming urbanized. China is 9.6 million square kilometers in land proportion. It's so big that statistics concerning China often tend to skew the data on a world scene. However, it is instructive at the outset to see what is happening in our universe. Until recently about 30 percent of China's 1.3 billion people lived in sizeable cities. But during the last few years the Chinese have been migrating from farms to cities at the rate of about 30 million per year. China will be 40 percent urban in about a decade.

Think about that for a moment. It is the equivalent of every single person in Canada relocating every single year. China assumes they can absorb about ten million people a year into expanding, existing cities. If you've been to China lately, you can see huge metroscapes emerging where medium-sized towns and cities existed only a few years ago. Where will the other 20 million internal migrants go? China has announced that it must create the equivalent of 20 new cities a year for the next decade, averaging a population of one million for each city. Just try to get your head around that statistic! It can be mind-boggling.

Let's compare this with the United States. The latest census data shows that a little more than 50 percent of our population lives in about 40 cities with more than a million residents in each city's metro areas. It has taken Americans more than 200 years of immigration, migration, and births to achieve those numbers. China, on the other hand, plans to create half that many cities of that population every year and be 40 percent urban in a decade. Because of the one-child policy and no immigration, internal migration alone will produce a new urban China.

Issues of every kind abound for China—from food to sewage. In the face of the urbanization of China, Christians must realize that churches also will be in migration inside China. At the very least this means we can expect many new kinds of churches to appear alongside reopened churches, most dating back to the earlier mission era. Catholic and Protestant structures, liturgies, and training approaches will be impacted in ways we can hardly imagine today. Given the historical reality of Western-style seminaries, which are structured along the lines of "memory banks" rather than research and development units, we should expect many new models of training to emerge, with specializations not unlike those we see in medical schools, law schools, education schools, and business schools.

A New Worldview Is Required

I am making the educated assumption that the new global urban model, like the one in China, the United States, and many other countries, is already a reality. There is no escape from its consequences. Fundamentally, for Christians, especially for church and mission leaders, we need a new way of thinking about missions, a new worldview or paradigm, if you please. Why? Because missions is no longer across the ocean and *geographically distant*; it is across the street and is *culturally distant*, in our cities and in cities on all six continents. In reality we have moved from a world of about 200 nations to a new world of some 400 world-class cities. Missions has moved to both ends of migrant streams—to, in, and from all six continents.

In addition to urbanization, where in a little more than 100 years we have moved from about 8 percent of the population living in cities to more than 50 percent living in cities, we also see the Asianization of the planet. Approximately 60 percent of the world is in Asia. More than two billion people live in India and China, just two of the nations in the Asian complex of countries. So, as the world turns, it moves from an Atlantic perimeter to a Pacific perimeter reality. Thus, urbanization and Asianization combine at this time in history to move the world in directions we could hardly have imagined just 50 years ago. This new worldview must incorporate thinking globally while living locally.

WHAT IS A WORLD-CLASS CITY?

Beginning with my doctoral studies on cities, I read the works of Lewis Mumford, Jane Jacobs, Phillip Hauser, and Brian Berry. In the old Chicago School of Sociology, made famous by Louis Wirth and Robert Park, among others, cities were defined as "places with static categories such as population, square miles, and density." Over the years this way of looking at cities began to change. Lewis Mumford wrote an influential article on cities in *The Encyclopedia of Social Sciences*, published in 1968. In that article he defined cities as follows: "The unique office of the city is to increase the variety, velocity, extent, and continuity of human intercourse."

In this updated definition, cities are defined by the roles or functions they have in regional cultures. Several years later, I read Jane Jacob's *Cities and the Wealth of Nations,* in which she demonstrates that when a city approaches a million persons, it becomes significant in economic terms far beyond its local reality. In short, large cities with a million plus in population begin to influence nations. The economies of many of these million-plus cities often are larger than the economies of many countries.

I decided to blend both schools of urbanology in my own definition of city and still keep the definition as simple as possible for my nontechnical audiences of mission, school, and church leaders. By world-class city, I mean "a city that has a population of one million or more persons and has international significance and influence." This definition blends cities as places and as processes.

By the 1980s we began to define cities around media definitions and also saw them in social psychological terms. With this development in mind, I added descriptors such as *urbanization*, by which I mean understanding a city as a magnet for sucking resources from the region. In addition, I understand *urbanism* as a sound magnifier—the city is like the woofer or tweeter of an amplifying system. A city propagates an urban lifestyle and values upon surrounding regions. So cities are dynamic and breathe in and out. In the early 1990s, writers such as Saskia Sassen of Princeton were reminding us that a gigantic three-legged stool sits like a colossus on this planet: New York, Tokyo, and London are the truly megaglobal cities that control the world, with influences that far transcend their national and linguistic boundaries in this economically organized world.

Over the years, many saw cities in our culture as poor and suburbs as rich, or cities as black and suburbs as white. I don't think such categorization is helpful. Rather I saw another trend that is now confirmed worldwide: cities are now homes to nations. We used to visit countries to see cities; now we find nations in our neighborhoods.

REIMAGING THE CITY

At one time in history, cities were defined by place, i.e., at the mouth of a river, at the foot of a mountain. Today's cities are defined by their roles and functions. Here are some to think about: political cities (Washington DC and New Delhi); commercial cities (Los Angeles and New York); and cultural cities (San Francisco, Rio, Paris, Chicago, and Bombay, now called Mumbai). All of these cities functioned as industrial cities previously but now are more recognized by their functional DNA than the location where they were built. Some cities have multiple roles today, and some, like Singapore and Monaco, double as a nation.

Cities also have personalities. Each city has a larger DNA, a personality type. However, world-class cities have multiple DNAs within the larger role or function of their primary DNA. If this were not complicated enough, we also know that cities constantly undergo dramatic change.

Such changes challenge the church. As a student of cities, I have come to see them as prophetic in their culture. If you want to know what your suburb, small town, or rural area will look like in 20 years, look at the nearest major city to you. Cities are the engines of change in this modern urbanized world. It is fair to say that the urbanization of the city urbanizes the communities around it.

How Should the Church Respond to Urbanization?

Grant for a moment that not only is the God of missions aware of exploding new cities but He may in fact be guiding this global reality in redemptive ways. In light of that, what should education for the church look like? Should cities be studied and classified as archaeologists and biologists study and classify prehistoric species that no longer exist? Of course not. We are all too familiar with seminaries that train pastors by using medical facilities and psych wards of mental hospitals to teach ministry skills. Why is that? Is it because the people in these facilities are so different from the rest of us that they need specialized attention? No! It is because the residents of these facilities are more like us than different from us. In these settings, behavior is easier to identify than in the general populace.

It is my opinion that seminaries, like medical facilities, should see and learn from the social exaggerations cities provide. Seminaries should study cities not because they are different from corncob Nebraska or resume-speed Kansas, but because the behavior in the city is exaggerated. Behavior is easier to see because city life is faster. Behavior is the same in rural Acme, Washington, and urban Seattle. It is just exaggerated in Seattle. Urbanization is when I am in Seattle, not Acme. Urbanism is when I see Seattle in Acme via media hookups. Urbanism is the invasion of urbanization into the rural.

My only problem with a clinical approach is that in most cases, young interns don't extend their critique to the hospital structures or the medical delivery systems in which they are doing so-called contextual studies. It can be argued, at least in America, that the medical structures in our time are "sicker" than the patients in the ward. The *New York Times Magazine* feature story on December 19, 2004, made that very point. The systems are sick. Clinical pastoral education needs a wider lens to provide tools for systems analysis.

The hospital discussion is not a passing comment. It is our contention that one cannot study models of ministry in a city in isolation from the cultures, structures, and histories of those cities. As we have stated, cities and neighborhoods have personalities just like people. Cities are not static. They change all the time. We look for patterns to emerge so we can continue learning.

Why is all this important? Because first, we must begin the process of getting comfortable with the world in which we live. And second, it is my conviction that the Lord is moving the whole world to cities for Great Commission purposes.

John Stott, the internationally known Anglican evangelical and pastor-scholar, has made popular the idea that preaching must bridge two worlds—the world of first-century Christianity and the contemporary world in which we must seek to apply that ancient but entirely trustworthy biblical text. Put simply, the old preacher could ask: "What is my text?" Today's preacher must also ask: "Who is my audience?" Seminaries are very familiar with the exegetical

> **The Lord is moving the world to cities for Great Commission purposes.**

tools for understanding the original intent of Scripture. Many of us studied Greek, Hebrew, and cognate languages to provide a thorough grounding in biblical literature and the cultural contexts from which our "divine library" emerged.

However, few seminaries have given us the tools to exegete the postindustrial cities in which we live and minister. These cities are the new context in which we must apply the ancient texts. It is a daunting task for most church and mission personnel because it has not been a priority in our theological education system.

I am writing this from my new base at a seminary, resourcing some 250 mostly doctoral-level leaders from 32 countries. We are not a stand-alone school in America. We are beginning a journey to create a virtual mall of perhaps a dozen seminaries in large cities on six continents that share a common curriculum. We are not inventing this curriculum but discovering it by observation and collaboration. We are identifying what the churches and missions are doing, and more importantly perhaps, what they are learning by what they are doing. We are not ourselves the experts in all aspects of what is obviously an interdisciplinary field of studies, but we are finding many who are, and putting them in touch interactively. Everyone in the program must go with us to cities in China, India, or elsewhere. Our style is not pure pedagogy. We seek to turn cities into labs and help, in an andragological way, prepare the next generation of emerging pastors and teachers.

EXEGETING A CITY

A walking tour of a world-class city includes moving around a city and interacting with people and places that make up the city. I have provided hundreds of these tours of many major world-class cities. They are important because they begin the process of exegeting the city. Let's take New York City as an example.

New York is the largest city in the United States. *The New York Times* featured a front-page story on Sunday, April 18, 2004, titled "In New York, Gospel Resounds in African Tongues." Scholars, like sociologist Tony Carnes of Columbia University and Mark Gornick, who is writing his PhD dissertation on this New York phenomenon at Princeton under the guidance of an Edinburgh professor, are cited in this article. Missions sent Americans to Africa, and the result is that Africans have come to American city neighborhoods to live and work. The gospel is exploding in African cities, of course, but also in expanded mission presence here.

Back in 1995, the same *New York Times* made us aware that people from more than 133 nations of the world could be found in one zip code area in Flushing, Queens, New York City. Think about that, nearly two-thirds of the nations of the world living in one postal zone in New York City. As we reported in chapter 3, the United States changed the immigration policy in 1965, and in spite of 9/11, nations export people legally and illegally into the cities of this country at a high rate. Dr. Sam Chetty, director of the American Baptist regional area that includes Los Angeles, said that 139 languages are spoken in the 141 churches registered with his denomination in that one city.

Europe has also entered this new reality. Here is one example. Two doctoral students from Amsterdam entered Bakke Graduate University to study global urban missions. They are Africans from two different countries, yet now residents in this Dutch city. One runs a European organization called GATE (Gifts from Africa to Europe), an emerging group of Africans pastoring in European cities, from the UK to at least as far as Athens, and probably beyond that by now. The other student runs an emerging seminary in Amsterdam with 40 African pastors studying for a degree while pastoring in a Dutch city.

The fabled British Empire comprised 52 nations. Now, of course, people from all these nations live in metro London, and increasingly in all other British cities. But did you know that there were 46 so-called Francophone countries on five continents? Now, the French certainly know that 14 percent of Paris is Algerian. Other French cities have even higher Arab and African percentages, and nearly all of us know how that impacts France culturally and politically, because it's front-page news.

We could travel further north to Oslo, Norway, do a walking tour on the east side of the Norwegian capital, and find 97 nationalities in St. Olaf's Parish, the oldest Catholic Church in Norway.

One finds more than a million Japanese in Sao Paolo, Brazil. You can hardly get further apart on the planet than north Pacific Japan and south Atlantic Brazil. How does this happen? Let's ask the question in theological terms: Is God urbanizing his world? We know there were 25 nations in the old Spanish Empire, but not only do you now find them in the cities of Mexico and Central and South America, you find everyone else there as well. Korean-speaking churches are common in Buenos Aires, Argentina. Jews and Arabs came on Spanish ships originally in the sixteenth century, and perhaps 20 percent of the Spanish and Portuguese vocabulary words are Arabic. The architecture of many South and Central American cities show the Arab influence of

Moorish (African) occupation of Spain and Portugal for more than 700 years. So in addition to new immigrants, older populations are rediscovering their precolonial roots. These cities are veritable flower gardens of colorful cultures. Newer churches, and even the oldest ones, cannot escape this influence.

In contrast to our narrow cultural, historical, and ecclesiastical boundary structures, God seems to be bringing the nations to our neighborhoods so everyone can hear the good news of the gospel up close and personal. We have always had the commandment to go and disciple the nations, but that has become expensive, and is often forbidden by walls and wars. It is extremely expensive to send missionaries around the world. The biggest bargain in the world is that folks are coming to cities at their own expense. The church living in an urban world needs to get into lockstep with what God is doing in the world. So God, who since Abraham has used missionaries as the point people on mission, may be at it again in huge and expanding ways on six continents.

We could do similar tours in Iberian Europe, Baltic Europe, Mediterranean Europe, Middle Europe, and Eastern Europe, and find the same phenomena everywhere. These examples demonstrate that urbanization is upon us and that it is imperative to learn what the urban culture is saying so the church can become more effective in sharing the gospel of Jesus.

Remember how God set the stage for the coming of Christ in the first century "when the time had fully come" (Galatians 4:4). That stage took centuries to construct. In order, Babylonians, Persians, Egyptians, Greeks, and Romans all played major roles and bit parts in its construction. Jews scattered throughout all the cities and learned all the languages of those empires, but kept coming back to Jerusalem for the Passover to Pentecost festival season. There in that context the Holy Spirit lit the match. The Greek Bible emerged in the ghettos of Alexandria, Egypt, and joined with the emerging synagogue or lay theology movements pioneered in Babylon. That urban Bible and portable structure could travel Roman roads and ships to the ends of the earth, and it did so with the planting and building of churches throughout the Mediterranean world, into Europe, and then west to the Americas.

That is our Western history, of course. Put simply, I believe today that same God is scattering Asians, Africans, Latinos, and others all over the cities of the world where they are incubating in new and powerful ways to articulate and contextualize the gospel of Jesus Christ.

We believe churches have two primary functions: first, to be signs of the kingdom of God, and second, to be agents for that kingdom in mission in an urbanized world.

WHAT IS MISSIOLOGY IN AN URBAN SETTING?

Missiology, as a word, evolved from German, Dutch, British, and American mission experience. The experience of missiology was then reflected upon in the theology faculties of several universities. For me it means two things: First, missiology is the *study* of the world mission of the church. Second, it is the *strategy* for the world mission of the church.

Church history is important. It has been recorded somewhere that if you don't know history you are doomed to repeat it. I would like to add to that adage that if you don't know where the church has been, you have no business telling it where it ought to go. Urban mission must be firmly rooted in the church's past. We cannot enter a building on the twenty-first floor. Nor can we enter cities without regard for centuries of previous urban church history. Such ignorance, and sadly, arrogance, goes on all around us, and the results run the gamut from the merely divisive to the massively futile.

City churches are not victims to be pitied or patronized by denominational subsidies. They are on the front lines of world mission. Like the famous starship *Enterprise*, they will be called to go some places where "no one has gone before."

A WAY FORWARD:
COLLABORATIVE CONSULTATION

We believe that "how we learn is as important as what we know," so later Jon will describe a way of studying cities and models of ministry, a process which we call "consultation," a collaborative effort of those who live and minister in a city. Today, business might call it "best practices."

Cities exploded in the 1980s in the United States with the combination of long-repressed racial injustices and anti-Vietnam protests in our streets. But underneath it all, the tectonic plates of global migration, massive new economic forces, and "cold war" doubtless fed the revolutionary fires. A good revolution will produce two good things: (1) it forces us to get informed, and (2) it forces us to set priorities. The days when a white male from Chicago or any other city could or should travel the world to tell church and mission leaders what to do is over!

Karl Barth is famous for the phrase "Grace is an outside gift." Truly there are things outsiders can do. However, coming into another city or country with outside agendas, hidden or overt, evokes suspicion at home and abroad. Pastors are tired of being manipulated or patronized by outsiders. Rather they respond favorably when they encounter a neutral convener and a more neutral approach to discovering what God is doing in their own cities.

Many ministries have lived and some have thrived under centuries of persecution. Now they are neighbors in our cities. They remind me of alpine trees, which live above the timberline and are all bent out of shape from spending most of the year under tons of snow. They are not good for making lumber, but after the winter snow melts, the imprisoned branches of the tree seem to come back to life after carrying tons of snow during the long winter months. The cycle goes on and on.

In a consultation, everyone in the body of Christ who is present has a part to play. This is often difficult because our churches have been separated into camps around theological issues and we have been taught to be against each other rather than for each other. To be a part of a collaborative consultation, however, does not mean compromising Bible faith or common sense. We know that the one who paints "Jesus saves" on the rock of a public park is breaking the law and making Christ unattractive for most of those who view such art. Yet their motive might be identical to, or more pure than my own as I do my ministries. William Temple, former Archbishop of Canterbury, should be remembered for many wise sayings, one of which is that "heresies are exaggerations of truths."

To borrow a phrase from Emil Brunner speaking of the Parthenon in downtown Athens, some ministries are "magnificent ruins." We can imagine what they were yesterday, and we can imagine perhaps how they could be renewed in whole or part. In an urban world, the range of diverse ministries expands on all sides. The Holy Spirit is there, teaching the church as He has throughout the centuries. We see ministries we might call Philippian and other ministries we might call Colossian. These books are side by side in the New Testament, but if you build your ministry on one or the other, it comes out quite differently depending on which paradigm you use, as we shall explain in a later chapter.

Isaiah 40:10–11 offers the image of God with two arms: the strong arm that rules and the tender arm that gathers the lambs and gently leads those that are with young. A collaborative consultation calls for pastors that embody two arms: one is a strong and secure pastoral theology around their community of faith, and the other seeks to embrace the physical community in which they minister. In an urban city there are congregational and community roles. The work of the city pastor is not just *in* the church, which is in the city, but *of* the church, which is for the community at large as well. It is a small shift of one's paradigm but a huge shift in pastoral and mission theology and strategy. Most every other book on pastoral care focuses on the internal life of the leader and the internal structures or strategies of contemporary leadership. I read those writers and hear those same speakers. I believe them. What I hope to add is that which is not said. If you only read this book, you will assume we are unbalanced in external or contextual directions. Please understand that Jon and I are *adding to* the best of contemporary pastoral and missional theological and ministry studies. We are also attempting to do so plainly and not technically, so that emerging and inexperienced leaders can grasp the ideas and apply the transferable concepts in their own urban context.

The world-class cities are urban; make no mistake about it. It often seems an overwhelming job to reach these cities, but if we change our paradigm and take a look at the street signs around us, it may become a manageable task. How? By focusing on the city as a parish, to which subject we now turn.

REFLECTIONS

1. How does your present paradigm about an urbanized city affect your present ministry in your city?
2. In what way is your city a world-class city or in what way does your city reflect the characteristics of a world-class city?
3. How can exegeting your city improve your awareness of the ministry to which God has called you?

Chapter 5

Learning to Embrace Your City as Your Parish

This chapter's purpose is to help you begin to think of the city as the parish. Generally Protestants think of their church as a group of people who meet to worship together. Roman Catholics, the Anglican Communion, the Greek Orthodox Church, and others usually think of their church as a parish, in the sense of the local subdivision of a diocese that has geographical boundaries and is committed to one pastor-priest who acts as a chaplain. I urge you to begin to think of the city as a parish where churches and their leadership function as chaplains.

CITY HISTORY IS IMPORTANT

Alexander Callow's work contributed a great deal to our understanding of cities. One study, "The Boss" describes how the famous Tweed organization worked in New York and helps us understand the Daley machine that thrived in Chicago. Perhaps even better known is the oft-reprinted collection of essays Callow edited titled *American Urban History*. His book contains information about how baseball emerged as the consummate urban game. Of course, this was interesting to me because of my early baseball experience. There is a fascinating chapter in Callow's collection on the historical conflict between the "lake cities" (i.e., Chicago, Cleveland, and Milwaukee), and the "river cities" (i.e., Pittsburgh, Cincinnati, and St. Louis). Among other things, you understand how these rivalries happened and how they attracted certain populations and created still-extant structures. As an illustration, you can also see how the new battle for Ohio goes beyond the recent presidential election. Given the growth of state capitals and universities and the declines in traditional economies, Columbus is winning because it has the two new growth industries—education and government. Ohio turns from facing out to facing its emerging center.

CITIES HAVE PERSONALITIES

Of greater significance to the theme of this book, Callow's second and third essays compare Puritan Boston with the Quaker origins of Philadelphia. The thesis is quite simple: Puritans had a public theology. Boston was to be a classic "city on the hill"; it was to model a theological worldview, not only in its sanctuaries on Sunday but in its cultural, economic, and political structures as well. Not surprisingly, in Boston there is a park called Boston Common, and the city exhibits a continuing support for publicly oriented services that came to be the agenda of the Democratic Party. Without trying to prove too much or be too simplistic, the authors in Callow's book point out that this has been the consistent legacy of Boston ever since—its DNA.

Meanwhile Philadelphia was founded by the Friends, or Quakers, as they are known popularly. Of course, they had egalitarian and democratic impulses, as any of us who've imbibed *The Journal of John Woolman* would surely know. Yet at its roots, Quaker theology is intensely personal. It works from inside out, rather than outside in, or maybe in Boston's tradition, from the top down. So, claim the authors, Philadelphia became the classic home city for insurance companies. Or we might call it the capital of privatized faith in the "citizen save thyself" American tradition.

It may be helpful to your urban ministry to read Callow's book, being careful not to press the details beyond recognition. But having said that, the two contrasting theological images are instructive. Two strains of DNA root deeply in cities of the United States dating from colonial times. Like the double helix, these two strains of what we might call "private faith vs. public faith" wind themselves around the American urban experience. Neither is all right or all wrong. In balance or in tension, they can self-correct. Let the debates continue!

Other grids may also shape our understanding. For example, Washington DC, New Delhi, and Brasilia function as capital cities. New York and Los Angeles in the United States and Mumbai and Bangalore in India clearly function as commercial cities. They drive national and increasingly global agendas, but do so differently than political capitals. People live and work in these various cities in vastly differing ways. On the other hand, we might describe San Francisco, Paris, and Rio as cultural cities, whose exports, near and far, are ideas, fashions, and trends. Other cities have industrial personalities.

Again, without pressing too hard on the details and exceptions, we can grant that Hong Kong and Shanghai, like New York, sit at the mouth of great rivers and on the edge of great oceans. In many ways, they have more in common with each other than each does with the other cities in their respective nations. Cities have personalities or spirit.

LEARN TO READ YOUR CITY'S ARCHITECTURE

Chicago is an architectural lab. Most of the city burned down in 1873. Pig iron had been invented shortly before, and the bridge builders of Paris were experimenting with it. George Eiffel, who built his great tower to show off the new architecture, used it as well. After the Great Chicago Fire, every architect with something to prove descended on that city.

Pre-fire Chicago was pushed into the lake to create what is Grant Park today, and new structures emerged, some on the waterfront, like Roosevelt University, literally floating on a raft-like sealed concrete foundation so effective it has hardly moved an inch in more than 100 years. But within two blocks of it you can see new uses of iron and steel creeping into the buildings. At first the builders didn't trust this new material, so they used it to decorate the windows rather than hold up the buildings.

All this reminds us of early attempts to use steam engines to power ships over the oceans. Pictures of the times show how sails lingered on until steam could be trusted. We have buildings in our cities like that. A giant contest was underway among the designers of our cities in those days. Every city wanted to be great. Obviously Greece and Rome were great, so many architects, often funded by the new rich, copied those models, even though the flat Illinois prairie was a unique piece of real estate.

Other architects, inspired by "organic metaphors," thought new designs and new materials should emerge in that new context. The structures of the city reveal a lingering battle over ideas of the great, the good, and the big. As we suggested in the last chapter, we need to be better equipped to exegete our cities, for in doing so we may find rich treasure that will aid our own ministries.

Take a Fresh Look at Ministry in Your City

Few things are more fun for a professor of urban ministry than conducting a walking tour at city center and then adjourning to a coffee shop to talk about ministry. Students see it clearly then. Some people think that to reach great cities, we should copy the big and well-known models we see in other locations. Transplants are everywhere. If we could franchise the model, given the spirit of America, we'd have a version of McDonald's and serve the same church menu from Anchorage to Miami. One size fits all. Seminaries in this model become a "hamburger university," where we learn the history of our model and how to run and market it. Let's be clear. We would feed a lot of people.

Some megachurch and mission thinking proceeds along these same lines. Customizing is very hard work, and especially daunting in the exaggerated scale of the modern city. Let me also admit that most of us will need to borrow from both schools of ministry thought to reach whole cities with God's good news about Jesus.

Bicycles and Jet Planes

Which is better, the bike or the plane? How shall we answer such a question? Isn't it readily apparent that it depends on where you are going and how many you wish to take along on the journey and other such questions?

Ministry model evaluations are like that question. There are certain gifts the classic "store front" and the contemporary "cell church" bring to the meeting, especially in a high-tech culture. More people than ever need a "high touch" ministry. People often ask, "What is the best model?" or "What is the most effective way to reach people (or the most people)?" The answers to these questions depend on other factors. Which people? At what time? At what cost?

Sectors Make Cities

There is no one city; but there are many sectors to a city. Here are some to think about: a commercial city, media city, ethnic city, political city, convention city, institutionalized city, theater and art city, athletic city, restaurant city, health and human services city, airport city, university city, commuter city, and so on. Huge, diverse populations live in these sectors. Add the mix of languages, cultures, religions, and the 24-hour reality of modern economics, and you begin to understand that one size does not reach all. We need "tall steeple" first churches and classic churches that speak to power and organize on behalf of the powerless. We need churches to be family for the lonely and clinics for the wounded, abused, and broken. We need all the expertise emerging in the body of Christ, and we need professors in our schools who can organize cities as laboratories where our newest pastors and missionaries can imbibe those kingdom specializations. How to create such labs is important to know and understand.

Some churches root ministry in the first sermon of Jesus (Luke 4); others organize their mission around the last sermon of Jesus (Matthew 28). Check your city and you will probably find many kinds of Matthew-style churches where the basic text for the church is the

Sermon on the Mount (Matthew 5–7). Some organize around the four action words of Matthew 9:35: visiting, preaching, teaching, and healing, which Jesus himself seemed to promote, as the following chapter in Matthew reveals. Still others are animated by the last days teachings of Mark 13 or the final exam judgment text of Matthew 25, which certainly motivated Mother Teresa, perhaps the most famous urban minister of our era.

Is your church a Great Commission or a Great Commandment church? Which is it? The question begins to resemble the bikes and planes discussion. Obviously we need the best examples of all of them. The tool kit for each is different. Each requires special gifting, calling, and for many of us, special kinds of teaching. We may only be beginning to apply Scriptures to our city discussion.

What Would Paul Do in Our City?

One of the Bible studies I often do with pastors, teachers, and students all over the world, is on Philippians and Colossians. I divide them into two groups, assigning one group Philippians and the other Colossians. I ask them to pretend that their book is the only Bible they have. I send them away for about an hour and ask the Philippian group to design their own approach to ministry in the city where they live with only the book of Philippians. I do the same for the Colossian group. They should answer the following question: What would your ministry in this city look like if this book were your whole Bible? Before they go into this study, I ask them to pay close attention to where Jesus is located in their book, and how He is described. I tell them this will be a major clue in their design for urban ministry based on that book. Then I give them an hour to study together, and when they return, to present their model for ministry.

When we convene again I ask the groups to report. Without fail, in our experience of doing this with students and leaders on several continents, two diverse ministry models emerge. The Colossians group will have noticed that Christ is seated powerfully at the right hand of God in the heavens. He can take on principalities and powers. He is the essence or glue that holds the cosmos in place. It is a classic Reformed theological picture: the public Christ of power. With such a Christ guiding and empowering us, the church can take on all the work of defeating Satan and his legacy of unjust systems and lingering principalities of ugliness, violence, and pettiness in our cities. We can take on hospitals that don't heal, police systems that don't protect, and banks that refuse loans to minorities. We can clean up the ports and school systems as well. Our Colossian group can discuss all this with relish and in vivid color. This is what Reformed Christians have done in cities since the sixteenth century at least, and often before that, if we care to do more remote studies.

Meanwhile, the Philippians in our midst are getting anxious. Their model emerges from the picture of Jesus who gave up power and dwells intimately in the human heart. They show little concern directly for the city; rather their focus is on the church in the city. They see it as the community of the faithful, living out fruitful and meaningful lives and sharing with other churches and other ministries in other cities. Amazing, isn't it? This is classic Wesleyan theology lived out in Wesley and his eighteenth- to twentieth-century descendants, and the Pentecostals or charismatic congregations often flourishing in our cities, sometimes with little apparent connectivity to the larger structures and institutions of that city. Then we have a delightful discussion. Which book is right? How far apart are they in the New Testament? Of course, both groups want to say that both books are right, and they notice they are back-to-back in the biblical canon.

At that point, I observe that in the United States at least, one part of the church took Colossians and made it their whole gospel. They did social and justice ministry. Meanwhile, the rest of the church reacted and took Philippians and made it the centerpiece of their ministry. It happened after 1920, and we've had a great theological cleavage ever since. Cities are in a mess because the church is ministering with only parts of the God-given gospel. I've spent much of my adult life trying to bring Philippians and Colossians back together again. These are two spiritualities in the New Testament. In this age of global power and massive injustice, we need a strong, transcendent Christology to confront systemic evil in the world. Yet in this high-tech world, we also need a very high-touch gospel, and Philippians embodies that for us.

That is taking two living church letters in the heart of our New Testament seriously, each with differing christologically-shaped ecclesiology, or what we might call the "nature and mission of the church." Cities are like labs of biblical texts frozen in time. Many young urban leaders have not been prepared for what they see in their communities. It is so easy to simply react and assume their irrelevance, but at a powerful level, we believe that also is to betray the Holy Spirit, who has been a faithful gift to the church now for some two millenniums. Cities are the "playing fields" of the Spirit of the living God. For sure, "traditionalism is the dead faith of the living, but tradition is also the living faith of the dead," and urban ministry leaders need to know the difference.

THE TRIBUTARIES OF EVANGELICALISM

Evangelicalism requires some definition in this day when the word implies many different things, positive and negative, to many people in our culture. Three branches of the evangelical river run through our country. Thinking historically, there are sixteenth-, eighteenth-, and nineteenth-century tributaries of modern evangelicalism.

The sixteenth-century branch came primarily from the Lutheran Reformation. Martin Luther's recovery of the gospel focused on salvation by grace alone and appropriated by faith alone for every believer. Luther understood that Christ's righteousness is not infused into us gradually over time as we do acts of merit, but is imputed to us by Christ the moment we confess our sin, believe, and receive Christ as savior. This tributary was strong on justification. The Reformed tradition, coming out of the ministry of John Calvin of Geneva, along with Scots and Dutch, widened this tributary, and Anglicanism included features of all these movements. There was a recovery of "common grace" in reformers such as Calvin. Saving grace, the primary work of local churches, is paid by tithe money. Common grace is paid by tax money, but it is all God's money. A city hospital, a good school, a strong wall to protect everyone, would be common-grace gifts. In this branch of the evangelical tradition, public ministry was affirmed, but sometimes in ways that oppressed people of other faiths.

In the eighteenth century, John Wesley, influenced by the Bible study groups he had seen in the Moravian communities of Germany, helped recover the sanctification side that made the gospel strongly personal. This recovery brought with it a new emphasis on personal devotion, community accountability, and the recovery of mission. Also Philipp Jacob Spener, August Hermann Francke, and Nicolaus Ludwig Zinzendorf on the continent of Europe, and Wesley's influence in England and the American colonies, added a strong mission influence that led to missions moving east to west and clearly branding Protestantism on the new American states. It would be fair to say the eighteenth century was the Methodist century in United States church history. The social impact of these movements resulted from masses of converts and changed lifestyles more than public or legislative actions.

In the nineteenth century, revivalism and dispensationalism increasingly defined evangelicalism. With the growth of cities and the Industrial Revolution, one can see churches moving to institutionalized programs and professional staffs in response to growing cities and alienated peoples. Also, when cities became bastions of Catholic immigrants, many from socialistic countries, people in England and America reacted and, one might say, retreated to churches, withdrawing from social engagement. These churches redefined the blessed hope of the Lord's coming to a rapture of believers from the earth. Yet one consequence was the clear withdrawal of many evangelicals from the very idea that Christians could be allied with others for public engagement and social change. Evangelization was reaching people individually or in citywide crusades with the good news that Jesus saves and forgives sinners while there is yet time.

These are broad-stroke descriptions, of course. I grew up in Lutheran pietism, which was the first tributary, influenced by the Inner Mission movements of the eighteenth century. This spread from Germany to Norway and influenced my family of "warmhearted Lutherans" who settled in Northwest Washington, as well as Midwestern states. Yet I was also touched by the third tributary, and relationships that influenced my attending Moody Bible Institute, Seattle Pacific College, and Trinity Evangelical Divinity School.

As an example, at Moody in the late 1950s, movies were forbidden for those of us living on campus in Chicago. Since I had grown up without television and theaters in my rural area, this was no great sacrifice for me. Hollywood was described as *evil* in many chapel talks. Twenty years after I graduated, a lifelong Hollywood actor, himself a divorced former president of the Screen Actors Guild, defeated a Baptist Sunday school teacher in the presidential race and moved into the White House. He was supported by many in the evangelical subcultures I knew well. In that election I sensed that American ideology had triumphed over theology for many in the third branch of American evangelicals. There was less emphasis on the immediate return of Christ and a sense that the United States had a divine calling in the world as a "chosen nation" to act for God in the world, in some ways as Israel did in the past. A return of the manifest destiny theology still holds some evangelicals hostage today.

FOLLOWING PAUL THROUGH CITIES

In former times and in many places, people could call themselves "Pauline" by becoming experts on what Paul had written. It is my contention that what Paul *wrote* is only half the truth. I wish to add that we should also pay attention to what Paul *did*, especially since he only went to cities on his mission. In so doing, of course, we know we are seeing Paul through Luke's eyes, for his Eurocentric eyes doubtless shaped what he saw and reported.

Nevertheless, try a fresh look at his second journey for starters. Coming out of the ancient version of the "gospel and our culture" conference of Acts 15, we find Paul in Acts 16 in Philippi, a European city, a rather upper-class place, named for Philip of Macedon, the father of Alexander the Great. In that city was a sort of pre-Christian women's Bible study fellowship run by Lydia and others. Paul joined his ministry to that women-led group. Women there apparently did not keep silent or wear coverings on their heads. It is interesting to note that Paul did not require that, nor did he end-run Lydia's ministry with his own "better model." He also did not ask that the newly converted Philippian jailer, or other males, replace Lydia or her descendants in the leadership of this newly formed community of faith.

The story moves to Athens, the cultural hub of the Mediterranean for centuries, but no longer the political center. Paul seems to have taken a cultural approach in his ministry in Athens. He visited sculptures and ruins, went to Mars Hill where scholars met, and quoted Greek poets in his message. That was appropriate there, but as we know, not for Corinth.

Corinth was an economic city, a century past its glory and power. Paul worked in the marketplace as a tentmaker so he need not be dependent on others, a marvelous choice for that context in Acts 18. That church plant became a divided congregation after Paul left. He repeated his work-ethic model in Thessalonica, perhaps the smallest city he ever visited specifically for ministry.

Ephesus was another great port city with economic and cultural roles in the region. Like many "third-world capital cities," Ephesus combined roles and functions. Paul wanted to reach his own people, the Jews. He did so for three months by meeting with them in the synagogue, the very place where you find Jews. After three months he was evicted. According to Acts 19:8–10, he rented a *scholae* (a theater) for five hours a day from the fifth to tenth hour (11 A.M. to 4 P.M.). He used a dialogical, Socratic method to communicate the story of

God to his listeners. It was question and answers for hours every day. That was quite different from the rabbinic method Paul used with Jews later in Rome (Acts 28:23), where according to Luke he argued with Jews from morning to evening about the kingdom of God.

What is the point of all this? Apparently, Paul, the consummate urban evangelist and architect of the church in the urbanized Roman Empire, adjusted his message, his methods, and his meeting places in order to reach very diverse audiences of every city he visited. He seems not to have had a single pattern, or a "one size fits every city" approach. His model should inform our methods, message, and meetings today.

DISCOVERING THE HOLY SPIRIT AT WORK HISTORICALLY IN YOUR CITY

Remember Lewis Mumford's definition of the city, one of many to be sure, but instructive for its brevity: the unique office of the city is to increase the variety, velocity, extent, and continuity of human intercourse. Let's think a bit more about this idea of continuity from a theological point of view. Up to this point, this chapter has focused on the city as parish, by using images from history, sociology, and Scripture.

The Orthodox scholar Michael Oleksa has spent his academic and pastoral life opening up whole new visits on the Russian contribution to the theology of mission and to our understanding of the work of the Holy Spirit. His doctoral work was published based on long-forgotten letters back to Russia, but you can also access his work in his book *Orthodox Alaska: A Theology of Mission.*

Put briefly, Orthodox and Catholics split in A.D. 1054. Differences preceded the open split for centuries. Why the split? The Western church (Catholic) added one Latin word to the creed that Eastern Catholics, Lutherans, and others recite every Sunday. They added the concept that the Holy Spirit comes from the "Father *and the Son.*" The Eastern churches (Orthodox) did not accept this addition for at least two reasons: First, historic creeds should not be changed. Second,

Islam surrounded the churches of the East with their creed "God is One...." At the risk of oversimplification, let us try to explain a missiological difference in how one might live out the difference of these two views in the missionary situation. We will take Alaska as our example for the moment.

Suppose Roman Catholics, Presbyterians, or most evangelicals had come to Alaska first. Viewing the villages of Eskimos and Aleuts, among others, they would have striven to learn the many languages, translated the Bible, and preached Christ to unleash the saving work of the Holy Spirit. That's a classic Western approach to frontier missions.

By contrast, the Russian missionaries who came with the explorers and fur traders noticed something else in those same villages. They saw the annual whale hunts where a 20-ton animal would surface in the bay and say, "Come and get me," or something to that effect. So the people rowed out to harpoon the whale. The rules of engagement were clear. The whale must stay put and agree to die on the surface. If not, everyone goes hungry and dies. After towing the animal sacrifice onto the beach, the people eat, build buildings, light lamps, and eat vitamin A for another year. They believe their god delivered all this from the depths of the sea. In fact, the celebration concluded with a small offering of animal remains placed back into the sea as a thank-you to the god who had made that animal sacrifice for the people.

The Russians became aware of this yearly hunt and wrote letters back home about it. They reported what the Holy Spirit was already doing in those villages before they arrived. They described it and joined it. By contrast, they did not write to the denomination headquarters and ask for pictures of sheep so they could picture Jesus as God's lamb slain for the sins of the world. They knew the Spirit was already there, giving them glimpses of the biblical concept of the God who ultimately sacrificed the Son for the people. By going from village to village in effect saying "This is that..." they were able to fill out the doctrine, and the Russian mission gospel spread from western

Europe, across Siberia and as far south as San Francisco, where those Russian missionaries ran into Spanish missionaries.

Those of us living and teaching on the Pacific Rim and on the edge of the Asian perimeter world, where two-thirds of the population of this planet live, must reclaim this theological heritage. Orthodoxy may be unknown to most Western Christians today, and seems cultur-ally strange to many others, who think of it in terms of liturgical "smells and bells," robes, beards, or beautifully domed church struc-tures only. Yet at its root, orthodoxy is charismatic, with a non-bounded view of the Holy Spirit. Remember, orthodoxy is trinitarian, but the Holy Spirit does not operate within christological boundaries. Let us recognize that in spite of many external differences, at root, these different approaches are profoundly similar. Both can be found in our cities. Sadly, for the most part, they seem not to recognize each other in America today.

WORLDVIEW SHIFTS

As I attempt to read the world, I see massive shifts in global reality. If the nineteenth century was the British and the twentieth century was the American, the twenty-first century is the Asian or Chinese cen-tury. I see a shift from an Atlantic to a Pacific perimeter world, of which Pearl Harbor and the attack by the Japanese in 1941 seemed something of a harbinger. As mentioned previously, some 60 percent of the world lives in Asia, and about 40 percent in two countries of Asia, both urbanizing at a rapid rate.

In the Pacific Rim, China is now the third-largest Christian nation, close to passing Russia, the second-largest, and by 2040 may pass the United States and become the largest Christian nation in the world. So when they become the leading nation in the world economically, matching their overwhelming population, perhaps Chinese Christians will be influencing both internal and external policies. (By the way, by 2020, we also think India will have passed China, because they have no one-child policy, and they have a much stronger agrarian base to feed that crowd. China has approximately 23 percent of the world's people and about 7 percent of the world's agriculturally appropriate land.

This may sound un-American, but we must remember that God is not an American. God loves the whole world and does not have any one favorite nation. In 1900, more than 80 percent of the world's Christians were white. Today the facts have reversed; more than 80 percent of the world's Christians are nonwhite, non-Western. The frontier has shifted. I am not anti–missionary movement, even though this kind of talk usually sounds like it. What we have now is missions in reverse. One hour out of Dallas, a Nigerian Christian group bought 100 acres to set up shop so they could evangelize Texas. They are building a 10,000-seat church. America is now being evangelized by both Christians and other religions. We have become the target of missionaries from churches and other religions.

EMBRACING THE CITY AS A PARISH

The primary burden of this chapter has been to provide a metaphor and motivation for pastors, educators, mission personnel, and lay leaders to embrace the whole metropolitan city as a parish into which your church or your calling to leadership is taking place. We are suggesting that when you see a Methodist or Holiness church, you thank God for John Wesley's legacy, now almost three centuries long. When you see a United Church of Christ (UCC) congregation, you are viewing four streams of God's action, one of which is rooted in Jonathan Edwards. You may be Protestant, but your spiritual roots go much deeper into Catholic and other forms of earlier Christian mission. All of this is for better and for worse, of course. We are surrounded by "magnificent ruin," legacies of the Spirit's work long before we came to our city. Face it, Glasgow produced the first modern rescue mission in 1826, and London gave us the Salvation Army. We owe a huge amount to such organizations. Long before Promise Keepers arrived to give hope and reconciliation to stadiums filled with men, D. L. Moody and John R. Mott traveled around the entire world seeking to plant YMCAs to bring about the salvation of our great cities under the banner "Win the world in this generation." When you look at your Y today, you might not see Moody and Mott, those city evangelists, both white, male evangelicals, but together and individually they shaped the evangelical and ecumenical movements of our time.

In the next chapter, we will follow these themes further. We not only ask readers to see the city as parish, but in very specific terms, we want to focus on the discovery of what we call signs of hope in cities.

REFLECTIONS

1. Can you tell a member of your community of faith the history of your city? If so, have you? If not, what would you have to do to acquire the story of your city?

2. What personality does your city have?

3. What does the architecture in your city teach you that would be helpful in your ministry? Which tributary of evangelicalism does your church live within and how does that effect your ministry within your city?

4. How do you respond to the news that God is not an American and America does not hold favorite-nation status with Him?

5. Where is the Holy Spirit at work in your city?

Chapter 6

Learning the Signs of Hope in Your City

In the last few chapters we have endeavored to provide a rationale for looking at your city in fresh ways. To do so you must cultivate a conscious eye for what the Holy Spirit might be doing in your city. You need the discipline to see beyond the structures of church buildings as you walk or drive by them and to ask yourselves which biblical text might have shaped the ministry of that particular church in its founding.

To discover "signs of hope" within a city, we must become aware of the common grace within a city, the grace God uses to animate architects, artists, prophets, politicians, and preachers alike, surrounding them with teaching and learning tools mediated to us by people who left the scene of human history long ago.

When we gaze at a gorgeous mountain and see nature, we celebrate God as Creator and enjoy that creation. Our ideas about God come directly or immediately to us in nature. Human beings, in fact, have added little to God's natural beauty. On the contrary, we may have damaged that environment. By its very essence the city is an artificial artifact or by-product of human activity. God seems less immediate there. However, God is mediated in structures and things people have created and built. We know that all people are created in the image of God. We also know that the perfect image of divine creation has been damaged by sin. Even so, we can learn to be amazed at what creative people do. Classical symphonies as composed and performed sometimes overwhelm me. The first responders to fires and tragedies who put themselves at risk often put me to shame. The people who volunteer to tutor and invest in kids never cease to amaze me. All of these and many more are what I call "signs of grace" within the city.

DISCOVERING COMMON GRACE IN YOUR CITY

The classic phrase for these activities within a city is "common grace" as opposed to "saving grace." The book about the prophet Jonah describes the behavior of the sailors on a ship in the middle of a storm. What was their response to these circumstances? First, they called an ecumenical prayer meeting (Jonah 1:5) and "each prayed to his own god." Jonah slept through this prayer meeting but was discovered later to be the cause of their impending doom. Jonah's solution to the problem was suicidal. He suggested that he be thrown overboard.

Notice the attitude and behavior of these sailors who believe in many different gods. First, they confront Jonah with the fact that he was holding out on them, that it might in fact be his God who could solve the problem. Implicitly they were believers. That is not all! They wanted to save Jonah from his own fate. They recognized his God was authentic and was dealing with Jonah's unbelief. Still they tried to save their shipmate. They rowed very hard (Jonah 1:13). Earlier they had thrown the cargo overboard to lighten the ship. They had sacrificed their "profits" to save this "prophet." Finally they acceded to his request, not in anger or glee, and tossed him overboard. The text is clear. Those sailors became believers in the true God and made vows in worship to the God of Israel (Jonah 1:16).

Those of us in the city are called to live with people who may have no faith or strange faith. We must cultivate relationships of common grace to live and grow in the city. A healthy person needs a healthy family, and families develop best in healthy communities. We need an ecological theology with a renewed understanding that God is Creator and that the cultivation of a good city is our business until the consummation of His kingdom occurs.

Many Christians function as Unitarians in their common grace practice. Some have a strong belief in God as Creator but downplay that same God's redemptive work in Christ, or the sustaining work of the Holy Spirit on our daily path. Psalm 48 reminds us that God has an urban address. God is praised in the city of the great king, and God is the sure defense.

Parks, schools, libraries, courts, jails, streets, and government are paid for by tax money. The ministries of our churches and mission agencies are paid for by tithe money. But in truth, it is all God's money.

RECOVERING A THEOLOGY OF THE CITY

Theology needs to recover what was lost from the Reformation. The reformers recovered the doctrine of common grace that was paid by taxes. Calvin asked the leadership of his church to monitor the hospitals of his city to make sure the poor were being taken care of. The hospital was paid for by the taxpayers. It was a gift of common grace. While we have private hospitals today, we still have county and federal hospitals subsidized by taxes. These are common graces in our cities.

Common grace includes a transit system, a health-care system, an educational system, or a sewer system. The city is a gift of common grace. The reformers believed that your taxes paid for common grace while your tithe money paid for saving grace, i.e., the church and its mission. Yet both graces derived from God's resources. This is not liberal theology, as it is often called, but a thoroughly biblical theology that is like a great piece of music held together by its harmonies.

As I listen to evangelical mission and evangelism leaders speak about cities, I detect a theological difference that may be slight, but I think it's real. Some people have what they call a theology of the city, but instead it is a missiology of the city. They are interested in and committed to urban ministry because they now know that cities are where the majority of the world's unreached peoples can be found. Such ministers, including many of my friends, take all the passion and salvation texts in Scripture and apply them to the urban setting, usually with a good practical dose of contemporary strategy development for their launch into cities.

By *theology of the city*, I mean something more biblically comprehensive, one that sees the city as a gift of common grace for people needing transit systems, health-care systems, education systems and employment systems. Cities are gifts to people with specialized callings. Rural life is generalized; cities allow for specializations. In the more than 1,250 biblical texts on cities, we learn that cities function as extended families and beacons of light for populations of vulnerable people who need all kinds of services. Cities, like families, should be governed well. God has many expectations for cities, as he does for individuals, families, churches, and nations. People are created in the image of God. To see a well-run and just city is to see God, mediated by people living out their creative or divinely appointed heritage. Within that context, we can see that God's agenda for the city is much more comprehensive than the multiplication of church ministries within it.

Thanking God for Those Who Steward Power and Resources

The five great lakes on the borders of the United States and Canada contain 20 percent of the surface fresh water on the entire planet. One of the challenges for the great cities that surround these lakes goes beyond the exploitation of this resource for drinking and irrigation. We know that all life is precious. Like most people of good will, Christians go to great lengths to prevent prenatal damage to preborn children. The sanctity of life is important. Surely then it is no leap of faith to see that Christians should back clean-air ordinances in cities surrounding these lakes from which millions drink, so that toxic wastes don't get into that water system and damage future generations of unborn children.

LEARNING FROM JOSEPH, DANIEL, ISAIAH, AND ESTHER

Joseph

The story of Joseph (Genesis 37–50) is about a Hebrew boy sold into Egyptian slavery by his own jealous brothers. By the grace of God, this foreigner rose to governmental responsibility for the economy and lands of Egypt. According to Genesis 41 and 47, he bought all the land and moved people into cities. Then he organized the government to prepare for seven years of famine after years of prosperity. In fact, this godly man used the offices and instruments of a pagan pharaoh to feed most of the Middle East, including God's people from the land of Israel who came for the food. Was Joseph a socialist or capitalist? It's a wonderful Bible study discussion question. He seems to have been rather eclectic in practice. He used elements of both.

Daniel

Daniel is one of two books in the Bible that take place in what is today Iraq. Jonah went to Nineveh, some 400 miles north of modern-day Baghdad, to preach. Incredibly, the greatest revival recorded in the Bible is not in Israel but in the land of Assyria, which today we call Iraq. Violent people had destroyed the ten northern tribes of Israel, but were offered grace and salvation upon repentance.

Daniel served 80 miles south of Baghdad in the city of Babylon. Daniel models how it is possible to master a pagan society while rejecting that same pagan value system. That is tricky. He moved into the palace and lived his entire life serving the very king and government that had destroyed his own city and Temple and killed Israel's king and many people in three different invasions over 20 years (606–586 B.C.).

Daniel's prayer of worship is recorded at length (Daniel 2:20–23). Clearly he accepted a sovereign God at work in governments and behind all regime change. Paul speaks of seeing through a shadowy glass in 1 Corinthians 13:12. Daniel saw mystery and God at work in the ordinary and extraordinary work of governments and structures.

Isaiah

Isaiah gives us a unique vision of the Middle East. Living in Israel, he saw two nations that had made war against his country: Assyria on the east and Egypt on the southern border. To government officials who believed in the true God at that time, Isaiah shared a divine insight: God has an ultimate plan. God sees a day when all three nations will come together united by a common highway. Mutual traffic will bless all nations. Here is the ultimate insight in the Arab-Israeli conflict.

God is trinitarian in foreign policy. Notice the language: "In that day Israel will be the third with Egypt and Assyria, a blessing in the midst of the earth, whom the LORD of hosts has blessed, saying, 'Blessed be Egypt my people, and Assyria the work of my hands, and Israel my heritage'" (Isaiah 19:24–25).

Suppose now it is your task to be on a government negotiation team responsible for bringing about a just settlement to the Israeli, Arab, and Palestinian issues in the region. Christians working behind the scenes know how God feels about each of these peoples and nations. They are parallel and all chosen peoples. Peacemaking is always an art, but Christians called to government service have a wonderful ordination. They have access to structures that can implement common grace in all society.

Esther

Esther is unique. She entered a contest to be Miss Persia and won first prize; she moved into the harem and eventually became the replacement wife for a pagan king. Her uncle, Mordecai, helped her practice theological reflection, which is what all public servants are called to do when the way is ambiguous and God is not known or named directly. Esther was called by God, as many laypeople are, to access power and to amend a very unjust law, an official law that made the annihilation of the Jewish people a government policy.

Of course she achieved the goal. She descended into the "black hole" of Persia (read Iran today), and had the law changed. Had she not done this lay ministry, Nehemiah could never have gotten his grant and letter of credit and inaugurated his government-sponsored city development plan for Jerusalem. Nor could Ezra have rebuilt the Temple or reinstituted the spiritual life of Israel.

These two laypersons, both working inside and with the pagan government systems, made the clergy person effective, as is so often the case today. Churches in the city ignore government too often, until they need the police, the school, the hospital, the traffic light, the airport, or a zoning variance for their church's expansion or building project.

LEARNING FROM SYMPHONIES AND COACHES

Organizing ministry in a complex world-class city requires some remarkable new styles of leadership and often equally complex physical structures. The city is a 24/7 reality. Obviously the church needs day pastors and night pastors, working in teams that can go creatively up to the power and compassionately down to the powerless, and do so with the battered and broken and in many languages. How do we do that? How do we teach that?

Symphonies are complex organizations, performing a range of technically diverse music, ancient and modern, on hugely different genres of instruments. All acknowledge that gifted conductors are rare, and they are in huge demand, rather like the pastors of large, complex, urban, cathedral-like churches.

Orchestras have a music director, who is the principal conductor, but sometimes a guest conductor is invited in, who may work very differently with that same orchestra. One might build the discipline into the symphony so that its precision is crystal clear. However, the guest conductor comes in and evokes color and emotion from that same orchestra. Leadership matters, but often it takes more than one style, even complementary but different styles, to bring out the best in a symphony so that a centuries-old score sounds vibrantly contemporary and relevant today. What can seminaries and churches learn about leadership styles from symphonies?

Athletic coaching has evolved as the money for sports has escalated. No doubt stadiums and arenas have replaced sanctuaries as real worship centers for many urban populations. Perhaps you've noticed that head coaches seldom coach the team directly. There are exceptions, of course, but today sports are so specialized that position coaches do most of the real coaching in the trenches of the game. Practically every position has a specialist. The range of skills and demands on talent are amazing.

When building leadership teams for urban ministry, we are moving in similar directions. Pastors are vision casters. Most of the work may be done by specialists in worship and communication arts, abuse, addictive behaviors, counseling, community development, housing, or other specialized ministries. We can learn from models all around us.

Shifting Mission Field

In the early '80s the frontier of mission shifted. As an example we stated earlier, every year about 30 million people leave rural China headed for the cities. This number is similar to the complete population of Canada, which is about 32 million. Think about it: the whole population of Canada moving from one place to another each year. Mind-boggling!

For years now, missionaries and mission societies have been locked on to tribal settings and unreached people groups, as American missiles were locked on to the USSR even though that country had gone out of business years before. I began this drumbeat in the 1980s, and it was difficult for missionary organizations to hear it, much less march to its cadence. I still beat the same drumbeat all these years later, and it is still difficult for missionary organizations to hear.

A generation ago, missions were geographical. They were out there. They were foreign. Today missions are no longer for distant, geographical spots on the world map; instead they are culturally distant and within American borders. As we have said before, the nations live within the shadows of the spires of our churches.

For years now I have led students to study supermarkets and maverick malls. A maverick mall is an inclusive mall, deliberately designed to attract diverse kinds of audiences. What have supermarkets learned that the church hasn't? Diversity. A generation ago you shopped in small markets, which sometimes were simple mom and pop shops. They served up fruit, vegetables, meat, sugar (especially after WWII), flour, bread, and all the main staples. Today the supermarket carries a diversity of foods. Why? Because the folks making their food purchases today are diverse. Supermarkets stay open 24/7. Why? Because folks work different shifts during the day. Where you used to get one or two kinds of rice (white and brown), you now choose from a large variety of rice in your local supermarket. Often I take students into a supermarket, ask them to look around, and then we get together and talk about what they saw. After a tour of the supermarket we drop by a local church to find its posted meeting time for Sunday morning on its marquee. What's the message? You get religion on our terms. You get it when, where, and how we want to deliver it to you. So be here at 11:00 A.M. Sunday morning and we will share it with you.

What if we had 24/7 churches that stayed open all day and night? What if we had meetings at many different and varied times? What if we had day pastors and night pastors? What if the church was more like the urban supermarket, hospital, or police department? Churches need to take a good look at themselves and ask what supermarkets know that they don't.

What Maverick Malls Teach Us about City Ministry

In *Downtown, Inc.: How America Rebuilds Cities*, authors Bernard J. Frieden and Lynne B. Sagalyn describe how people like the late James Rouse came to design and build malls that increase the possibility of reconciling diverse peoples: black and white, rich and poor, locals and tourists. It is filled with fascinating case studies on Underground Atlanta and Inner Harbor, Baltimore, among others, and includes a chapter about a smelly old fish market a few minutes' walk from Bakke Graduate University in downtown Seattle. (For those who do not know, Pike Place Market is one of the premier tourist attractions in the Northwest and the "natives" love it, returning often.)

For several years now, we have taken our doctoral students from around America and the world on a stroll to that market. They enter two by two and emerge in an hour. More often than not, we must go and rescue them. It's an incredibly compelling environment. We then discuss some questions:

- Why does this mall work? It is, after all, a rather smelly place, with a bit of shabbiness here and there. Believe it or not, one of the design and operating principles is "slightly scruffy by intent."
- Why is this now the largest tourist attraction in the Northwest? That is a true statement. Space Needle, museums, gorgeous scenery abound on every side, but tourists come in droves to experience this market.
- Why do the locals hang around? Obviously the artists come, but so do the homeless and all manner of age and ethnic groups. No sign says, "We are inclusive," but all feel welcome.
- Why do different musical groups play in rotation all around the buildings? Clearly the mall welcomes a variety of musical languages. It is a sensate experience, both inside and outside.

We share with the students that when Seattle tried to get rid of this shabby mall years ago, one person had the vision to save it. His crusade paid off, but he had to confront city hall to do it. City government, like church government, is often shortsighted.

Learning from Maverick Downtown Malls:
A Worksheet

What would churches look like if we were as serious as the Pike Place Market in Seattle, Washington, about attracting diversity? Page 128 begins a worksheet with some thoughts and questions that I use when helping students exegete Pike Place Market.

Finally, consider also that athletic coaching and symphony conducting, like today's supermarket and maverick mall development, are almost always cross-cultural and complex institutional tasks. All should be obvious urban pastoral models for the church in a contemporary urban culture.

LEARNING FROM FOOD BUSINESS IN THE CITY

Exegeting a modern supermarket in any city or suburb today can be a phenomenal learning experience. Forty years ago stores opened in the morning and closed at night. They sold local or national brands. Then came 7-Eleven with the promise of opening as early as 7 A.M. and staying open until 11 P.M. They focused on convenience in selling food items, especially those things needed in emergencies at home. Now supermarkets sell international products and prepared foods, provide a bank and video rentals. We have a food mall, open 24/7. Appropriately, the management system pluralized. The dairy and some other divisions are outsourced and specialized. Managers work in shifts.

Walk a few blocks in each direction from most supermarkets in a city and you will find an amazing array of specialized food stores, from ethnic to mom and pop, all serving products in ways the big store cannot match. Obviously the supermarket has created the space for many others to specialize.

It does not take theological or mission students long to draw comparisons to churches, especially when they see the sign "Morning Worship: 11:00 A.M." in one language. "As it was in the beginning, will now and ever shall be, world without end, Amen" right?

To learn what food businesses teach, we ask students to reflect on a couple of obvious questions:

- How did that supermarket overcome the famous seven last words—"we never did it that way before"? Presumably, without the Holy Spirit to help.
- What could that church or other churches look like in this same community if we were as serious as those markets in serving those same populations?
- What barriers keep the church from doing what we all know it could do about it?

The last question is the most telling. Perhaps 90 percent of the real barriers to effective city ministry today are not in the city; they are inside the church. Our leadership and our people are unprepared or unwilling to risk. We are afraid that our denominations will label us liberal and/or cut our funding. We have learned by doing consultations in more than 200 cities around the world that this is a worldwide reality. Right motivation and right information alone will not change city ministries to bring about effectiveness. Something must be done about the intimidation issues, internal and external, to the leadership.

LEARNING FROM THE SLUMS

Several decades ago, Janice Perlman wrote *The Myth of Marginality*. She produced groundbreaking studies on slums in Brazil. She modeled a brilliant ethnographic approach to local communities, but the thesis of her work is embedded in the title of the book. It seems most middle-class Brazilians believed two facts about the urban poor, which turned out to be myths unsubstantiated by facts.

Myth #1. *Slum peoples are basically incompetent and unprepared for city living.* On the contrary, she found that these peoples were incredible organizers and could work together for long periods of time. They gathered boards, cardboard, and metal scraps; explored

sites for potential occupation; and organized their governing structures. Then, overnight, they could invade and occupy, build, sleep, and
eat. With no budget, they could create instant communities on city
land, doing it all while the government was asleep or not looking.
Whatever you may think of this, we don't call that incompetence.
Brilliant may be a better word!

Myth #2. *Slums drain public funds like parasites.* The truth turned
out to be totally different. Most of the new jobs in cities are developed
in these so-called slums. They are entrepreneurial to a degree that we
can hardly imagine, something microenterprise studies now reveal all
over the world.

Obviously migration presents challenges to cities. Nevertheless,
in spite of the obvious squalor and many other tragic realities, slums
worldwide are not the problem. They are indeed symptoms of much
deeper issues about land-title policies, health care, political conflict,
or economic issues. The point is not about them but about us. Rather
than react with the equivalent to "Isn't it awful?" we suggest you find
the community gatekeeper who can take you inside so you can see
"the signs of hope" within your city.

A SIGN OF HOPE IN CHICAGO: THE CHICAGO HIGHER EDUCATION SYSTEM

One of the signs of hope in Chicago is a collection of 12 seminaries in
the greater metropolitan area under the rubric of ACTS (Association
of Chicago Theological Schools). Other cities have similar educational signs of hope, such as the BTI (Boston Theological Institute)
and the GTU (Graduate Theological Union) in Berkeley. The beauty
of the ACTS system is that you can cross-register at any school to
take any course. Often a school will have one or two great professors,
which is a great gift to the whole educational community. You can
register for a course at a different seminary from the one you specifically attend and receive credit within your seminary for the course.
Corean used this system when she decided in 1984 to go to Northern

Baptist Seminary (where I was teaching and she had the spouse benefit of free tuition) for a master's degree in theology and again when
she moved into doctoral work for her doctor of ministry degree from
Chicago Theological Seminary. What a blessing! She was able to put
her own curriculum together using all the available seminaries. She
was able to build her own specializations out of the total curricular
offerings of all 12 seminaries.

This idea provided me with a watershed concept in my own teaching. I took a class of 20 students and we met on campus the first week
of the quarter, then at various other places within Chicago—city hall,
the top of a bank, a Catholic parish, a prison, or public housing. Each
of these was a mini-seminary where we learned what it had to teach.
In addition, I required my students to stay in my home for one weekend during the quarter so we could talk candidly about raising kids
and not being overprotective, not hemorrhaging emotionally in the
ministry, and various other ad hoc topics. We all know that environments are not neutral. When students live in campus housing, usually
in an up-market urban or suburban setting, and take courses only in
classrooms, they take away more than the course content. The
"medium is the message" as we all know.

A SIGN OF HOPE:
TURNING AROUND OLD URBAN FIRST CHURCHES

Turning around an old downtown "first church" is a "sign of hope"
within a city. Bakke Graduate University has chosen to locate in
a historic downtown Seattle church. First Presbyterian spawned 27
Presbyterian churches in the greater Seattle area, of which 19 still
remain. The first pastor, George Whitworth, founded the college that
bears his name in Spokane, but he also served in Washington state politics, led the Indian Affairs bureau, and helped to found the University
of Washington. One of his successors led the city to clean up the infamous "skid row" red-light district and championed the creation of
Harborview Medical Center, the public hospital through which King

County offers free medical care to the poor and indigent. Obviously George Whitworth and his famous successor, Mark Matthews, believed in *common grace* and *saving grace*, incorporating them both into their ministries in Seattle. Their legacies continue to bless the whole city today, including the suburbs of Seattle. Seattle, as most cities, is filled with landmarks, which when you scratch them, reveal evidence of designers who cared about us and others they never knew.

Old first churches became the Protestant equivalent of the Catholic cathedrals at city center. Each denomination planted a flagship church as close to the town square as they could get property. Old *firsts* were never local churches; they were regional from the start. Their members were "boulevard people, not side-street Christians." Power was concentrated downtown in the old days, and old first churches were chaplains to those in power. Those pastors met weekly with mayors, university presidents, and other civic leaders, often over lunches in the clubs reserved for the elite of urban communities.

Then cities changed. Power fled the city and town centers and old first churches resembled large beached whales when the tide went out. They were kept alive by endowments, often without many people. Every mainline denomination has them.

In the late '70s I received a small grant to set up my Lausanne Urban Office in Chicago (Leighton Ford ran *the* office in Charlotte) while I was still pastoring. During that time period, I began to research what could be done to turn around old first churches.

When I joined the faculty at Northern Baptist Seminary, which served some 1,500 churches in eight states around the upper Midwest, I was often invited to preach at the anniversaries of some of the old Baptist first churches and sometimes other denominations also. It is often easier to "run to the suburbs" than to salvage old first churches. I once preached in Cincinnati in an old first church, and as soon as I finished preaching, the congregation held a vote to close the church, sell the building, and relocate to the suburbs. In that case and in many others, I could see that pastors were often the key influencers in such discussions. In most cases, those pastors had no understanding of the

city center community and when they did, they had almost no experience in turning churches around in that environment.

Like medicine, law, or other business, ministry has growing specializations, and pastoring old first churches within the city center is
clearly a new specialization. It requires a strong historical understanding, a capacity to think biblically and theologically, a sense of symme-
try and perspective with the city as a whole, and a commitment to be
in dialogue with other churches in that city and in cities around the
country. Moreover, I also suggest that a first-church rejuvenator needs
to read widely in the emerging literature on business turnarounds.
Above all, those called to turn around old first churches need a strong
ego and sense of call, because there are no guarantees that they will
experience visible success, at least in the short term of a decade or
less, most of the time.

I finally convinced my friends at the National Ministries Board of
my American Baptist denomination to sponsor an "old first churches"
consultation and research process. We organized, I chaired a gifted
committee, and we set up the consultation in Pittsburgh. As part of
that process, I had the privilege to work with Dr. Sam Roberts, an
African American colleague who was then academic dean of Virginia
Union University School of Theology, a sister seminary to Northern
Baptist. Sam was a researcher with a strong social-science background who did the primary research for us. He designed the instru-
ment we used with 150 of the 650 old first churches we identified in
our denomination.

In that three-day consultation, we worked with the themes of history, first-church features, and their contemporary response. After the
consultation we studied the cases to see what we could learn from the
surveys we had gathered. We were amazed to discover eight things
one has to do in order to turn a dying old historic church into a live,
vibrant, growing church. Those became the chapter titles in my book
The Expanded Mission of Old First Churches, published by Judson
Press in 1986.

Just before this first-church consultation, I gave a series of lectures sponsored by the Oxford Centre in the summer of 1984. Riots had broken out in 20 of England's cities in previous years. In response the Archbishop of Canterbury convened a commission to hold hearings all around England about the churches in their cities. Their report, "Faith in the City," changed many things for Anglicans and others in England. About 20 of those commissioners signed up for my Oxford lectures, which were later put into print and published in England as *The Urban Christian: Effective Ministry in Today's Urban World*. A student and an urban missioner from Liverpool, Jim Hart, took copious notes, which became the foundation of that book. A year later InterVarsity Press published the book in the United States.

REFLECTIONS

1. What are your impressions about common grace and saving grace?
2. Which does your church spend the most time thinking and talking about? Why?
3. What did the small overviews of Joseph, Daniel, Isaiah, and Esther help you learn? How can you expand your study around those thoughts?
4. Take some friends and go exegete a maverick mall in your city. What did you learn about diversity? How can your church become more diverse in its city ministry?
5. What are some of the "signs of hope" in your city?

Should the church have a commitment to save the best of the old buildings?

The church: Add architectural historians to your church planning team.

How can we learn from international models (e.g., Tivoli in Copenhagen, Underground Atlanta or Inner Harbor, Baltimore, and James Rouse's reconciliation malls)?

The church: Expand our worldview nationally and internationally.

Commitment to partnerships. Notice how many organizations work and cooperate in the mall.

The church: Urban church ministry cannot be done in isolation from parachurch and other community organizations.

What new structures of decision making, funding, and communicating make each urban maverick mall project unique?

The church: Require adaptive policies or flexibility to changing environments and even seasons.

Multiple cultures and ethnicities are normal in Pike Place Market.

The church: If malls and schools can adapt, can the Holy Spirit help the church do this also?

The mall operating style expects crises.

The church: City pastoral ministry could hardly be more contrasting with traditional rural or suburban ministry. Crisis is a norm for us.

Pike Place Market had to overcome a negative community image, both real and perceived in the Seattle community. One University of Washington professor had the vision to save it.

The church: Urban pastors must understand that the major barriers to effective urban ministry are seldom in our cities. Rather they are in us, our churches, our denominations, and our mission agencies. Just as with Pike Place Market, a single pastor can make a difference inside and outside our churches.

Urban mall creators and directors have great political skills needed to mobilize community support.

The church: No question about it, this is a city pastoral skill set. "Politics is the art of the possible" by definition.

Patience. These city malls normally take much longer than planned to become successful.

The church: A decade of planning may be the norm rather than the exception.

They make deals with the city.

The church: A public, environmental, institutional, and common-grace theology must accompany our traditional salvation message.

Maverick malls are using new patterns of funding, like TIF (Tax Increment Financing) grants.

The church: May need to explore foundations and other options.

Pike Place Market is a blend of theme park, theaters, open-air plans, and parking options.

The church: We must opt for similar mixes in liturgical and pastoral strategies.

Pike Place Market is "slightly scruffy by intent." They want the local artists, vagrants, and street people to come. Local artists decide who is welcome. All have "a right to be here," said one Pike Place executive.

The church: Use inclusive arts, murals, music styles, banners, and architecture. Tourists love Pike Place Market because it is "untouristy." Note the raucous character of the maverick mall in contrast to the quiet, restrained, and correct atmosphere in so many of our churches.

Malls have learned how to serve low-income customers without turning away the middle class. Consider this summary statement of why Pike Place and some other maverick downtown malls work.

> The pulling power of Rouse's malls depends upon an intricate blend of light-hearted good taste and restrained but canny design that makes them fun. . . . The atmosphere was refreshingly honest in part because Rouse avoided many tasteless shopping center clichés such as Muzak, fountains, plastic plants and gimcrack fakery to evoke nostalgia. The formula is a mix of location, design, tenant mix and excitement.
>
> —From *Downtown, Inc.: How America Rebuilds Cities,* Bernard J. Frieden and Lynne B. Sagalyn, (Cambridge, MA: MIT Press, 1989), 204, 220.

The church: So-called "maverick developers" may be models for urban pastors.

Chapter 7

Crusades, Conferences, and Consultations

It's time to take our cities for Christ!" The city is a target for evangelists and evangelistic campaigns, and this is not a new idea. As we pointed out earlier, the apostle Paul "followed the contours of the urbanized Roman Empire." Paul knew cities were important to the spread of the gospel. It seems obvious to almost all leaders by now that cities are where the most people are, so they become the object for reaching masses of people.

Some religious groups focus their concern on the poor, while others opt to focus on the lost. The truth is, by a host of criteria, most of the lost are now the urban poor.

The whole idea of "taking our cities" or "target group" thinking creates conflict in the mind of many, if not most, city pastors or leaders of specialized ministries. The image of "taking" connotes battle-ready troops ready to assault or "take the hill." For these pastors the military image doesn't square with the idea of incarnation, the One who became flesh and lived among us.

For others, the phrase "take the city" seems to imply that there is no church in the city and the taking must come from the outside. The assumed audience of this concept is usually outsiders who come in with a solution to the city and take little time or effort to join those already present in the city or even to learn how God is presently working in the city.

STRATEGIES FOR URBAN ENTRY

City pastors will recognize the following description. The phone rings and you receive an invitation, along with dozens or perhaps hundreds of other pastors, to a special breakfast in a major downtown hotel. The purpose is to hear how God will do a new thing in your city next year. A major organization has identified your city as a special place where God plans to work. Pastors show up to hear all about it, and the dates of the event are announced. You hear testimonies and know this will be good for your city. You hear the old drumbeat that "church participation is critical for the success of the event."

When you look around the room, one thing is immediately clear. The outside organization has leveraged their power to call insiders to the meeting. All kinds of diverse networks show up. Young pastors look around the room and know they don't have the power or sheer chutzpah to approach those insider senior pastors and learn from them. The room is full of individuals trying to figure out what their church will get out of participation with the outsiders' events. Younger pastors and older pastors usually don't engage in mutual strategic planning. More than likely the older ones will not engage in planning or gift sharing because they are asked to agree to work on the agenda of the outside group producing the event. Some pastors within the city just don't show up because they are so jaded by the regularity of such experiences. The meeting concludes, and while driving home you hear that the "deal" is done, and some organization is coming to your city for a great crusade. Now you have to sell it to your people.

In this oft-repeated scenario, we are implicitly told that the agendas some pastors were praying and working on are probably not important and won't happen. We have been taught to be good soldiers, and because we need to survive in our community of faith, we join the crowd.

Another scenario comes from denominational mission executives: "Our denomination's missions department has been asked to plan an urban or specialized track for a major international event, which we have decided is genuinely strategic. So we are writing (or calling) you as a mission executive who has gifted colleagues working in the field, and asking you to contact them about this opportunity. We know they could add a great deal. We want nominees or experts to read a paper, speak, or lead a workshop."

That mission executive may be the most gracious leader in the world, but soon the event planners hear something like this: "You know I really respect you, and I believe this could be a truly significant international meeting. But I must tell you that if I give you these names and permission to invite them, they will write me immediately and ask for funding so they can go."

Or the tension rises in this response: "You know, we have five international conferences or congresses this year, including the one our own organization is planning. All of them are asking for my people and my budget commitment."

Or you may hear a quiet response of resignation: "The only way some of these organizations know how to justify their existence is to hold expensive international meetings."

The late Ed Dayton of World Vision was full of aphorisms, including: "A point of view is a view from a point." To react negatively to the obvious through veiled frustrations of that city pastor at the hotel breakfast, or to the hard-pressed global mission executive, misses the point. From their perspective, all these good intentions and outside gifts frustrate rather than facilitate their perceived calling and, in many cases, previously announced commitments.

CRUSADES

Modern evangelistic crusades have been identified in America, and throughout the world, with Billy Graham since 1948. Though he did not invent the model, city ministries specifically and the church globally, will be blessed forever because of the faithfulness, effectiveness, and integrity of Billy Graham. I acknowledge that. Yet the very mention of "crusade" evokes anger in Middle Easterners with long memories. Candidly, *crusade* is a word that has probably outlived its usefulness, whether used by churches or governments.

Evangelistic crusades are fundamentally event-driven. When they are planned and executed, they have the capacity to grab the whole church, symbolically if not actually, for a small moment in time. Small, scattered, and battered Christians do need to feel big sometimes. Honest studies of such events over the years may reveal that while the goal was to reach many outsiders or nonbelievers with the gospel, the larger benefit was the unity it brought to the churches in a common witness.

While many have wished Graham might have been more prophetic at times, we should never underestimate the social benefits of such events, both intended and inadvertent. For example, President Clinton spoke about and to Billy Graham at his first presidential prayer breakfast soon after his first inauguration in 1992. He reminded the audience that Graham had come for a crusade in Little Rock, Arkansas, when Bill Clinton was 12 years old. His Sunday School teacher took Bill and his class to hear Billy Graham. Meanwhile, the White Citizens Council had asked Billy Graham to segregate the stadium to keep blacks from whites in the choir and the congregation. He refused. All his public meetings, choirs, and platforms would be integrated. The President testified that the impact was so significant on him personally at the age of 12 that he sent small offerings to Graham for years after that.

Broadcasting or Narrowcasting?

Another theological paradigm shift came out of the Chicago meeting in 1971 with the Billy Graham team. I realized that between 1964, when Graham first came and filled Soldier's Field, and 1971, something had changed. Television was now prominent in the crusade. I realized that those in attendance were like a present *Oprah* show. We were the studio audience. Billy was not only talking to the folks within view, he was now speaking to a much larger audience, so he spoke into the camera to the multitude of folks watching in the comfort of their homes, places of business, hotels, and so on.

In 1971 the Chicago Billy Graham crusade was held in McCormick Place. I watched all the suburban types who fled the city years before come back into the city for the crusade. What kept going through my mind was the phrase from John's Gospel, "The Word became flesh and dwelt among us" (John 1:14). I thought we were losing the Vietnam war for the same things I was witnessing within this crusade. In Vietnam we had decided to wage an air war, where bombers came from a distance and dropped their payload. At the same time we pulled out the ground troops. I realized the same thing was happening in evangelism. You pull out the ground troops and move them to the suburbs. Then you rent a building and turn on the TV cameras and everyone watches from afar. They see both Graham and the audience. However, the real audience is not the live folks in the arena. The real audience is the invisible people sitting in myriads of places watching their televisions. This is the exact opposite of incarnation.

Is evangelism the message (i.e., Jesus saves)? Or is evangelism a method, like the incarnational way in which Jesus reached His world? Jesus spent lots of time with a small group of people. This led me to an understanding that to reach the city, one had to focus on *narrowcasting* versus *broadcasting*. This was a huge shift in my thinking. In Any City, USA, folks read the same newspaper and watch the same TV stations; they are reached by broadcast, from the typesetter to the telecaster. I began to see that in the city we needed to focus on a narrowcasting medium. The bigger the city, the narrower the focus; the more personal and relational evangelism must be. This is the reverse of the way folks think, which is big city, big meetings, and big strategies. But the opposite is true: the bigger the city, the smaller the focus. By putting all our emphasis on broadcasting, we lose cities at the cost of millions of dollars, under the delusion that we are reaching a large group of people. Nothing could be further from the truth.

The years 1970 through 1972 were real yeasting years for me. As I sat in the 1971 Graham meeting in Chicago, I had no dream of consultations, but I did begin to think about how outsiders carried a tremendous amount of power when they came to the city, and how that all needed to change. However, I didn't have a clue how to do it or know that I would eventually be involved in the process.

After that crusade experience, I requested that a group of seminaries in Chicago allow me to prepare a course whereby the city of Chicago would become a laboratory in which we would turn students into detectives who, with a large amount of curiosity, would discover what was happening in the city as a way to bring the gospel to the city in a different way.

This is similar to the idea of "best practices" in business schools. I was unaware of anyone in the religious community using this concept at the time. A best practice in business management is a generally accepted "best way of doing a specific thing." Best practices are formulated after specific business or organizational case studies are examined to discover the most widely effective and efficient means of performing a function or organizing a system. Best practices are disseminated through academic studies, popular business management books, and "comparison of notes" between corporations. This term became popular in business and professional management books starting in the late 1980s with its most famous proponent, Tom Peters, in the book *In Search of Excellence*.

CONFERENCES

While crusades may be event- or calendar-driven, conferences are product-driven. The inviters have planned a benefit for customers. We are all familiar with conferences of many kinds. It is the age of specialization, after all, and there is no end to varying conference styles and content. We participate in many and have all benefited from them. Yet we all know the rules about conferences: we pay for the product, and the platform controls the agenda. Conferences come in all sizes for all ages and both genders these days. Traditionally, denominations hold regional or national conferences. Some denominations, in fact, have the word *conference* in their name. Conferences can be hierarchical in nature or they can be a gathering of ministry networks functioning as trade associations. Others use *congress* to label the event, but generally they are all the sponsor- and platform-driven events with which we are all familiar.

CONSULTATIONS: WHERE DID THEY COME FROM?

The idea of consultation began to germinate over the years as I found myself attending crusades and conferences in which "outsiders" came to town, in this case Chicago, to show those of us ministering in the city what their organization could do for us. During the 1971 Billy Graham crusade recruitment breakfast at the Hilton Hotel, I remember thinking, *I wonder what it would be like if Billy Graham (or Bill Bright or Bill McCartney or Bill Gothard) came to town and asked, "Could I bring my team here to your city and learn from you how to reach the lost in your city?"* But alas, it never happened.

I often fantasized about this concept during these crusades or conference planning and recruitment meetings, as I looked around a room filled with area pastors, some from large churches pastoring important people in our city, like the mayor or other city officials, and others from small churches who were just pastoring common folk as I was. I was young and only beginning my pastoral journey and never had the strength to speak out in such an auspicious group and ask why they always brought their agenda from outside to tell us what God was going to do in our city.

The power of the outsider is that he or she gets to set the agenda, whether they are from a large organization such as the Billy Graham Association, or representing a smaller organization. I began to realize that these crusades were usually event-driven. I asked myself, "What if there was a process in which we could teach each other what we were doing and learning?"

Later, out of those experiences in my early days, a model evolved for working *in* the city *with* those who ministered. Both World Vision and the Lausanne Committee liked this new model, and we decided to call it *consultation*. A consultation is a time when the churches in the city get together to discover each other's gifts and the signs of grace God is already doing in their cities.

The plan I created, done in cooperation with World Vision and the Lausanne Committee, included planning cycles that kept Corean and me on the road internationally for three months each summer. We provided consultations for an average of 20 cities a year, often on two or three continents. Dr. Sam Wilson, who headed up the MARC unit at World Vision, led our organizing team, and usually traveled ahead of us to the cities we would visit after my regular teaching assignments ended at Northern Baptist Seminary. Sam had a PhD in urban sociology from Cornell University and had served in Peru as a missionary for 11 years. We had a great partnership with Leighton Ford, Billy Graham's brother-in-law, who chaired the Lausanne Committee for World Evangelization, and with Ed Dayton, a senior leader of World Vision.

WHAT IS A CONSULTATION LIKE?

In those days a consultation usually lasted about three days. We requested that ministers and ministries in the city gather case studies about churches and other ministries in their city so that before we arrived in the city where the consultation was held, we could begin the process of understanding what was already happening there. Day 1 of the consultation consisted of the whole gathered group examining all the case studies that had been collected and learning from them where God was already working in their city. Day 2 was spent visiting these ministries to help the attendees process what a specific ministry was doing. You can see it on paper, but you also need to see it in action with your own eyes. When we returned that evening to a central meeting room, we interacted with the group, asking them what they had seen and learned. These sessions were amusing at times. These pastors and ministry leaders thought I was brilliant, but all I was doing was helping them teach each other what they had discovered themselves. These discussions generated great excitement as they began to see their city differently. They saw things God was doing about which they were totally unaware. One of the biggest concepts they discovered was that it was really okay to have more than one kind of church, one kind of worship, and one kind of pastoral strategy in their city.

I began this process believing that all I had to do to help these folks was provide them with the necessary information and some motivation to accomplish what they needed to do in their city. I thought, *If they just had the correct information and motivation, they could turn their city around.* About 50 cities into the process, during a visit to Cairo with 50 pastors from different denominations, I had my eyes opened about my presupposition.

During one of the Cairo sessions, the participants were asked to define the ten barriers to effective ministry within their city. I asked them to talk about how these ten barriers might be at work in their city. One group of pastors sitting in a corner of the room began to laugh. I walked over to inquire what they were laughing about. They told me they were too old to cry, which I thought was an interesting answer to my question, so I inquired further, "So tell me why you want to cry?" They told me that the exercise had helped them discover that the ten barriers were not in the city but in their churches, every last one of them. They realized Cairo was not the problem; Cairo's churches were the problem. That was an "A-ha!" moment for me.

We have all read or heard about the seven last words of the church: "We've never done it that way before." What I learned that day was that no amount of right information or motivation could get the job done. Why? Because the pastors were intimidated by their own church congregations, which might think them silly and send them packing; or by their boards, which might think them crazy and cut off funds for favorite projects; or by their denominational leaders, who might frown on doing something radical and blacklist these pastors from climbing the denominational ladder. I heard these fine ministers say things such as, "Our bishop would never let us do that." "Nobody would fund that." "Seminary did not prepare me for this." As I analyzed their responses on that warm day in Cairo, I discovered that all the barriers being voiced were, in fact, internal ones from within the framework of the church, not from the structure of the city of Cairo.

In October 1984, I took my research public. I wrote an article for the *International Bulletin for Missionary Research* (IBMR) entitled "Urban Evangelism: A Lausanne Strategy since 1980." In the article (p. 154), I suggested that 85 to 90 percent of the barriers to effective ministry are inside the church, not outside. Here are some of the common barriers as I presented them in that article:

1. The lack of organized prayer for the city.
2. The lack of properly trained leaders: lay or clergy.
3. The lack of vision, motivation, or burden for the lost on the part of the majority of evangelicals.
4. The rural mentality of churches and pastors.
5. The failure to use the opportunities we do have for witness.
6. The ghetto existence of Christians, and the loss of non-Christian contacts.
7. The lack of cooperation among churches.
8. The busy lives of Christians compounded by many church meetings.
9. The generation gap. Existing leaders are over 55 years old. Emerging leaders are still younger than 30, but no leadership in church or society was between 30 and 45.
10. The lack of appropriate buildings or facilities.

Not much has changed! Today, I would make that number well over 90 percent. This created quite a buzz then, as it does now.

Consultations: A Process-Driven Focus

Everyone is familiar with consultants. In this age of rapid change, outside gifts are on call to insiders. We use the word *consultation* to describe a process-driven focus. Of course, consultations are still events, but the center of gravity of the event and the starting point is the city itself. An outsider may be called to help form the agenda, and the event is controlled, and hopefully financed, by those inside the city.

Community or city entry should begin by creative and intentional listening. Leaders who lead many other leaders are asked to identify their own favorite ministries. Everyone has favorites. When a group is asked the simple question "Where would you take me to see that God is alive in this city?" predictably, a huge array of responses follow. If we continue with that tour metaphor, the outsider will be taken to all sorts of places, people, and programs that many others in that same room did not know existed. Inevitably you will see people taking notes. Put simply, they have already begun to teach each other about their own city.

Perhaps we can arrange to follow up that initial meeting with an announced tour of some previously identified "signs of hope" in that city. Another variation on that might be to ask, "Could someone take a camera around to those places, so we could produce a CD or video that could be shown in all our churches to our new- and not-so-new members classes. Wouldn't this be a great way to share with each other what we are learning in our own ministries?"

Some might also suggest that we organize a tour for church leaders, perhaps on the weekend when many others may be available. Still others may wish to bring these ministry models and leaders together for a day or more for mutual encouragement.

We know from years of watching cities, that some of these people are the "Michael Jordans of ministry" in their context. They have invented programs to reach their communities and created ways to fund them, or structures and how to build them, or ways to "scratch people where they really itch" in the name of Jesus. What I have discovered in this process is that some of these people have never analyzed or taken the time to reflect on what they do or what they have learned. Professors at Bible schools and seminaries need to be exposed and then teach what these urban practitioners are learning about ministry in their many different contexts and denominations.

We know that some of the world's best athletes make terrible coaches. There is an old expression: "When the tide goes out, each shrimp has its own puddle." So it is with many leaders of urban ministries. They are reimagining, even reinventing the church in significant ways, but have no access to the networks where it can be shared. This is where professors and teachers come into the picture.

Consultations, then, are processes rooted in relationships across the city. They connect the powerful with the powerless, and people of need with people of resource. Likewise they connect people who have learned by experience with professors who are instilling the next generation of emerging leaders with the need to learn. This is all about turning cities into labs.

WHO ATTENDS CONSULTATIONS?

Senior pastors usually don't attend consultations. Instead, usually senior associate pastors or assistant pastors attend. A senior pastor will come to an executive meeting with other senior pastors. I guess birds of a feather do flock together. They do not attend because either they want to protect themselves from being used by outsiders, or they think the consultation will be a waste of time. What is their disease? They see themselves as givers and not receivers. Listen up, senior pastors! Your urban ministry depends on your ability to see where the culture is going and getting in lockstep with it. Consultation may help you in this area. Are pastors being helped by consultations? Yes! We know this because of the testimonies we receive that describe how their paradigm of ministry in the city has changed.

SOME LINGERING ISSUES

By now we hope you see that outsiders can be gifts of grace to insiders if they come without a prepackaged agenda for the city. They can be neutral conveners. Real partnerships have never been more valued or needed, be they local-global or city-suburban. In nearly every city now, God seems to be graciously providing neutral bridge builders to bring us together, so we can teach each other what God is teaching us.

Furthermore, we all know now that mission is in the migrant streams to, in, and from all six continents. We cannot really do our ministries locally in most cities without the capacity to connect with our newest neighbors. The local city church is often the global church. So we need people to set tables of resources, and then call us to sit and learn together. Doing that both sensitively and competently must be one of the highest callings in city ministry.

What most outside organizations have is "power," but that is precisely what many insiders, like our frustrated city pastors, laity, or mission executives, feel they lack in contemporary situations. Some see both triumphalism and paternalism in outside organizations, or even in church leaders who enter the city to "plant" their own stuff. Others see such approaches as flat-out racist. How often have you heard the complaint, "They didn't care about this community for 40 years, and here they are all of a sudden with a 'miracle cure' for our spiritual ailments. In fact, when we moved in, they took their church and business and left. Now their kids moved back in, so they want to return." They may not be the exact folks who left us, but they are the new "pharaohs that know not Joseph." It's another common experience, but it evokes bitterness instead of blessing for many.

Modern organizational gurus remind us that this is the information age. To survive, every organization should be a "learning organization." After listening to hundreds of urban workers in many cities over the years, some great suggestions have emerged. We should all be in a continuing educational model of ministry as we continue to listen in dialogue with each other.

Women have emerged as the signs of hope in most of the cities we know about. It seems that the more violent the community, the more necessary it is that women lead. Gangs, as we know, are not the problem. Like the temperature in the body, gangs form as a visible sign that something has gone wrong in a community. They "turf" to control their space when all other mediating institutions cease to exist. We know that women cut right through to the core of problems. Their vulnerability is their power. Male church leaders often threaten emasculated men in such communities. Unless we learn to follow these women, we might as well write off these communities for evangelism or church ministry.

Consultations require relationships, and the best relationships create sustainable partnerships. Another phrase from the late Ed Dayton of World Vision comes to mind: "God can do great things if we don't care who gets the credit."

Up to this point we hope you have noticed that a theory of cities and a theology of ministry work together to benefit ministries within a city. With St. Dominic we affirm that ministry is "loving God with our minds," while at the same time we affirm with St. Francis that ministry is "faith in action." So we have tried to provide academic thought with a desire for action on the part of the reader to work within their cities with a newfound paradigm.

We now switch gears as Jon takes over the remaining chapters of the book. First, he will share his journey from Index to Seattle. Then he will give us a view of the spirit of a consultation facilitator and take us through the what and how of facilitating a consultation in your city.

REFLECTIONS

1. Do you agree or disagree with the overview of crusades and conferences? How do you agree or disagree?
2. What are your thoughts about narrowcasting and broadcasting?

3. How many of the barriers to effective ministry are in your church? Is your percentage close to my prediction?

4. If you are a senior pastor, what would be the reason(s) that you would or would not attend a consultation?

Chapter 8

Index to Seattle: My Journey to the City

An engineer blows his whistle as the train moves along the tracks, pulling a long line of boxcars on its journey through the Cascade Mountains, past lonely little towns and winding rivers and the snow-capped peaks of the Pacific Northwest. Some of the towns the train rolls by are barely a whisper anymore, but they were once thriving communities built around logging companies and mining operations that spread throughout the green, wooded valleys of cedar and fir. Kids used to stand in the schoolyard and wave at the engineers, brakemen, and hobos as the trains rushed past. Mothers stopped to notice too, before going back to the laundry they were hanging on their clotheslines.

This idyllic setting was shattered one day when the railroad inspectors showed up at our school and talked to us about a serious crime occurring in our schoolyard. They suspected that some of us were the culprits! My schoolmates and I used to stand in the schoolyard and throw rocks at the trains, thinking it was great to have a moving target! I guess we didn't fully comprehend that migrants (we knew them as hobos in those days) were riding in those boxcars, and that our rocks could have been deadly. For a little kid in a small town, this was one of my first introductions to the reality of the poor being real people, not just passing images of despair.

Little did I know that one day my life would be given to help bring healing to the cities those wandering rail riders were trying to escape. All these years later, I'm able to look back and see the winding road that brought me out of the mountains and down into the city, far from the place where I grew up, and I'm amazed at the journey. Having a lifetime rearview mirror sheds light on how we arrived at this present space in our lives and the environments that shaped us. Parents, siblings, cousins, uncles, aunts, teachers, coaches, friends, rivals, and our communities: they shape our lives. How did we get here?

MOUNTAINS TO CITIES

Although we eventually ended up in the cities, Ray and I were both raised in rural settings. We came from valleys where little towns were built along the railroad tracks that dotted the highway. I was born in Albany, Oregon, in 1950, and moved with my parents, my brothers and sister and three cousins to Index, Washington, in 1953, where my parents, Cameron and Medora, and my Aunt Laura Mae Mooney purchased Garland Mineral Springs.

Garland Mineral Springs was a mountain resort with a rustic old hunting lodge and a row of neat little cabins all built around bubbling mineral springs. My parents had long dreamed of owning a place like Garland, a place that would serve as a "retreat unto the Lord," and so I watched as they sacrificed everything they had in order to found this Christian retreat center that could minister to "any and all who would come."

My dad always described our home as "living in the heart of the Cascades," the range of mountains running through Washington State. Growing up at Garland, my house was a 33-room hunting lodge built during the prohibition days, and the 40 acres of property that surrounded us was my playground—endless acres of mountains and woods and streams. Even though the setting was ideal, the constant flow of people was often overwhelming. I found myself surrounded by guests, the resort staff, friends, cousins, and others just needing a place to be loved and accepted (my parents often took in all kinds of young people in need of a loving environment, or even alcoholics needing a "dry place" to recover). Although there were times I resented the intrusion into my life, growing up in the middle of this thriving Christian retreat center and witnessing the ministry that took place there helped shape my own concepts of ministry, service, and what it means to provide both love and rest for others in desperate need of help.

JESUS HAS A BIG TENT

Groups of all kinds flocked to our retreat center each summer, aching to breathe the mountain air and soothe their bodies in the warmth of the hot springs. As each new group arrived, I watched them with interest and then I withdrew into my world as my parents became busy with the Herculean task of meeting each guest's needs. I remember feeling that I didn't really have a home like most people, with a nuclear family and the sanctity of my siblings and my parents, but that I had to share my life with hundreds of other people. However, moving unnoticed through the crowds, I learned in those years to listen to the groups, to observe them, and to enjoy the variety of Christian expressions I witnessed: the Pentecostals jumping up and down and praising God, the Christian Reformed elders enjoying their Christian liberties—smoking cigars and discussing theology—the holiness groups committed to prayer and the avoidance of Christian liberties. These images were burned into my heart and mind. At an early age I learned that Christians came in different packages. Little did I realize this was my preparation for a lifetime of embracing Christians from every segment of the church.

The mix of people, a wide variety of religious expressions, and the ebb and flow of my early life is the very ground God uses to help me live and minister in large urban environments today. Within the urban context, people and places are constantly facing contrasting ideas, cultures, and systems, competing for the same space. The idea of "one size fits all" does not work in the city.

CHAOS AND CHARACTER

We had many devastating experiences during my childhood years, but when you are young you don't often realize these events are unusual. When I was four years old we were "snowed in" under a white blanket of six feet of snow. My uncle couldn't make contact with us and called the sheriff's office, which sent in the National Guard to rescue us. Our family was featured on the front pages of Seattle newspapers as a "rescued wilderness family." When I was ten years old a major flood ripped through our property and destroyed most of our resort grounds, filling our lodge with several feet of mud. When I was eleven, our beloved lodge burned to the ground, and we lost almost everything we owned. Fortunately we were taken in by the good folks of the nearby town, Index. Within a few months we returned to our property and lived in our small resort cabins along the wild river. During this time we might as well have been living in the nineteenth century, as we had to go to the creek every day to get water for cooking and toilets. Many years later reflecting on the chaos of my young life, I realized God was outfitting me to do my best work where chaos and crisis situations were evident. Today's urban global realities, driven by the travel-information phenomena, offer this chaotic environment twenty-four hours a day!

LESSONS FROM SMALL PLACES

We lived thirteen miles beyond the little town of Index, so to get to school we had to travel down a long, treacherous gravel road that wound through the woods beside the river. We often found ourselves dodging logging trucks, tourists, and county road crews on our daily run to town. Sometimes it was an education just trying to get to the place where our education was supposed to occur. Drivers often ran off the road and up onto the ridges of gravel as they tried to dodge a logging truck on the way to the mill, or they got stuck in a ditch, or even worse, down in the river. Thirteen miles of road, five days a week for eight years, tucked between siblings, cousins, and friends, gave me plenty of time to observe the behavior of others and of course to think about my personal journey.

Mabel Steinman was a visitor at our retreat and had the misfortune of being our requisitioned driver of the day (my parents had a way of putting everyone to work). On that particular day Mabel was given the keys to my aunt's new DeSoto and started off down the road with great zeal. As we neared our destination, the left tire of my aunt's new DeSoto hit a gravel ridge, and Mabel, our fearless driver, literally threw up her hands and yelled "Oh no!" as we flew off the road and rolled completely over and down into the gully. We all survived, but within a few short days my brother Cameron honored that straight stretch of road with the new name "Steinman's Straightaway." It was a miracle that we lived through all the automobile spinouts and breakdowns, and all the long walks home after accidents. Mabel's story represents a long list of folks who found their way into our lives and became the grist for object lessons on life. Mabel's story reminds me to not just let anyone take the wheel when the mission is important and lives are at stake. Any organization or movement can veer off course and go into a roll when an ill-equipped leader under pressure throws their hands up, and exclaims, "Oh no!"

My school in Index, Washington, was a little two-room building that served as the "academic fount" for our area. The school only had two rooms: a small room and a larger one. Graduating from the little room to the big room was a huge deal! Two teachers governed the 20 or so students (on a good year). It seems all our teachers came from teacher's colleges in North or South Dakota, and I'm sure they found our little school district a last resort in their occupational placement. My sister Janis, my cousins Ray, John, and Barbara all attended this little school for eight years in a row. Although Ray, John, and Barbara were cousins, they were really more like brothers and sisters at the resort. We have many common stories to tell from those two rooms! For some reason the local folks of Index took pride that their little school was also an independent school district, and I'm sure the smallest in the state. We always felt as if we lived at the end of the road.

We had challenges, being from a small town with few resources, but we learned to work around them. We learned to play tackle football on a rock-filled field behind the school where we had to keep one eye on the trains as they rumbled by on their way over the mountains. In the little concrete gym we learned to shoot baskets with missile-like flat shots to avoid hitting the low-lying rafters! As meager as they were, the gym and the field became my relief from hours of boredom in the classroom, and sports became the arena where I found my role models.

I remember when my brother Curtis came home from college in San Francisco and brought me a bat signed by San Francisco's incredible hall-of-fame baseball player, Willie Mays. At that point I became a Giants fan. I was never able to watch the Giants play, because they were so far away, but I soon found local sports heroes as well. Since we couldn't get any television reception in our remote mountain home, we listened to radio despite our spotty reception as the airwaves bounced off the mountains. I remember being glued to the radio as we listened to Seattle University's legendary all-American Elgin Baylor as he led his school's team to the NCAA basketball finals. I lay awake at night dreaming of flying through the air like Elgin Baylor, with a basketball in one hand, and then slamming the ball through the basket as the crowd roared.

It didn't occur to me in those days that my chosen sports heroes were African Americans. The youth of the '50s and '60s in the Seattle area virtually grew up outside the racial conflict taking place in most of the urban centers of the United States. It wasn't until the '70s that many of us became aware that our own racial insensitivities were due to a lack of engagement. It is easy to think you are not racially insensitive until you actually live and work with others from another race or culture. I remember a friend telling me once that he has the most unity with those he keeps at a distance! Knowing the emotional pain we all experience as we cross racial and cultural barriers makes me appreciate those early black athletes who crossed the color barriers in a hostile environment. Building holistic ministry in the city requires building meaningful relationships with those from diverse cultural backgrounds and being willing to be uncomfortable when others don't understand your culture or make assumptions about your journey. Being one in the spirit is hard work!

From primary school days all the way through my time at university, I pursued sports as a way to fulfill my dreams. Sports coaches became my models as they instilled an attitude of perseverance, hard work, determination, and competition within me. I remember Coach Clifton in particular. He had been an All-American basketball player and came to our little town for his first coaching job. He knew what it took to play at a high level of competition. He trained us well, and finally took our little country team to within one game of the state tournament.

The first night of our district play-offs, we were defeated by a superior team, which later became state champions. After that game Coach Clifton left notes in our lockers instructing us that we were a group of sorry losers, and that we didn't know

Being one in the Spirit is hard work!

how to pull ourselves up and do what it took to win. That day we determined to fight back and we reached for that 110 percent effort to re-enter the tournament, and did quite well. Coach Clifton instilled a new toughness in us.

Sports provided me with incredible lessons about teamwork and determination that helped shape who I am today. Cultural icons in every neighborhood, whether it be coaches, teachers, pastors, or youth pastors, shape who we become. They provide the ground for our life lessons. However, the sports world wasn't the only place I found role models and learned life lessons. I was also blessed to meet some incredible saints of God at an early age.

ROOTED IN THE SPIRIT

I cannot escape the powerful effect on my life of my parents' spiritual journey. A few years ago when tracing John Wesley's and Ray Bakke's lives and ministries I could not help but notice the family environment that so heavily influenced their rich lives. In the 1930s my parents were a young couple living in Wenatchee, Washington, when they came in contact with the holiness movement and the influence of pastor Fred Landis and his wife Gwen. Pastor Landis was the epitome of decorum. His six-foot four-inch frame, his gentleness, and his well-mannered lifestyle all appealed to my parents. They saw the love of Jesus Christ and the discipline of a godly lifestyle working hand in hand in this man's life and were intrigued. Because of his influence, both of them soon made radical commitments to follow Jesus Christ. They also emulated his lifestyle of grace and etiquette. In the late '40s my dad, Cameron, after many years of business, would become an ordained minister in the Christian and Missionary Alliance denomination and pastor a country church near Albany, Oregon, and then later when living at Garland he would become the "parson of the valley," marrying and burying people who did not find their way into a church home.

When they moved to Garland Mineral Springs in 1953, my mother, Medora, proved she was also a spiritual force with which to be reckoned. Whether in the coffee shop, restaurant, kitchen, or great room in our lodge at Garland, she always engaged others in conversation about following Jesus. She had a unique outlook on life and people. She believed that everyone she met would eventually be won over by the grace of God and submit to the love of Jesus Christ. In her view, all anyone needed was a little love and encouragement. Her evangelistic zeal and rate of conversions proved her theory true. People seeking to fish the river near our resort soon found themselves hooked! My mother's kitchen became her pulpit. When I reflect on my mom's unique life, I like to say, "For dinner, the rolls were burned, but the souls were saved." My mom lived in a time and in a

Christian culture where women could only minister in their home or in Sunday School or schools with primary students. Due to this cultural constraint she learned how to cross boundaries by turning our home into the biggest hospitality center possible. Legislators, business leaders, and pastors found their way to my mom's kitchen. At her funeral the Methodist pastor shared that when he came to his congregation he did not know Jesus Christ but that when he met Medora Sharpe she led him into a personal relationship with Christ.

My mother's faith was not lost on me. When I was very young she began to talk and pray with me about giving my life to Jesus Christ, and I followed her example. My dad was a preacher as well as a resort proprietor. Between his moralistic preaching and my mother's tenderhearted spirituality, I began to develop a tender conscience toward God and a love for seeing people grow in faith. In the home of Cam and Medora Sharpe, everyone was welcome at the dinner table.

Another factor that undoubtedly had an impact on my view of how God works with us was that series of catastrophic events: first the snow storm, then the flood that tore through our property and destroyed the beauty of our resort. The damage was devastating. I watched as my parents tried to put things back together, but realized they were struggling and that life had become unusually hard. Then within two years of the terrible flood, came the fire that burned our lodge to the ground and was the last blow for the retreat center. My dad worked hard to find ways to keep the ministry going, but the flood, fire, and lack of insurance coverage put an effective end to the ministry. Although my mother had Scriptures and hymns for every occurrence—"some through the water, some through the flood, some through great trials, but all through the blood"—the reality is that we were a family without a home, without a ministry, without a business, and living in the wilderness.

In spite of all this, my parents kept focused on the reality that God was leading them and that somehow all these events would lead to the glory of God and the furthering of His ministry.

PENTECOSTAL EXPERIENCES, GLOBAL REALITY

During this bleak time in our lives we began to have "Pentecostal experiences." These began with visits to little Pentecostal prayer meetings and churches as we were searching for people who were seeking and finding the "filling of the Holy Spirit." The next few years, as we lived in cabins on our property, rented houses in the little towns of our valley, or traveled long distances to meetings, I watched with keen interest as we joined a band of people looking for supernatural intervention. Crisis has a way of turning us outward, away from our normal experience, as we grasp for some new hope, something to hold on to. Our family began to seek a fuller dimension of the Holy Spirit.

Although we were not aware of the timing, we were part of a new wave of people from mainline and evangelical churches embracing Pentecostal experience without being bound by the rigid doctrinal stands so characteristic of many Pentecostal denominations. Instead of being identified with these Pentecostal denominations, we were identified as charismatics, and rather enjoyed identifying with these folks and this movement with the likes of Dennis Bennett the Episcopalian, Joseph Fulton the Roman Catholic, and others who experienced new-found freedom in the Holy Spirit. The new friends we'd found convinced us that these fresh experiences were God's answer and hope for us.

As I travel the world following Ray Bakke's broad trail and see people involved in ministry touching the hardest places and the hardest people in our cities, I find that many of them have some touch with the Pentecostal phenomenon. I agree with Philip Jenkins and Harvey Cox when they take notice of the Pentecostal Century impacting the church globally.[1] Although people in Mumbai or Manila may be Anglican, Roman Catholic, or evangelical, a great majority that we engage seem to be able to point to a Pentecostal experience. The sociologist David Brooks notes that the Pentecostal movement was the most significant social movement of the twentieth century.[2] Brooks also notes that the seemingly knowledgeable middle-class American would have little knowledge of this fact. The Pentecostal wave swept over a hungry planet promising healing, power, and an experience of the presence of God in incomparable fashion. Although many can question some Pentecostal theology and practice, churches involved in the largest urban centers must seek to understand the appeal and the hope provided by this movement. Pentecostal reality and urban reality often go hand in hand.

CALLING

In 1962, when I was 12 years old, I read the biography of Governor Mark Hatfield of Oregon. I was impressed and told my mom I wanted to be the governor of our state. I also remember thinking it would be great to be a dictator of a small island or a banana republic, and that Washington State seemed about the right size for a takeover at that point! Around that time, my mom asked me to sit down and talk about some other life matters beyond my takeover plans. We began to talk about a life committed to following Jesus Christ and how I could make the greatest impact in life by serving Christ. Out of that table conversation I recognized the significance of giving my life to serving Christ and not simply choosing a career. I have been able to look back on that conversation many times as a milestone in my life path. I can't help but track my calling to my mother's prayers and input.

The little town of Monroe, Washington, was the first place I had the opportunity to teach. I was 16 years old when a church invited me to come share some spiritual nuggets with other teenagers. I remember my preparation as I looked for every available piece of information. I finally settled on a little pamphlet widely used in evangelical Christianity at the time, *The Four Spiritual Laws*. When it came time for my first sermon, I stood behind the little pulpit and proceeded to break into a cold sweat, and then I almost passed out while hanging on to the pulpit! Thanks to the pulpit, I stayed on my feet. Since I had already made a fool of myself I went on to wax eloquent for the rest of my allotted time! As radio preachers often reminded us through the years, "this vital ministry of faith and power would not go off the air," or let go of the pulpit!

EDGY CHURCH

As I moved toward my college years, my sister introduced me to a church in Seattle that was becoming a haven for youth. There I eventually met my wife, Laila. I arrived there in 1968. The war in Vietnam was not going well; Richard Nixon had just been elected president of the United States; and growing numbers were discovering marijuana, psychedelic drugs, a new form of protest music, and sexual freedom. I entered college that year with a sense that my entire world was being turned upside down. Friends experimented with drugs and were active in the raging war protests. During this tumultuous time, I began attending an urban church my sister had recommended. This church under the leadership of Pastor Ralph Sander and his musically gifted wife, Darlene, had discovered an edgy music style that was a bridge to the emerging culture. They introduced a blend of gospel and soul that made their ministry appealing for youth looking for something with power and energy for that challenging time. New gospel music stars like André Crouch were discovered at this church, which fed a youth culture that was hungry for something new and was tired of the tame, contemporary music offered by Christian youth organizations and Christian movies. Our church was the closest thing to a multiracial church you could find in the late '60s and early '70s in Seattle. The pastor was an urban pastor with a heart for youth and for the African American community. He had cultivated relationships throughout the city with many black leaders. I had the opportunity to build deep friendships across racial lines and to share in the life and plight of the African American community during a tumultuous time. My early years of urban ministry were formed during that time. We celebrated in a multiracial congregation where women led in ministry long before we had words to describe it.

The lessons learned during this time keep on teaching me. Jesus is edgy and an encounter with Him is not simply a rehash of old information or comfortable platitudes. Scripture reveals that Jesus is radical in just about every dimension, bringing comfort to those who seemingly have no hope and confrontation to those who think they had things wired. Today, when I consult with churches I encourage them to quit playing it safe and to think about taking risks and providing an environment where people will be challenged and confronted.

PENTECOSTAL NUANCES IN A TIME OF TURBULENCE

The peace movement and the Jesus People movement both found their fertile soil in this tumultuous cultural setting. While students were rioting at Kent State University in Ohio, or tripping out on drugs in Berkeley, California, or protesting on the freeway near the University of Washington in Seattle, others were finding new freedom in an anti-organizational church movement that has now been identified as the Jesus People movement. Youth attracted to this movement were often just coming out of the drug culture and were desperately searching for something to fill the hole in their souls. Others had been raised in a church culture that was, in their opinion, void of emotional and spiritual meaning. The Jesus People movement tended to have a strong emphasis on the work of the Holy Spirit, like the earlier Pentecostal movement, and it dovetailed with the growing charismatic movement of which my family had been a part. Both movements could be identified as Pentecostal in expression.

I was constantly in contact with both the peace movement and the Jesus People movement, but along with many of my friends, I found myself caught up in the Jesus People movement. Perhaps what pushed us toward a "seeking faith" in those days was the desperation of the Vietnam War, a sense of cultural loss, and the promise of fulfillment that came from following Jesus outside the formal bounds of current religious systems. I remember one terrifying night as a group of us sat in our dorm and watched the draft lottery on television to see if we would be called up to serve in the Vietnam War. As the numbers were called out based on our birthdays, one student jumped up and shouted, "I finally won a lottery!" as his low number was called, but it wasn't a good feeling. Still, the Jesus People movement provided a sense of hope; it introduced us to risk and adventure and seemed much closer to the exciting experience of the first-century Church than the staid North American representation we'd experienced in our short lifetime.

I was attending Bellevue Community College in Washington in 1970 when one of the leaders of the Jesus People movement asked me, "What are you doing for Jesus on your campus?" I remember thinking, *Nothing, I'm not doing anything for Jesus.* His challenge captured my imagination, and I determined to start an organization on my campus that I dubbed the Christian World Liberation Front (CWLF). I had learned that another group had used this name at Berkeley on the campus of the University of California and were able to get school funds to preach the gospel. This sounded great to me, so I did the same thing at my college. Soon I found myself with other students sitting at the student government table utilizing state funds, much to the school administration's consternation. Through CWLF we promoted the most radical music concerts on campus! Our rock and soul groups were cutting edge for the time and with newly converted, ex-druggie rockers pounding out the sounds, it

> "What are you doing for Jesus on your campus?"

didn't take long before we had a strong following and people identifying themselves with Christ on our campus.

It was during this time in college that the pastor of our church asked me to join him in ministry. Over the next four years he encouraged me and endorsed my ministry as college kids started following Jesus and experiencing the life of the Spirit.

Looking back on my college days and on the Jesus People movement, I realize these were formative years for a lifetime of ministry.

Most of our meetings during that time were simple, worshiping God together singing, reading Scriptures, sharing our stories and sharing our bread. We cared for each other and watched the Holy Spirit touch down on us.

Today I observe this same kind of spirit in believers who are making a dramatic difference in the city, serving with the poor. There is simplicity and an earnest seeking of God's life and power, which is vital to those who bring about change. Recently on one of our trips with doctoral students in Mumbai, we observed the Teen Challenge ministry to the children of prostitutes and found a vibrant spirit there. In fact, most of these little children, safe for the night as their mothers roamed the streets, were singing, praising God, and praying for one another. We all marveled at the simplicity and faith of these workers and children who were caught up in the presence of God in the midst of a desperate and dark place. When I encounter this kind of vibrant spiritual life, it reminds me of my own journey.

During those formative college days, in the midst of that vibrant spiritual explosion, I met and married my wife, Laila. She was born in northern Norway, and her family lived on a beautiful remote island. My sister Janis met her first and then told me she wanted me to meet this "beautiful Norwegian girl." Through our college years Laila and I explored the work of God together, and I found a soul mate who shared the same passion to serve Jesus Christ.

After 34 years of marriage, I can reflect on how God brought us together and grafted our gifts together. Laila is highly organized, a vocalist, an artist, and a caring wife and mother. When we pray about direction, I always know that when God speaks to her it is the "green light" to move to the next assignment. I trust her wisdom and her ability to hear God. The journey teaches us that God gives gifts and whether we are male or female we need to make room for the gifting of the Holy Spirit in each other. So many key urban leaders are women who can and do go into difficult places where men are not welcome.

LESSONS IN COMMUNITY BUILDING AND LEADERSHIP

During the mid 1970s a group of us formed a new fellowship, seeking to build a community of believers who were disciples and not just churchgoers. This was the closest thing to a tight-knit Christian community I've ever experienced. Most of the people in the fellowship were young couples, and we had the joy of raising our children together for several years.

Building community is not easy, and working through the crash of a community is painful. This young, gifted group of people was living out an ideal. We believed we were on the front end of a great movement to see the Kingdom of God ushered in. We proved that you can lead people in the church to dramatically shift their theological views, but that changing the color of a carpet can tear a church apart! Our leaders were young, educated, and bright. As a whole, the community prospered, as everyone was motivated to grow and become all God called them to be. We also took on the attitude that a "spirit of poverty" should be rejected, which meant we should all become successful and preferably wealthy. Most of us thought this was a great idea and a marvelous theology!

Perhaps the turning point for our community was the advancement of the idea that as Christian leaders we knew what was best for the rest of the Christian community. We began to think of ourselves as knowing what was best for others in all things, including occupation, spouse selection, even finances. We played with the dangerous practice of replacing the need for the Holy Spirit's counsel in the believer's life with dominant human leadership. As our fellowship began to break up over some of these issues, some of us stumbled onto the little book *Life Together* by Dietrich Bonhoeffer, and we realized his comments on Christian community were certainly on target for our brief journey, and were cutting and timely for a group of people who'd gone off target.

God hates visionary dreaming; it makes the dreamer proud and pretentious. The man who fashions a visionary ideal of community demands that it be realized by God, by others, and by himself. He enters the community of Christians with his demands, sets up his own law, and judges the brethren and God Himself accordingly. He stands adamant, a living reproach to all others in the circle of brethren. He acts as if he is the creator of the Christian community, and his dream binds men together. When things do not go his way, he calls the effort a failure. When his ideal picture is destroyed, he sees the community going to smash. So, he becomes, first an accuser of his brethren, then an accuser of God, and finally the despairing accuser of himself.[3]

During this community breakup the issues of incarnational leadership were burned deeply into me. Incarnational leadership, which we often teach in our courses at Bakke Graduate University, describes leaders who live alongside others, sharing in common life, both joys and plight. I began to reflect on the kind of leadership needed at various steps in Christian development. When do we need the strict discipline training (crossing the *t*'s and dotting the *i*'s), and when do we need coaching and leadership that creates a vacuum and platform for growth?

My journey took me away from a tight management approach to a coaching, nurturing leadership approach and then eventually to the "create a vacuum" time of letting people go and letting the Holy Spirit become the teacher. If people do not reach this level in their growth they are dependents and not adult followers of Jesus Christ. If Jesus really is our model then we have to follow His example.

During a ten-year time period from 1975 to 1985, I worked in the marketplace and was able to gain experience in management, sales, marketing, advertising, and business ownership. Looking back, I see this ten-year experience as proving ground for my future work.

THE SECOND CALLING

On one particular day in 1983, I was having lunch down by the ship canal near Seattle Pacific University, and I began to ask the Lord to send me anywhere He chose. I prayed this way: "Lord, I'll go anywhere you want me to go, anywhere in the world, as long as you fully use me." I realized I was under-challenged at that point and that I wanted to be commissioned and stretched. I suspect millions of people pray that same prayer each day. I remember getting the impression that God spoke to me by the canal. I do not know how God speaks to others or even how we discern God's voice, but I went away from the canal that day believing God spoke to me. My hunch is that we know when God speaks to us. We cannot avoid the still, small voice or the glaring writing on the wall! We know when we know. The word came to me really as a question: "How about Seattle?" Up to that point I was thinking somewhere exotic like Tonga or Uganda or Cambodia. When I thought of Seattle, I began to laugh! I reckon this is how Sarah felt when God told her she would have a child in her old age.

Within a few short weeks, driving through the downtown corridor of Seattle, I was observing the skyscrapers and recognizing the power of human genius represented by those bold architectural lines and height, and the line of a song from Handel's *Messiah* came to me,

> The kingdom of this world is become
> the kingdom of our Lord and of His Christ,
> and of His Christ.

At that point, a new picture of Seattle flashed before my eyes. I caught a glimpse of a city so radically altered that it reflected God's glory. From that time until now, my prayer turned toward seeking God's heart for Seattle. Little did I realize that one day we would be holding city leadership consultations in our city, and that Ray Bakke and I would link up in a global, urban educational ministry.

REFLECTIONS

1. What are your spiritual roots and how have they formed your present ministry?

2. Can you identify the time and place of your calling to ministry?

Chapter 9

Called to Seattle and Beyond

In 1984 I was reading the book of Nehemiah when I began to reflect on the book in relationship to Seattle and to see it as a guidebook for city transformation.[1] As I read, I noticed that the work of Ezra, the teacher and prophet, preceded the work of Nehemiah, the governor. Ezra was responsible for bringing the refugees back from Babylon to rebuild the temple of God. While in Babylon, the Jewish people had submitted to the laws of the Babylonian system, but now they were returning with the legal decree of the law to rebuild their center of worship and their community, the place for which they had longed. Most of us think they began to build the walls first, because in the book of Nehemiah the walls are the focus. However, many biblical scholars believe that they started by building an altar and offering a sacrifice to the living God (the chronological order is debated by scholars). After offering the sacrifice, they began building the Temple, and finally, under Nehemiah's rule, they built the walls.

The story from Nehemiah's time gave me fuel for thought, and I began to work on analogies from this story. What does it mean to offer sacrifice in our cities today? What does it mean to build the Temple, and what are the city walls? I began to ask, "What transferable principles can we appropriate?" The altar of Ezra has significant application for us as we think about offering ourselves to God for a city. Wasn't the altar a place where priests and people offered them-selves to God? A place where they asked for forgiveness of sin and pledged their lives to a new walk? Perhaps the refugees asked for for-giveness for their ill treatment of the poor, their lack of regard for the widows, their hardness of heart toward their own families and God's covenant in general. Perhaps they pledged that in the New Jerusalem they were going to give themselves to the poor, responding to the words of Isaiah the prophet as he called them to "pour out their soul for the needy" (Isaiah 58). What if people in our modern cities began the same kind of repentance and offering of themselves for the pur-poses of God in our cities? I saw this as a mandate for the church. Build an altar! Call the churches to repentance. Call the people of God to repentance, and as an offering give themselves to their city!

Next, moving in a linear fashion, the refugees under Ezra's leader-ship began to build the Temple. The text mentions that the Temple did not have the same status as the original Temple under Solomon's rule. This was a different time and place with different resources available. In a sense, each temple built has to reflect the builders' capacity and resources. However, the Temple speaks of a place to worship God and a gathering of God's people. Jesus's discussion with the woman at the well in the Gospel of John, chapter 4, conveys a message that Jerusalem is set aside as a place to worship God. Place is important to God. The prophets also mention that the house of

> **The walls of our cities must be built in record time and with God's help.**

God shall be a place of prayer for all nations gathered (Isaiah 56:7). As we look at our cities and think about the Jerusalem Temple, how do we build an atmosphere of worship and prayer that gives God glory in our cities? What does a temple equivalent look like in the postmodern megacities of today? Perhaps our temple is the people of God gathered, connecting, communicating, loving, and living to see the glory of God in their city. In Seattle we have worked with the principle that we should know those among whom we minister. The church of Jesus Christ should be about knowing each other, ministering to each other, and building up the body of Christ within a city. When this happens, the ministry of the church in the city will have the spiritual and relational equity to engage the whole city and challenge the systems and powers.

Finally, Nehemiah came to Jerusalem on a mission to make the city safe and strong for the citizens of Jerusalem. He was concerned for Jerusalem after he heard that it was still a disgrace even after the renewal of holy sacrifices. Jerusalem was a weak city without any defense. The city without walls defined the city and defined the governmental responsibilities for those ruling and those governed. Cities without walls were cities without government and power. Today a strong city is defined by its ability to create an environment that produces jobs, homes, transportation access, safety, and services. These urban environmental issues are the contemporary "walls" of a city. Nehemiah was a builder and wanted to make his city strong. He saw this as a vital issue for the glory of God. This is a compelling issue for the church today as we look at a planet moving toward the urban future. At this point, more than 21 megacities, with anticipated populations of ten million or more by 2015, struggle for the resource capacity to provide the necessary infrastructure for the teeming mass in urban migration. We firmly believe we have a biblical mandate and that the Nehemiah story gives us the tracks, as it were, to unleash the church for the task of city development. The walls of our cities (the infrastructure) must be built in record time and with God's help. The church together, fully engaged in a city, can make the difference and provide the families for each section of the wall!

After processing the Nehemiah passages of Scripture I began to teach about the city and how the church could be involved in the renewal of the city. At the same time that I reflected on the work of the church in the city, most of our friends were moving into home-schooling, private schools, and suburban schools, and our city was shrinking. Families were vacating Seattle and the public school system because several social experiments were being implemented in the district. A shrinking public school population left vacant school facilities, which were sold and then became community centers and churches. Many Christians were not focused on rebuilding the city. They didn't seem to have a concern for the city at all. Rather, they seemed refocused through a rural lens on lifestyle and living. I noticed instinctively that American Christians followed a rural exegesis of Scripture as they plundered the Scriptures for lifestyle texts. Abraham, who stayed out of cities, became their model for Christian living. Poor despicable Lot chose to live in the city, and look what happened to him! Living in the city was tantamount to seeking the wild nightlife! I remember one time when I was lecturing about how Jesus often kept his eye on the city and left Galilee to go to the city. One of the members of the class immediately exclaimed, "And look what happened to him!" Actually the North American lifestyle motif has been primarily rural. Early Americans saw themselves as a farming nation, not necessarily a group of urban dwellers. During the war for independence from Britain, American colonists marshaled an all-volunteer militia that was primarily an army of farmers. The British were frustrated, as they were able to occupy colonial cities but soon realized large populations didn't live in the cities, and conquering a city in America was not like conquering a European city built around the old medieval town system.

Contrary to what was happening around me, I began to realize that Scripture is an urban book. Take cities out of Scripture and it's like taking the words of Jesus or the apostle Paul out! Ray reminds us that the Bible contains 1,250 references to cities. Take the stories of Nineveh, Sodom, Corinth, Thessalonica, Ephesus, Athens, Jerusalem, and Babylon out of Scripture and you have an executive briefing, not a book!

I had just finished some teaching regarding rebuilding the city, speaking at Cornerstone Christian Community Church in Seattle, where I was a teaching elder at the time, when Laila and I were invited to a house meeting. I was dubious about attending this particular meeting because we were told a lady would be prophesying for those in attendance. At that point in life, my regard for prophetic utterances was pretty low. I thought most of the utterances were *pathetic* rather than *prophetic*. Our years of involvement with the charismatic and Pentecostal movements had worn me out. Too many so-called prophets crashed and burned around us. We were left to make sense of their rubble. I was often reminded of Jeremiah's words from God to the prophets in Jeremiah 23:16–18.

> Thus says the LORD of hosts: "Do not listen to the words of the prophets who prophesy to you, filling you with vain hopes; they speak visions of their own minds, not from the mouth of the LORD. They say continually to those who despise the word of the LORD, 'It shall be well with you'; and to every one who stubbornly follows his own heart, they say, 'No evil shall come upon you.'" For who among them has stood in the council of the LORD to perceive and to hear his word, or who has given heed to his word and listened?

I told my wife as we entered the home, "If I hear one more goofy prophecy, I'm going to start despising prophecies!" This was in reference to the apostle Paul telling the Thessalonian church, "Don't despise prophecy" (1 Thessalonians 5:20 KJV). As the evening progressed, the woman who was giving words to people about their personal lives gave the standard "the Lord will do wonderful things through you," and so on. I listened with skepticism as she worked her way around the room. I was pretty sure her words for me would be the same generalizations I was hearing all night. Finally she came to me. As she began speaking, she quoted some verses and then said, "The Lord gives me the book of Nehemiah and says you are like Nehemiah and the Lord has called you to Seattle." My wife says my head dropped as these words sunk in. I walked out of the meeting that night knowing that somehow God used these words to speak to me and to confirm my calling to Seattle. I remembered the day down by the ship canal. I still wrestle with prophetic words and I am not always sure of their validity in each situation, but that night those words moved my heart toward a city. Of course, I knew that from that point on, if God was in this and if this was a word from Him, it would be confirmed by open doors and the Holy Spirit's movement. I remembered the apostle Paul receiving his call and then, by some scholars' accounts, having to wait at least 14 years for the fulfillment of God's word to him. Paul's first trip was to the desert, and then he could fulfill his prophesied calling.

With the call of God stirring in my heart, I began to pray about whether I should stay in the building-products business or start moving toward this next phase of ministry. For about a year Laila and I asked the Lord for direction. I was approaching a crossroads in my world. Business was good, and at age 35 I knew I was either going to be doing business the rest of my life or I was to turn my energy and focus to living outside the security of an "accepted career."

I am firmly convinced that being in business is a legitimate ministry and that each of us must follow our particular calling of God. I know that politicians, businesspeople, physicians, and educators are called to make an impact as ministers. In fact, the church has been remiss in not recognizing these and other calls in the marketplace. Each one of us has to be obedient to the call on our lives and the affirmation of the Christian community. Some have been called to the pursuit of life that is often called "full-time ministry." I think the reality is that each of us has to work this out before the Lord, directed by the Holy Spirit. Our family has always honored those who are called to serve in their occupation as God's ambassadors. We also honor those who have been called to ministries that network, serve, evangelize, teach, educate, and pastor.

In early 1985 Laila and I chose to leave the security of our business world, load up our children (at that time Jonathan was seven; Katrina, four; and Christopher, two), and go to L'Abri in Switzerland.

Francis Schaeffer founded L'Abri in Switzerland as a place to study, pray, and seek wisdom. I had just read Francis Schaeffer's works and decided I needed some wisdom from other voices in the church to study and gain discernment for the rest of our journey. We ended up spending six months in Europe traveling and ministering in churches across the continent. It was a life-changing time for us.

PLANTING A CHURCH ON THE WAY TO THE CITY

Later in 1985 we returned to the US, and through the counsel of friends and advisors, we decided to pioneer a new congregation for the Christian and Missionary Alliance (CMA). We began the Antioch Alliance Church in Lynnwood, Washington. Although I knew the city was calling, I also knew I could not respond to God's call until the timing was right. When I make decisions, I have learned to look to the biblical narrative and biblical characters for reference points. At this point in our decision making, the example of Paul waiting 14 years in the desert to realize his calling and Abraham having to wait for the promise of Isaac became my life-giving stories. In light of counsel

> **God is a Father who provides, guides, and affirms our lives.**

and our circumstances, we pioneered a church and pastored it for the next 12 years. This was a second time for me to learn about community from the ground up. During our time at Antioch Alliance Church, we learned that God is a Father who provides, guides, and affirms our lives. We also learned that community is built by the grace of God and not simply by our hard work or vision. Antioch was a wonderful time to raise our family and to embrace our dreams and limitations. I can look back now and realize how God gave us community. During that time many people came to the Lord and to an understanding that God loves them unconditionally.

In 1997 I sat in a room with the key leaders from our church, listening to their stories. Couple by couple shared their spiritual and church journey. As they shared, it began to dawn on me that I was pastoring a much different church than the one I had pioneered. Five years prior to this retreat, another congregation approached us, asking to merge with us. At that point our fledgling congregation consisted of young families, new to the suburbs, looking for a Christian community where they could raise their families. Many were new converts. The church, although small, had grown rapidly in the first five years. When the other congregation approached us, we realized they would immediately add strong middle-aged families and leadership to our church. At that point we were struggling to raise leadership with so many young adults. The promise of a merger was also the promise of increased resources, something we desperately needed.

Five years later it dawned on me that when the merger took place, we did not really have a marriage of two congregations or even assimilation, but we simply exchanged cultures and congregations. I remember a friend once saying, "two plus two does not always equal four." I had moved from pioneer leader and pastor to chaplain pastor of a different church. Many of our original young families had drifted away within a two-year period of the assimilation while the congregation we absorbed began to take leadership and ownership. This was a tough lesson to learn about culture! Churches have cultures, people develop cultures, and where cultures are strong, they will rule the day. I can now see that the culture of our original church plant was still being formed when we invited the other group in, which had a strong identity and long-term culture.

Within a few weeks of that retreat, I knew it was time to move on. I began to ask if it was perhaps the time to transition to the city where God had called me. This was not an easy decision. I had to wrestle through philosophic issues that I had developed around our ministry. I had started the church with the ministry philosophy that churches were like families and that pastors didn't just come and go, but they were a part of the DNA in each congregation. My philosophy was, if a pastor left, it should be on a mission from the church and not a disassociative move away from the church. So I began to work with the leaders of the church to move together toward an urban venture in Seattle.

I remember thinking the leaders would surely want to move in this direction, but I discovered they did not have the vision for this. One day, sitting in my new office (the result of a yearlong facility expansion), I felt the Lord say, "It is time to go." I knew at that point that it was time to go to the city. However, it was tough to leave the church I had pioneered and the honor of being their pastor.

On a Monday morning as I read Oswald Chambers in the devotional *My Utmost for His Highest*, I read these words: "When Jesus says go, don't stay." Chambers didn't use those exact words, but they were written on the wall in 3-D for me that morning.

> He comes where He commands us to leave. If you stayed home when God told you to go because you were so concerned about your own people there, then you actually robbed them of the teaching of Jesus Christ Himself. When you obeyed and left all the consequences to God, the Lord went into your city to teach, but as long as you were disobedient, you blocked His way. Watch where you begin to debate with Him and put what you call your duty into competition with His commands. If you say, "I know that He told me to go, but my duty is here," it simply means that you do not believe that Jesus means what He says.

Up to that point, I felt as if the Lord was prying my hands off the congregation, leading me away from the ministry I pioneered and into which I had poured so much. Yet my commitment to my philosophy of ministry was holding me back. I think many ministries lose their sensitivity to the Holy Spirit when they cling to their philosophy. This was true of King Saul in the Old Testament, who was committed to his earthly kingdom even after God removed His anointing. I finally realized that no matter how strongly we are committed to our vision and philosophy of ministry, our passion, vision, and philosophies must bow to the leading and direction of the Holy Spirit.

CITY REACHING ON THE WAY TO THE CITY

God sends angels along the way in our otherwise clueless lives. One of my professors in graduate school captured my imagination with the idea of saturation church planting. He shared stories of the church being the visible, tangible expression of Christ in each neighborhood. The model came from the Philippines, where saturation church planting was taking root. It was seen as a way to reach a nation. My professor, Jack Dennison, was translating the principle of reaching a nation to reaching a city.

As I began to process how God was leading me to the city to finally implement my long-term call, I phoned Jack and asked him for some counsel. He invited me to take a trip with him to Houston, where I heard him share his assumptions for the kingdom of God and the city. Dennison had synthesized much of Ray Bakke's work and the work of others in missions to build a case for the work of the church in the city. I would say that Ray is process-oriented and that Jack is strategy-oriented. Dennison worked on the concept that you could mobilize the church toward a fixed end or city transformation. In his model you started with a vision and then developed a strategy (indigenous) and pushed toward the goal.

Armed with the new information, I began to mobilize leaders in the Seattle area around the vision of a transformed city. I networked with people who could connect with pastors and leaders throughout the metro Seattle area. Doug Engberg was leading Promise Keepers in Washington State, and he became a friend and a guide, leading me to relationships throughout our city. I called Doug and asked him to introduce me to people, shared the vision of a transformed city with him, and the vision resonated with his heartbeat. Soon I was meeting African American leaders who were seeking to coalesce a movement to transform Seattle's urban areas.

Developing networks is much like entering a war zone. You have to understand the existing networks and their domains. Much like the Internet, where everyone is concerned with domain, networks have territory and personalities. Multiple networkers inhabit cities and see their work as key to the life of their constituents. When you enter their turf, they expect you to enter through their door, only with permission. Most often the gatekeeper for a particular area of ministry wants to be your guide. There are prayer-focused gatekeepers, racially-focused gatekeepers, reconciliation gatekeepers, neighborhood gatekeepers, youth gatekeepers, urban ministry gatekeepers, political gatekeepers, marketplace ministry gatekeepers, business gatekeepers, and on and on without end. I moved into a city ministry seeking to catalyze the whole church with the whole gospel for the whole city. I soon found out the city was made up of multiple turfs. People who had labored for years in one area of the city or within one segment of Christ's church were not always eager to see new players. Often the challenge of maintaining ministry and resource can become a competitive venture in the city. Learning to serve those who have already given their lives to the city is vital for any newcomer.

The prayer gatekeepers believed all we needed to do was pray more and make sure that all pastors were in committed prayer meetings. The racially focused gatekeepers believed that the main issue of any work in the city was racism. The reconciliation gatekeepers believed that reconciliation around race was the primary focus. Those working with the homeless were sure that their work was the most important and the hottest issue of the city. Every gatekeeper had a particular special priority.

Tipping-point personalities are needed in the city. Networkers need to be supported, especially if they have a Barnabas spirit. There are at least two kinds of networkers: the networker with a huge ego need and the networker with a Barnabas spirit (see chapter 10).

With the encouragement of Doug Engberg (a Barnabas-spirit person) we began catalyzing a group. We started identifying this group as the Envisioning Team for Seattle and built it around three elements: (1) the vision of a transformed Seattle (whole city), (2) mobilizing the whole church in the Seattle region, and (3) implementing a saturation of churches and ministries in the city. It was a unique time, a time full of hope. A significant group of networkers, pastors, and ministry leaders came together each month to envision a transformed city. As this group prayed and discussed the direction, a decision was made to call a group of pastors from a variety of churches together to work and pray toward unity in the city.

I well remember the day the entire Envisioning Team called me out and laid hands on me and commissioned me to pull a group of pastors together for this purpose. I realized at that time that it was my Paul and Barnabas moment, much like when the Antioch leaders laid hands on that team and sent them out. I had waited for this for a long time. We believed at the time that pastors working and praying together would result in some significant changes in our city. Aaron Haskins, an African American brother, volunteered to help catalyze the pastors, and from that point on we began making contacts. We identified several pastors across denominational lines, representing African American Pentecostals, Baptists, Episcopalians, Pentecostals, Presbyterians, and Independents.

At one of our first meetings, Dick Leon, the pastor of Bellevue First Presbyterian, expressed the opinion that we should work under the nomenclature of Serve Seattle. All of the pastors agreed as they bought into an incarnational approach to our city. It was a joy to report back to the Envisioning Team that the pastors were coming together and seeking to identify Seattle as a place of common service and commitment. We were dreaming of a transformed city!

PROPHETS, PRIESTS, AND KINGS

I remember a prayer meeting in our city where the prayer facilitators were talking about being the leaders of the church. As I participated, I realized that although they were earnest, few in the church followed these faithful prayer warriors. As I prayed (I am usually convinced that when you think of something in prayer, it is God speaking to you), I got the thought that perhaps prayer facilitators were like priests, and pastors of large churches and organizations were like kings, and people like me were like prophets (we bug everybody by questioning the status quo). It can be said of the prophets that they can run a revolution, but they can't run a government!

Two remarkable experiences took place during this time. The first was an overnight retreat held in a five-star hotel in downtown Seattle. Pastors and spouses were invited to come together to tell their stories to one another. As we sat around a table, we sang, shared our stories, and wept together. Years later everyone in that room referenced this as a special time and place. Spouses talked about the loneliness in ministry while pastors talked about the realities of their ministries. I believe this was a glimpse of a preferable future God allowed us to see. Yet only about a month or two later this group broke up due to a breakdown in communication and relationships. When relationships began to fragment within the Serve Seattle leadership, it became apparent that we had a leadership capacity issue in our city. Leaders were not able to solve the relational problems and simply walked away from the issues, knowing it would be difficult.

As I reflect on this difficult experience, I am thankful that this circumstance was the middle of my story and not the last chapter, that the relationships built during this time are still intact, and that each of these pastors still believes God is doing something very special in our city and that it will continue as God enables. I also recognize that Paul and Barnabas, after their calling, sending, and affirmation in Antioch, had to split due to a relational conflict. The rest of the story is that God will keep working, and if we allow Him to work with us, we will see fruitfulness. After a five-year interlude of pain and waiting, we have seen forgiveness and healing in most of these relationships.

The second meaningful experience during this time was the first Serve Seattle Ministry Summit. Jim Hayford, pastor of Eastside Foursquare Church in Bothell, Washington, came up with the idea of having a summit where ministries were invited by leading pastors to share what they do in ministry. Seventeen ministries spent the day sharing what they do with congregational leaders. It was a first! Many of these ministries had spent years trying to get their message out to congregations, and in one day they had the full attention of these congregations. It was a wonderful day as ministry after ministry walked through their particular gift within the city. We all walked away believing the Lord was doing a new work among us.

I have found it difficult for ministries and leaders within cities to take the time for conversation that doesn't further their particular ministry objectives or personal learning curve. So it is vital to provide places and spaces where leaders can connect to others around the issues that most concern them. However, it is also important to hold people to conversation and not just projects. Some folks find it difficult to turn off their "project mode" to build relational capital.

EDUCATION IN THE CITY

Moving into the city and seeking to be a conduit of God's grace across sectarian lines is a challenge. However, the challenge is also a great way to grow and learn. I would say that this last phase in my ministry had the steepest learning curve. From 1998 until 2006, I've had the opportunity to serve the Baptist General Conference as a church-networking director helping rescue two urban churches from certain extinction. I also was able to serve a large suburban Foursquare church as their global urban mission pastor, helping cast vision and energize their 3,500-member church. During the time with the Foursquare church, we found that exposing congregations to the city, to signs of hope, and to effective ministries was life-changing.

Ray Bakke entered my picture when we found ourselves serving together on an urban education committee called the Association for Urban Studies (AUS). AUS was initiated by Dave Hillis, who was executive director of Northwest Leadership Foundation. For about 18 months we worked to develop an urban educational program to reach out to urban ministry folks, building a bridge from a certificate-street level to a doctor of ministry level. Dave had been dreaming about this for years and had laid a good groundwork with churches and urban ministries.

We reached out to the local Christian universities and colleges in the Seattle and Tacoma areas, seeking schools that would lower the drawbridge for us. Although many schools are well-intentioned, the chasm between higher education and most urban ministry is deep and wide. Dr. Tim Dearborn announced to a group of graduates at Seattle Pacific University one day that they were "the privileged one percent of the world's population with college degrees." As the AUS committee met and wrestled with how to make this educational dream a reality, we found the going tough. It is difficult for the academy to stop long enough to build a bridge, and it is difficult for those working in urban settings to be patient, as educational systems builders are slow.

At the time we were meeting at the AUS table, Rick Kingham, the new pastor of the Overlake Christian Church (OCC) in Kirkland, Washington, was just beginning his ministry there. OCC had founded and was maintaining a graduate school called Northwest Graduate School of Ministry (NWGS). In conversation with Rick one day I asked, "What are you going to do with the school that Overlake sponsors?" Pastor Kingham's response was, "I don't know. Do you have any ideas?" Of course I had many ideas. I approached Dr. Ward Gasque, a wise and seasoned theological education veteran, about meeting with Rick and his ministry team regarding the future of Northwest Graduate School of the Ministry. The chairman of my board (the Serve Seattle group) was Tom Adelsman, who also served on the staff at Overlake as the strategic networks pastor after ten years of leading the mission effort at Overlake. Tom was at the meeting as Ward and I met with the church staff. During that meeting Ward suggested the school get new leadership and a new focus. Within a short time, Tom Adelsman was appointed president of the school, and long-time president Bill Payne moved into the academic dean role. Bill's experience with the school was legendary by this time. He served in practically every role available. One of Tom's first steps as president was to bring Ward Gasque and me onto the Academic Affairs Committee and ask for our input regarding the direction, marketing, and new programming for the school. Ward's wisdom and my enthusiasm helped start the school in the direction of city reaching and church planting as a focus.

Meanwhile the AUS committee had linked its vision of certificate to doctoral level urban education with Ray's vision for a global doctor of ministry degree, which he entitled Transformational Leadership for the Global City. AUS saw this venture as a global seminary mall, offering a joint doctorate with seminaries in India, the Philippines, and other parts of Asia. This effort was dubbed the Transpacific Alliance. At one historic meeting the Transpacific Alliance was moved under the leadership of the AUS Committee.

Ward Gasque and Corrie DeBoer helped Ray jump-start the first doctoral cohort in the Transpacific Alliance with Carey Theological College in Vancouver, British Columbia; Asia Graduate Seminary of Theology; and Northwest Graduate School as partners. Students were recruited to enter the program and select the school of their choice for the degree.

Sometime during our first two weeks of courses, Tom Adelsman came to me and said, "Jon, I think Overlake wants to sell the Northwest Graduate School of Ministry, and I think we could buy it for $200,000. Tom and I had discussed the possibility that such a thing could happen and thought that perhaps churches in the Seattle area would want to be a part of this school if it were owned by several churches rather than one church. That evening, as our first doctoral group of students sat together, I shared with two pastors about the possibility of buying NWGS. One pastor was an African American and the other a suburban white pastor. Both told me that their churches would commit $20,000 the first year to help us out. The conversation continued through the night, and Ray Bakke said he thought perhaps the Mustard Seed Foundation, a Bakke family foundation, would help us too. That night we polled the members of the AUS committee and decided AUS would be the best organization to house the school.

Within just a few days, Ray, Tom, Ward, and I had lunch with Rick Kingham and some of his staff and approached them about buying the school. Over the next few weeks Rick Kingham led his board to the place of actually giving the Association of Urban Studies the school. In my opinion, this decision by Rick was based on the reputation of Ray and Dennis Bakke. Overlake forgave the $200,000 paper debt, and that only left approximately $17,000 owed to Overlake. Within a year Overlake forgave that debt also!

I was asked by AUS to direct the transition of the school from Overlake to an urban location, and we began to work with the AUS committee to see how we could refocus the school utilizing Ray's vision and focus of global urban transformational leadership. Over the next few months, Tom Adelsman, Ward Gasque, Bill Payne, Jeorily Martin (Bill, Jeorily, and Tom were the NWGS team at that point), and others rolled up their sleeves to make the transition complete.

Ray would often put growth challenges in my path. One of his first challenges was, "If you can get Dave McKenna, the former president of Seattle Pacific University, Asbury Seminary, and Spring Arbor University, to work with us, I'll really get involved." I knew that my wife, who was coordinating and directing the alumni events at Seattle Pacific University, would be able to find Dave for me. Sure enough she came up with his phone number and I called him. Within a few weeks Tom Adelsman and I met with Dr. McKenna, and he eventually became our first chairman of the new board of directors.

Since that time in 2000, I have served as the senior vice president, the vice president of church relations, academic dean, and now professor of global urban studies and director of the doctor of ministry program for what we now call Bakke Graduate University. Thanks to Northwest Leadership Foundation and Dave Hillis, the executive director, I was funded for an entire year to direct the transition. During that time I was also able to complete my doctoral degree under the mentorship of Ward Gasque and the editing of Corean Bakke, analyzing the global consultation process employed by Ray.

That's my brief story of a journey from the rural town of Index, Washington, to the urban city of Seattle and the ministry I now enjoy. Now I turn my attention to several important issues in the ministry of "city consultations." First, I begin with an overview of the spirit and nature of a city facilitator, using Barnabas from the New Testament as a model. Then we will turn our attentions to the consultations themselves, and how they may benefit your own city.

REFLECTIONS

1. How does the reading of Nehemiah in this chapter help you identify a clearer need for ministry in your city?

2. Are you prophet, priest, king, or . . . ?

Chapter 10

Barnabas: The Spirit and Nature of a City Facilitator

What provokes us to live sacrificial lives? This question is difficult to answer because God works with all of us in such unique ways. I know I don't have the answer but I do have many stories to tell of people I have encountered on my journey who lived this out in their daily lives.

THE STORY OF JOHN HAYES

John Hayes graduated with degrees from Princeton and Yale and had a bright future. He was in business developing a global venture in Japan but was dissatisfied. He grew tired of his self-centered drive for success. He decided to make a 180-degree turn in life and moved into a Los Angeles neighborhood looking for a way to give his life away. Once there he consigned himself to listen, learn, love, and be loved by the community in which he had chosen to live. He began to submerge himself in the culture of the community, allowing himself to be shaped, molded, and informed so he could bring healing and love to its people. John has a strong personality, but he decided to bring the love of Christ to these people out of his weakness rather than his strength. He founded INNERChange, a Christian order whose followers live among the poor. This approach was risky, and he knew he would likely be misunderstood, ridiculed, violated, or killed.

In the beginning, John visited this community over and over until some Cambodian families finally invited him into their homes and hearts. As he built trust, they helped him find a place to live and began to accept him as one of their own. It wasn't an easy transition from the halls of Princeton and Yale to living in the midst of cocaine addicts, gang bangers, and immigrant families just trying to make it through another day on the streets of Los Angeles. He demonstrated a spirit focused on others, willing to give up privilege and spotlight to bring the message of the kingdom of God to this community.

This short story about John, as well as others that I have met along my journey, exhibits what I call a Barnabas spirit—an ability to read, listen, and love a community and be willing to give oneself to and for it. John's own journey provided riveting insights to my understanding of the Barnabas spirit. Here are the thoughts he shared with me as I asked him the following four questions.

First, I asked John what he learned about entering a community and finding gifts there. He told me he discovered that when a group of people appreciates and recognizes God's Spirit as a creative agent, extraordinary ideas and solidarity occur. While living among the Cambodians he learned to appreciate the process and outcome of the Spirit's work. He gained patience because it took patience to watch the gifts of the Spirit interlock and begin to coordinate within a community. He observed people who were single-minded and accomplishment-driven struggle when others received affirmation for their contribution to the community. The outcome of this slow process was a love and appreciation that men and women began to have for each other as truly fully functioning people within a community. John believes that this is the most important thing in sustaining the forward vitality of a community.

Second, I asked John if he thought having a Barnabas spirit included the tendency to underestimate the risk of entering into a relationship or community with a primary role to empower and encourage others. He found that he continually underestimated the cost of engagement in terms of time and energy, even when he soberly tried to count the cost. John finds something magical about investing, watching someone begin to shine, and as he is drawn into that relationship, he forgets how much time and effort it takes to make the shine permanent. The lesson here: those who operate with a Barnabas spirit should take time to value the process and not just the outcome, and that will take incredible time and energy.

Even when one counts the cost of time and energy, what they see at the beginning of the relationship is usually only the tip of the iceberg of the real sacrifice of time and emotional energy to come. Choosing to become fully involved in mentoring others includes the decision to *not* do other things that may also be vital. John's illustration of this point occurred in the late '90s, when he chose to mentor a group among the poor, which meant he did not have the time to develop INNERChange. When a person risks something to empower others, she or he often misses out on other unique experiences or opportunities in other arenas. In the world's eyes their choice may look like mundane work, but in the eyes of God it has significant value.

Third, I asked John if he'd ever risked his life for anyone in this new kingdom venture. Comfort is a high value to those living in the United States. Risking bodily harm for the sake of others may happen with a rush of adrenaline in a spontaneous moment, but it's not coveted as a lifestyle. John shared the following story with me about the risk of life and limb:

> In December 1990 I was driving back to my apartment on Minnie Street from the gym, looking for parking on our crowded street. Three young Cambodian men, who had become disciples in our ministry, waved to me as I passed by. Only later did I realize, by the expressions on their faces, that they seemed preoccupied. I drove another 100 feet and was trying to squeeze into a parking space in front of my apartment when I glanced into my rearview mirror. I was shocked at what I saw. Sophal, Sith, and Sampasong were in a

wild fight with about 10 to 12 members of "the Loper's gang." Sith had been pushed against a car with his jacket pulled over his upper body so he could not fight back and was absorbing vicious blows to his head and body. Sampasong crouched for cover as four guys alternately kicked and hit him. Sophal, the biggest and strongest, edged out into the street, with blood on his face, the only one more or less holding his own. I double-parked, threw open the door, not bothering to shut it, and ran purposefully into the middle of the gang fight, pulling guys apart. I shouted, "In the name of Jesus, stop!" I said it several times, almost as a mantra, and remember being a bit irritated several hours later that the Spirit hadn't given me something more compelling or uniquely articulate to declare. Yet after I shouted that phrase several times, everyone not only stopped but froze. The Loper's gang leader had an extraordinary firm face—the look and bearing of an ancient warrior. He was bigger than I realized. I told the gang who the Cambodian guys were to me, who I was, and why I was on the street. I think they struggled a bit with my English, as Spanish was the primary language for most of them, but they seemed to get the message. The leader respectfully began to pull his guys away. I remained planted in the middle of the sidewalk as a barrier between the Cambodian and Latino young men, and ordered Sophal, Sith, and Sampasong to walk down to my apartment. As I turned to watch them move toward the apartment, from out of nowhere someone hit me so hard with an uppercut that I was dazed and fell to the ground. As I got up, I saw the gang leader yelling at this young man, "Not him, not him," and then they all quickly ran up the street.

When I hear John tell that story, I realize that risking our lives is usually not a plan we craft but an action we take when the Holy Spirit prompts us.

Finally, I asked John, "What have you learned about building platforms for others?" He replied that when one builds platforms to help others to move to a different life, the result is life in a group of quality relationships with exciting and caring people. John has said, "The fruit of acting as a platform builder for others in a community, in my case, a worldwide one, feels like a down payment on the Hebrews 12 'cloud of witnesses.'" One must have a high tolerance for short-term misunderstanding and also the ego strength to be underappreciated and undercelebrated. John Hayes certainly demonstrates a Barnabas spirit with qualities of leadership worth emulating.

Barnabas Had Big Faith

Barnabas was a giant of the faith. He is listed in Scripture as an apostle. We often think of the big twelve as the apostles, but the facts suggest otherwise. To be listed as an apostle in the first-century church was no small task when you think that they shared the title with men who actually saw Jesus walk on water, turn the water into wine, and raise the dead! Barnabas was a latecomer to the Jesus-follower scene. Some believe he didn't show up until after Stephen's stoning. By most historical accounts, Barnabas was a Levite, a special class of religious folks committed to the Temple faith in Jerusalem. These men could track their roots back to the first Jewish priesthood. Levites possessed pedigree and status among those who cared about religion within the Jewish community. To the secular Jews, however, they were an annoying group of angry bigots!

The group with which Barnabas affiliated was typically offended by Jesus. The Temple faith was supported by funds from the people, and the Levites had turned it into a large money-making "faith enterprise," much like some televangelism of today. When Jesus entered the Temple, these folks really got under his skin. Most of us have a hard time imagining Jesus slamming tables, whipping people, and causing general mayhem. But the Temple leaders really got to him on one occasion. I have been tempted a time or two to punch out a strutting worship leader or televangelist when they enter into an abusive groove (I've kept my cool so far).

Barnabas rose to leadership apparently by being a risk taker and encourager. Once he chose to follow Jesus, he moved outside of his comfortable levitical setting and into a new culture and neighborhood.

Antioch was an exciting place to do ministry. The crossroads of the world intersected at this large urban center, a city where many nations, tribes, skin colors, and languages overlapped. Although Barnabas came out of Jerusalem and religious privilege, he adapted quickly to this new environment. The other apostles must have had confidence in his ability

> **Too often our view of mission puts boundaries around God, as if we need to protect Him.**

to connect with the community because when they looked for a leader to send to this new church, they chose Barnabas. Perhaps the apostles had seen his open style when he welcomed Paul at his first signs of conversion, while others were afraid of this new convert. Whatever the reason, the choice was a good one because Barnabas's leadership provided an environment of acceptance for many new converts from diverse backgrounds. Risk taking was part of Barnabas's life.

Barnabas was a forerunner of an Eastern Orthodox missiology that observes the Holy Spirit at work within a culture before the missionary arrives. Barnabas could see God at work in Antioch prior to his arrival. Michael Aleksa, writing in *Orthodox Alaska,* noted how the Russian Orthodox theology of mission in Alaska allowed them to appreciate the work of the Holy Spirit within the Alaskan people prior to Christianity arriving. These early Russian Orthodox missionaries drew attention to the symbols within the culture already pointing people to the true God of the universe and His son Jesus Christ. All too often our limited view of mission puts boundaries around God (as if we need to protect Him), which keeps people from entering the kingdom. We set up arbitrary exercises and rules to assess where people are in their spiritual journey and miss the beauty of the Holy Spirit working in others. Barnabas and the church at Antioch did not miss it. They began to proclaim the gospel to the Greeks and also to others outside the Jewish community. In the words of Tevye, from the play *Fiddler on the Roof*, "Unheard of, unthinkable!"

In Mumbai, India, Pastor Joseph leads a large cell-driven church of more than 18,000. An estimated 200,000 adherents participate in this church movement throughout the whole country. One of the toughest groups in India to reach is a community of transvestite eunuchs living primarily in Mumbai. Pastor Joseph and others felt the Holy Spirit calling them to this group, and they now have developed a fellowship among this once-rejected group within that society. Pastor Joseph, as Barnabas, follows the Holy Spirit as the Spirit opens lives and eyes in dark and uncharted territory. Some of Pastor Joseph's cell churches observed the Holy Spirit working among this despised social group and followed. Traditional Christian mission often finds it difficult to step outside the well-beaten path of evangelism to our kind of people.

Not only was Barnabas a risk taker relationally and culturally but he was also the coaching type. He loved to see others excel and to witness their gifts being used. Barnabas had an eye for talent and sought ways to help others develop their talent to make a spiritual impact. For example, it was a big risk to introduce Saul (Paul) all around town. Saul would not be easy to introduce to the family or the young church. He was a suspicious character with a spotty past, an outsider. He was a notable home wrecker, famous for breaking up Christian homes! When Saul was converted, the early church was convinced he was an undercover terrorist working for the bad guys. Many Christians thought he would infiltrate their fledgling movement and perhaps carry out what would have been equivalent to a suicide-bombing mission! The apostles and young church members were not willing to risk their lives at the hands of Saul.

The early church in Antioch was no different than we are today. Our theology and practice is built primarily on our experiential value system, and it takes the work of the Holy Spirit, often in dramatic ways, to break through and move us to take risk. For some reason Barnabas was able to reach beyond his own experiential frame of reference early in his life. He didn't need a "Balaam's ass" to pry his heart open. Other apostles, such as Peter, needed a Holy Spirit encounter, like the story of Peter's rooftop vision in Acts 11.

When Barnabas is first introduced in the biblical narrative, we see him open and available to the movement of the Holy Spirit. Barnabas could be described as "an early adapter" rather than a "later adapter" in the social science of innovation diffusion.[1] Early adapters are like people who enjoy sitting in the front seat of a roller coaster! They seek new opportunity and potential rather than moderate risk and adventure.

Barnabas was a relational risk taker who saw the benefit for the kingdom of God of getting Saul (Paul) involved in mission of the church. Barnabas saw potential written all over this young, zealous Jewish leader. He apparently connected to Saul's heartbeat.

Barney, as I'm sure his friends called him, continued throughout his biblical story to notice people with potential and bring them along. He was not egotistical about his own leadership as much as he was immersed in the kingdom of God and an appreciation for people with good spirits.

When I was completing my doctoral work, a portion of my research involved surveying urban leaders who have effectively facilitated consultations. In that research I found significant energy around the characteristics of a successful facilitator in any given city. This energy may partially be due to the people who completed the survey, many of whom described their own efforts and what they felt about themselves and respected in others. They knew that a city-facilitation role was a pivotal and significant responsibility in the city, drawing people together in meaningful ways. In my opinion these urban leaders highlighted the life and ministry of Barnabas.

When Barnabas went to Tarsus to recruit Saul, he instinctively knew additional spiritual gifts were needed in Antioch. As an apostle he was aware of the social capital necessary to create momentum for a new movement. Individuals can be moved with individual determinism and persuasion, but to motivate a whole community or movement toward a new goal takes more than lone ranger leadership. The movement must attract gifted leaders, who in turn engage multiple social strata. Barnabas had a way of searching the landscape for gifted people. I often wonder how the first multiracial church in Antioch was put together. Did Barnabas go out and actually recruit this unique blend of leadership? I bet he did. Perhaps someone told him there was a new convert from Africa in the city who could work with all the new converts from that area of the world. Perhaps another person mentioned that a Persian guy just entered the movement and he would be great too. However he accomplished it, Barnabas was a gifted networker who loved all of God's children.

Barnabas was a kind of maven, with a strong networking gift. A maven, as described by Malcolm Gladwell in his book *Tipping Point,* is a resource investigator and must be "in the know." Mavens are the consummate "I know where we can find that or them" people. Such a personality always remembers people and places and categorizes them as resources to be utilized at the appropriate time. Barnabas was apparently not looking for leaders who would follow him as much as he was looking for people to add some measure of grace and strength to this new and growing church in Antioch. Barnabas was "other focused." He had a wonderful outlook on life, where others had significance to him because he could see their potential for the kingdom of God. Rarely do we find leaders who think about others and how God is developing emerging leaders. Far too many leaders see others primarily as a good support team for their own personal burgeoning ministry.

INCARNATIONAL LEADERS

The term "incarnational leader" is an appropriate way to describe Barnabas. He was fully present and following in the footsteps of John the Baptist when John said of Jesus, "He must increase, but I must decrease" (John 3:30). Jesus gave a clue to the value of incarnational leadership when He quietly and firmly informed His disciples that He would leave them permanently and that it was necessary for Him to go away. Peter and others could not believe Jesus was saying this. They must have thought it was a bad dream or that Jesus doubted himself. I can hear Peter mumbling to himself, "Jesus, is so *down* right now, we need to cheer him up." His *downer* message was not well received by the disciples. As Jesus prepared them for His departure, they could only believe He was having a few miserable days. Peter tried to stop Jesus from this "bad self-talk" but Jesus strongly rebuked him and even put Peter in the place of standing with the devil. Jesus's words, "Satan, I rebuke you," spoken to Peter face-to-face must have been a shock. Most of us would never recover from such straight talk. However, Jesus had a mission, and part of that mission was to create a vacuum so God could introduce the Holy Spirit, who would fill that vacuum as the disciples' ruling guide. Jesus's message was clear, "If I don't go, the Holy Spirit will not come."

Bob Lupton: An Illustration

Bob Lupton, founder and president of Family Community Services (FCS) in Atlanta, Georgia, is one such gifted incarnational leader. He has spent a lifetime raising up young leaders and promoting them. When Bob entered Atlanta as a young man committed to live his life out in tough urban communities, he sought to find others who could grow with him. Today, some 30 years later, Bob has effectively turned a large, effective ministry over to Chris and Rebecca Gray and is watching the ministry flourish, enjoying the fruit of "setting the stage for others." Bob shared with me some of the joys and pains along the way when a leader is stretched to live out an incarnational life:

> After 30-plus years of frontline urban ministry, I felt the wear and tear on both body and spirit. My calling to serve among the poor was as clear and certain as it had ever been, however, my stamina at age 58 was not what it once was. I was ready to let someone younger take the reins of the organization I founded.

Fortunately I was spared the difficult task of conducting an executive search. Chris and Rebecca Gray, career Air Force officers, had experienced a call of God to leave the military and join with our staff and were obviously equipped to assume significant leadership roles. Over a five-year period the Grays emerged from being community chaplains to administrative directors to executive directors of our organization. They learned a variety of roles quickly and gained a thorough understanding of community development from both living in our urban neighborhood and leading development efforts (organizing, building affordable homes, managing programs and properties, and so on). Their leadership was received well by most of the FCS urban ministry staff, and it was obvious to me and our board that either of them could assume the CEO position. Because they performed so well as a ministry team, we elected to promote them as co-CEOs. I retained (and still hold) the president's position but have relinquished all operational duties for the ministry.

In the first year the Grays led the organization, they attempted to maintain the status quo and run the ministry much the same way I had. But their leadership styles were quite different from my somewhat laissez-faire mode. Having spent eight years in the military, they were much more comfortable with a chain of command and expectations of subordinates following orders. This did not go over well with some senior staff who had been used to doing things their own way. A major crisis arose during the second year of the Grays' leadership when it became apparent that the comptroller and administrative director, both with years of seniority, were simply not going to salute their new bosses' directives. The showdown came when the Grays hired a new CPA to head up finances and a younger administrator, effectively demoting these older faithful employees and dismantling the accounting and donor-management systems they had designed and managed for years. Both women quit, along with a young assistant whose attitude they had contaminated. The shock waves that radiated through the organization caused a lot of anger and fear among the rest of the staff. Rumors of people being unjustly fired, dictatorial regime changes, and whose head might be next on the chopping block spread like wildfire. It took several months for everyone to get used to the new CFO and COO, younger competent people with new ideas of how the organization could run more efficiently and effectively. In time the staff came to appreciate the improvements and the cooperative, supportive attitudes of these new leaders. The pain of transition has now faded into the past and the organization has a fresh, exciting feeling that everyone appreciates. The Grays' leadership has been firmly established and is well-respected.

The transition of leadership was clearly more difficult for the Grays than for me. They faced all the staff conflict and criticism while I remained uninvolved, except for the occasional intervention when I had to step in and remind folks who was running the organization. It was difficult for me to watch loyal associates struggle under new leadership and turn to me to rescue them from these new managers who must have seemed immature and unorthodox. Rescuing my former employees, however, was not my job. If they could not adapt to the new realities and become genuinely supportive and affirming, I told them they should leave sooner rather than later. Some of them did, which was hard; it damaged long, valued relationships, but was necessary.

Because the Grays value me as a person as well as for my experience in urban ministry, they view me as more of a coach than a competitor. I am available to them but do not impose my thinking on them. I have to let go of my ideas on how best to run the organization, let go of ministry directions I would choose, let go of my preferred methods of raising funds, and let the Grays learn the way I did—by trial and error. They treat me as a corporate asset to be used for the benefit of the organization—my celebrity, my books, my contacts. That makes me feel valued rather than used. Because I was so ready to be relieved of the CEO responsibilities, I am more than willing to let someone else lead the ministry, even if it is with priorities and methodology different from my tried-and-true ways. If they were less secure, they could feel threatened by my presence. If I had greater control needs, I would find it difficult to let them take the reins. But instead, I have the freedom to focus on things that give me life—writing, teaching, strategizing with other ministries, and taking on an occasional new vision.

The risk for me is seeing the support base (relational and financial) gravitating away from me and toward younger, more energetic, perhaps more visionary leadership. My limelight could diminish as theirs increases. In time it probably will. Sometimes I think about this, but I believe it is worth the risk. As long as I stay on the urban frontier and engage in frontline work, my instincts will remain sharp and my stories fresh. My writing will keep my credibility current. But it wouldn't take long for me to lose my cutting edge if I were to retreat to the academic world. I need to stay actively engaged.

Conventional organizational wisdom says that if the founder of an organization stays around too long, his influence will at some point begin to retard its progress, and finally reach a point of diminishing returns. The shadow of the founder can stunt the growth of new leadership. I was encouraged by wise counselors some years ago to leave the organization, so fresh leadership could take it to the next level. History will reveal whether I harmed FCS by staying around for 35 years. I like to think I gave the ministry my best creative energies, and at the appropriate time (I am age 61 at the time of this writing) stepped aside to let others take control while still remaining involved. I am sure the Grays may have a different perspective on this and I would defer to them. I still am president of the board and hold 51 percent of the social stock. But that is changing, slowly but surely, and it feels like a good process.

Promoting Emerging Leadership and Creating a Vacuum

Bob Lupton apparently understood the role of the incarnational leader, no doubt somewhat as Barnabas did. An incarnational leader is to come, serve, build, help establish the mission and vision, promote emerging leadership, and then execute an exit strategy for himself or herself. The incarnational leader seeks to have followers moved out from under his or her leadership and onto a dependency on a God-breathed, Holy Spirit encounter. Barnabas was willing to let Saul take the lead when the time came; as the story goes, Saul increased and Barnabas decreased. The same was true in the story of Bob Lupton.

In the book of Acts, Paul was called Saul until he and Barnabas were sent on their first mission together. It appears that this was when Saul was finally released to the unique call of God he had been commissioned for some 15 years earlier. Barnabas was clearly the leader until they left Antioch on their mission. However, once they were confronted on the road, away from Antioch, the home base of Barnabas, Saul moved into a new calling and identity. From this point in the narrative, Luke, the writer of Acts, refers to Saul (Paul) as the leader and Barnabas as the sidekick. Notice the change from Acts 13:1–7 to Acts 13:9–13:

> Now in the church at Antioch there were prophets and teachers, Barnabas, Simeon who was called Niger, Lucius of Cyrene, Manaen a member of the court of Herod the tetrarch, and Saul. While they were worshiping the Lord and fasting, the Holy Spirit said, "Set apart for me Barnabas and Saul for the work to which I have called them." Then after fasting and praying they laid their hands on them and sent them off.
>
> So, being sent out by the Holy Spirit, they went down to Seleucia; and from there they sailed to Cyprus. When they arrived at Salamis, they proclaimed the word of God in the synagogues of the Jews. And they had John to assist them. When they had gone through the whole island as far as Paphos, they came upon a certain magician, a Jewish false prophet, named Bar-Jesus. He was with the proconsul, Sergius Paulus, a man of intelligence, who summoned Barnabas and Saul and sought to hear the word of God.
>
> —Acts 13:1–7

Clearly Paul is still being identified by his original name, Saul, traveling with Barnabas. Barnabas is still considered the leader at this point in the narrative. However, the next passage in Acts finds the spiritual leadership juices flowing in Paul as he sheds the old name, Saul. He was released from his old identity. Note verses 9–13:

> But Saul, who is also called Paul, filled with the Holy Spirit, looked intently at him and said, "You son of the devil, you enemy of all

righteousness, full of all deceit and villainy, will you not stop making crooked the straight paths of the Lord? And now, behold, the hand of the Lord is upon you, and you shall be blind and unable to see the sun for a time." Immediately mist and darkness fell upon him and he went about seeking people to lead him by the hand. Then the proconsul believed, when he saw what had occurred, for he was astonished at the teaching of the Lord. Now Paul and his company set sail from Paphos, and came to Perga in Pamphylia. And John left them and returned to Jerusalem.
—Acts 13:9–13

With Luke's words "Now Paul and his company set sail..." it is apparent Paul is now the leader. Barnabas is not even mentioned! Barnabas is only mentioned as one of the company. He was the leader, the one people noticed, but now he was simply in the company of Paul. Few leaders would put up with this kind of leadership rearrangement and dramatic identity shift. Going from primary leader to one of the group is not considered upward mobility in modern leadership lore.

Tim Svoboda: A Barnabas-Style Leader

Tim Svoboda is another Barnabas-style leader working in the country of India. Tim and his wife, Karol, traveled in their Volkswagen bus from Amsterdam to India in the early '70s. They were early pioneer Youth with a Mission (YWAM) missionaries and had to pay a dear price for pioneering. Here is a short interview I did with Tim.

Jon: Do you have an example of a time when you took a risk with an emerging leader?

Tim: Yes, I can think of several. There was one guy who quite a few were concerned about. He came from a management background and was in YWAM. He was an Indian, and at that time YWAM was so foreign-led that turning things over to an Indian was scarier for the Indians than the foreigners. They would be concerned what kind of Indian got leadership. I believed this guy would be the right person to replace me as the national director. We started getting to know one another in 1989, and I was able to turn my job over to him in 1995. However, it actually took about two or three years for my peers to accept him and endorse the decision. That's the short version of the story.

Jon: What did you see in him that made you want to take the risk?

Tim: First, he had a tremendous mix of management skills I saw we needed to make us more goal-oriented. Second, YWAM India was growing so much that we needed a leader who was more vision-ary than I was. I am a visionary, but in the confines of a place, namely cities, where I get satisfaction from hands-on participa-tion. YWAM India was growing so fast that it needed a person who could lead by vision, not getting his hands in the mud so much. I was not that person, and started recognizing this in 1992.

Jon: How did you handle others who were critical of that risk?

Tim: Lots of times I had to slow down the turnover process to make sure those whom he would be leading were part of the process of bringing him into power. That took time because others involved were still skeptical. Therefore, we had leadership meetings where we discussed my turnover, the implications of this new person taking matters on, and letting people freely voice their concerns. I had to learn to listen, keep checking out why I felt this was the right direction, and then practice what Stephen Covey calls "seek-ing first to understand and then to make yourself understood." I had to do this to those whom he would be leading, not to the person to whom I was trying to give my leadership. I had the advantage of working with this potential leader closely enough to know his strengths and weaknesses. The others did not have that advantage. So I had to become an advocate of his character and leadership to those within the groups who had questions. Not all groups had questions; however, a few did, and sometimes "the few" can be powerful, especially in an organization such as

YWAM, where we do not make decisions by voting but by consensus on large matters.

Jon: Was there a good outcome?

Tim: Yes, very good. He was immediately able to identify our blockages as a mission that kept us from further growth. He came up with structural changes that would take us forward and was able to implement them. We went from 22 locations in India to approximately 100 during his leadership. He broke the country of India into separate structures related more to people groups (South India, North India, and so on), rather than trying to be one large entity. He became the last national director of YWAM India, which was his goal. He initiated a plan for YWAM India to be led by five associate national directors and his position would be eliminated. Today those goals have been achieved and each area functions on its own steam.

He also helped me in my new role from 1996 to 2003, helping me grow YWAM as an urban mission in Chennai. Though not an urban person, his management skills helped me implement a decentralized structure that brought growth to us in the city.

Another good outcome was that he was a gracious leader. I stayed in Chennai during his leadership, and though he could have ignored me and kept me out of his way, he constantly brought me into meetings with him, even though his inputs and leadership were much more effective than mine. Though it is always hard turning something over to another person when you still stick around, he made it quite easy by making the effort to keep me in the loop of communication, bringing me into meetings (even when I didn't want to go), and sharing with me the structural changes for which he was dreaming and planning, as well as harboring an atmosphere where I could ask questions for clarification.

This story sets the principal characteristics for the ministry of a city facilitator. An effective city facilitator serves the city with a Barnabas spirit.² Barnabas types find gifted leaders and nurture them into prominence. The facilitators gather people with gifts just as Barnabas did, and they "set the platform" for others to follow. Effective facilitators will often find themselves in behind-the-scene roles, opening doors for others.³

Wes Anderson in Seattle, Washington, is one of those gifted leaders. Wes works with government leaders and business leaders in Seattle. He brings people together for discipleship groups and for mayoral, gubernatorial, and presidential prayer breakfasts. Leaders throughout the city know Wes. Recently I asked Wes if he would speak to a group of doctoral students from around the world about public ministry. As we discussed the needs of the students, he asked if he could bring a guest. Of course I responded that he could. The day of his lecture, he brought the former chairman of the board of one of the leading companies in the United States.

As this corporate executive shared and the students were profoundly impacted, Wes stepped out of the limelight, as he has so many times, and let the students learn from another gifted leader. What the students did not see was the years of discipleship and care Wes had given this man. They did not realize Wes was setting the stage for another. He was making room for gifts of the Spirit through another person. This is the ministry of a facilitator living out the Barnabas spirit. May his kind increase.

CHARACTERISTICS OF A CITY FACILITATOR

Several characteristics are helpful for an effective city facilitator to have. She or he must: (1) be able to cross sectarian lines, (2) have meaningful relationships, (3) be a natural-born networker, (4) be a humble servant leader, (5) have knowledge of city ministries, (6) be strong in commitment to individuals, (7) have a long-term vision for the city and concern for the welfare of the people in the city, (8) be prayerful and practical, (9) exhibit risk-taking, creativity, and perseverance, (10) have the ability to listen and learn and be an incessant student, (11) have a passionate spirituality that knows how to live in the city, and finally, (12) read the Bible with urban glasses.

Able to Cross Sectarian Lines

Corrie DeBoer of Manila models a life of crossing boundaries. Corrie is a professor, social activist, spiritual director, and Christian. She has completed two doctorates, started a ministry for homeless children, and connected evangelicals and Roman Catholics for ministry to the poor all across Manila. Her gentle and loving spirit, coupled with a profound pastoral care for each person she meets, helps her walk into any setting and be received. She does not come across as a threat but as a blessing and fresh breeze of the Holy Spirit. People of goodwill in each section of the church respond to her calls to work together. She is equally comfortable with Roman Catholics, evangelicals, and Pentecostals. She brings out the best in each group as she helps them focus on the love and compassion of Jesus Christ. Corrie is involved with us on our board of regents at Bakke Graduate University, and we watch with amazement as she enters areas where others fear to tread.

In contrast I have watched many Christian leaders actually turn red in the face and become agitated when someone mentions to them that an orthodox priest or a Roman Catholic priest may attend a meeting and they may have to interact with such a guest. I have even watched evangelical pastors get concerned when they hear that a Lutheran or a Pentecostal pastor may join in fellowship! Although all of us have limits as to what we need to embrace (outside of orthodox Christian boundaries), a person who seeks to mobilize the church and the city must have a gracious heart and understand that personal limitations are not God's limitations.

Barnabas was not afraid to embrace people on the other side of the aisle. In fact, it would be interesting to know how much of the vision and passion for the Gentiles that Paul so passionately carried actually emerged from Barnabas's ministry. Barnabas was the leader in Antioch, the first church where the gospel was preached to the

Gentiles. It was Barnabas who brought Saul to this place and introduced this devout Jewish leader to the growing Gentile congregation.

Attempting to work within a city will test your sectarianism. As soon as you think you have a broad reach, you will be tested. You will soon discover whether or not your convictions are biblical or sectarian, orthodox or cultural. Recently I was working with a group planning a consultation, and as we moved toward the actual date of the consultation, one of the members questioned whether or not we could actually hold the consultation in a church that was considered controversial in the city. The committee met and decided it best not to start at this location because it might send the wrong message to the rest of the church from the beginning of the consultation. In this particular city more than 60 percent of the church would have objected.

Crossing sectarian lines can be costly on every side. As that consultation team worked through this tough issue (they did a good job of navigating this rough water), we recognized that living between factions and sectarian views is painful. Perhaps the first lesson learned when you seek to serve in a facilitating role within a city is that you will be misunderstood. It reminds me of the question Jesus asked his disciples: "Can you be baptized with the baptism I'm baptized with?" (see Mark 10:39).

As I mentioned in chapter 8, I had the privilege of growing up in the mountains at a resort where diverse groups of Christians came to retreat. We watched the Pentecostals jump and shout and the Dutch Reformed discuss theology while puffs of blue smoke rose from their pipes and cigars. I observed Roman Catholics serving and giving sacrificially and holiness folks giving themselves to prayer as if this was normal Christianity. God planted a love for the whole church in my heart at a young age. Sectarian lines never mattered much to me. I was always surprised when churches and leaders took such strong stands against others, especially when it was not for a clear-cut biblical reason. Somehow it didn't make sense to me that brothers and sisters would treat each other with such little respect. It still doesn't.

A characteristic of a city facilitator is one who loves the whole church and is not afraid to be in the mix of it all.

A Person with Meaningful Relationships

Recently I was sitting in my living room as we entertained a prominent Christian leader in our city. During the conversation of the evening, he said, "You know, I'm reading a book, and it's really convicting." After he told me about the book, I asked him if he remembered that about four years prior we sat at a restaurant as the author of the same book tried to talk to him about the issues of the book and he refused to listen. He looked at me and said, "No, that wasn't him, was it?" Having relationships with key people in leadership means you are with them when they fail to understand, and you are with them when understanding breaks through! You may not be seen as the authority in any area, but when you need to access them, the door is open.

A Natural-Born Networker

Networkers continually find people and things and put them together. They envision how people come together. They look for connections at every point. Networkers keep people, organizations, and resources on file for the appropriate time. When they see a fit, they facilitate the connections.

Malcolm Gladwell, in *The Tipping Point*, explained the networking genius of Paul Revere, the American patriot. Two men had similar assignments on one historic night in American history. Samuel Dawson and Revere were to travel through the countryside at the inception of the Revolutionary War with England and alert the American militia that the "British were coming." Revere went one direction and Dawson the other. Gladwell points out that Revere was grafted into the Boston community's social web, involved in many activities, clubs, church activities, and so on. He was a well-known Boston figure, or as we would say today, "well networked." Dawson, on the other hand, was not as well networked and was not widely known. As history records the story, everywhere Revere went sounding the alarm about the British military advance, militia were activated, while the areas Dawson traveled to, militia were noticeably absent. Dawson had the misfortune of many would-be city facilitators. He wasn't well-known; he had not been exercising the gift of a networker. Revere, on the other hand, did what so many good networkers do. They spend time with people. In many cultures this can be described as "having one more cup of tea," rather than rushing on to accomplish a task. Networking is about people.

I often picture this story of Dawson and Revere as Revere traveling through the countryside and everyone shouting, "That was Paul Revere, get ready!" However, after Dawson traveled through their communities, they looked at each other scratching their heads, saying, "Who was that?" The message was lost through the messenger. This often happens in the kingdom of God. The message of the kingdom is obscured by a messenger who has not developed strong relationships.

The apostle Paul instructed young Timothy to, "Know those who minister among you." Of course, Paul was speaking of knowing a person's character, but the meaning transfers to the necessity of being known. Being known and building appropriate relationships is a key to motivating others. Barnabas was known in Jerusalem as a "good man." His reputation preceded him as he went to Antioch.

Doug Engberg, US director for Viva Network, an organization confronting global child trafficking, prostitution, and slavery, is a Paul Revere type. Organizations and movements thrive when he starts spreading the word. Watching Doug and his wife, Margo, build and maintain relationships is amazing. We attend their annual Christmas celebration at their home, and it is a feast of relationships across the city and region.

I remember talking to another acquaintance of Doug's about how many phone calls I receive from Doug in a day or week and he exclaimed, "Well, you and about 30 other people!" For Doug to have authentic relationships, he must convey his love, care, and personal commitment to all of these people. A Barnabas type spreads pastoral care over multiple relational spheres. I asked Doug what he thought were the keys in relationship. Here is his response. A networker

- needs to have the gift of leadership.
- must not care who gets the credit.
- must have excellent facilitation skills.
- has the ability to quickly understand other cultures and how to navigate through them.
- is a level 5 leader (a level 5 leader has a strong resolve to succeed and has humility).
- loves to connect people together and is able to walk away and encourage them in their relationships. The networker does not have to control.
- has the ability to make friends quickly and gain trust.
- cannot come in with his or her own hidden agenda.
- is able to adapt and go with the flow. This means they have the ability to change and still keep their eyes on the goal.
- is all about kingdom building.[4]

A Humble Servant Leader

I have had the privilege of working with all types of leaders. I have observed two kinds of people who hang out with them. The first are people who get ego strokes by being around people of notoriety. They lavish praise on a well-known leader and then use the overflow for their own benefit. They borrow power continually. Such folks have huge ego needs. They serve to glean some of the glory and cannot simply serve. These folks impede the work of the Holy Spirit, because they need to be recognized or control the environment. If they are not mentioned or their plan is not utilized, they begin to sabotage what God is doing within a city or ministry. We all know people like this; as soon as something is outside their control, they attack others. Furthermore, we all have a bit of this ego in us.

Every city houses those who want to control. This is quite prevalent in urban ministry in particular. Perhaps it's because few people
served in urban ministry for many years and they had to fight for
every inch of funding, when churches and denominations primarily
focused on foreign missions and left urban ministries to the rescue
mission movement. Many veteran urban practitioners often impose
their leadership on newcomers and want others to work only through
them. It is difficult for some urban pioneers to trust the next wave of
workers who seemingly come in at the eleventh hour and do not have
to pay the same price the pioneers had to pay. This is often manifested
by the pioneers establishing litmus tests for newcomers, reminding us
of the Galatian problem in Scripture where a certain group of religious leaders required others to be circumcised by them. These pioneers wanted others to recognize their authority. Urban litmus tests
are often established by defining the neighborhood you live in, the
church you attend, the clothes you wear, the car you drive, the school
your children attend, the racial balance of your group; the list goes on.

Often these "gatekeepers" are offended when others begin working on their turf, and so they try to limit others' access. This was the
very attitude Paul addressed to the Galatians. Barnabas, in contrast to
this attitude, drew people together. He brought in new talent to the
city and the vibrant growing ministry of the church in Antioch.

The second type of people I have observed are those who know
how to serve. They recognize varieties of gifts and are happy to step
aside when they see a gift blossoming in someone else. They love to
promote others, whether big or small. They receive pleasure from seeing God work through people. This type of leader is a person God can
use in the city. Unfortunately we see few models of this in contemporary ministry. It is a rare leader who allows God to do things outside
his or her own domain and still applaud it. I think this controlling
"gatekeeping" is one of the major blocks to transformation of the city.

Rita Nussli, executive director of New Horizon Ministries in
Seattle, working with street kids, demonstrates a servant and gracious

heart toward other ministries. I have found Rita always willing to assist other ministries and promote her own staff. Rita's grasp of giving away leadership is uncanny. She sits on various boards throughout the city of Seattle because people know she really cares about others, not for the status.

Larry Winn facilitated a consultation in the Miami neighborhood of Overtown, and in the end determined there was not the heart within the leadership of the community to bring about transformation. He found that Christian leaders were primarily self-centered and myopic when it came to working together. He also determined that few of the Christian leaders were actually willing to live in the community; they were "drive-in" leaders! His experience in that area left him discouraged about the lack of a Barnabas spirit among the urban mission leaders in the Overtown community.

Knowledge of City Ministries

When God finally released me to the city, I knew my growth curve would be steep. I had been out of contemporary urban life and in the suburbs for quite some time, but I was determined to learn. I began to visit ministries and listen to people's stories. Soon I was aware of many wonderful signs of hope in our city. I am reminded that a city facilitator must be one who learns, listens, and remembers what God is doing.

The time we take to know ministries and Christian leaders within a city is vital. Viju Abraham in Mumbai, India, helped us facilitate a course for doctoral students, where we explored the nature and mission of the church in the Indian urban context. At BGU, we require all of our doctor of ministry students to travel to a world-class city with a group of fellow students to explore world-class cities, mission contexts, and urban ministry. Viju exposed us to ministries working with prostitutes and their children, church planting in the slums, ministries caring for the poor and dying, and social spiritual movements. As we visited one ministry after another, it became apparent that Viju had spent over 30 years building relationships with a wide spectrum of people and ministries. Ministry after ministry referenced Viju and his work and spoke about how he helped them through the years. Many of them had been in touch with Viju since the '70s. Viju is a leader who takes time and critically assesses ministry involvement in his city. Through years of relationship building, he has connected and resourced many ministries. When people need to find assistance, he can often be counted on to point them to the right resources.

Strong Commitment to Individuals

Barnabas was committed to individuals, not just movements or mission. When Paul and Barnabas had their big fight over John Mark, recorded for us in Acts 15, Paul thought Mark was a flake. On their first mission journey, Mark had quit about halfway through the trip and returned home. Paul thought Mark did not have enough stamina to serve, because John Mark quit when things were tough. Paul was developing a habit of leaving wimps behind. He later said, "Demas has forsaken me, having loved this present world" (2 Timothy 4:10 NKJV). I often wonder what that looked like? Did Demas do something terrible, like adultery or sodomy, or did Demas simply want a break? Did Demas grow tired of countless long hikes through the mountains, fighting wild animals, losing sleep, spending time in prison, having to run for the door when the constant riots broke out? I picture Demas coming to Paul one day and saying, "Paul, I found a little cottage on the Mediterranean and I think I'm going to settle down there and get a good tan and take the winter off." In a sense, he may have been the forerunner of snowbirds going to the desert or the beach!

John Mark was in a similar place. He couldn't take it anymore; he was going home. At that point Paul said, "He is not fit for the ministry or at least working in my ministry." Barnabas, on the other hand, saw promise in John Mark and realized that through time and experience Mark would make a good leader. The ministry approach of Paul and

Barnabas was diametrically opposed. What Scripture records is quite interesting; they had, "a sharp disagreement" (Acts 15:39 NIV).

From this story, we see Barnabas emerge as a disciple-maker of broken, imperfect people. We see a man committed to individual lives at the expense of his relationship to Paul. The spirit of a Barnabas is necessary in our cities. We need people who will look beyond their own ego and their own time frame, and be apostolic in encouraging and strengthening others for the kingdom of God in their city. In one sense, we can say it takes a Barnabas spirit to consult a city.

A Long-Term Vision for the City and
Concern for the Welfare of the People of the City

Jesus talked about the good shepherd. The shepherd cared for the sheep and did not run when the natural enemies of sheep appeared.

> I am the good shepherd. The good shepherd lays down his life for the sheep. He who is a hireling and not a shepherd, whose own the sheep are not, sees the wolf coming and leaves the sheep and flees; and the wolf snatches them and scatters them. He flees because he is a hireling and cares nothing for the sheep.
> —John 10:11–13

When the money dries up and the fame is gone, city facilitators are still there, caring about the city, the people, and God's heartbeat. A vision was burned into their soul somewhere along the line in their journey, a vision that said, "This is your town; love it and let God work here through you."

Prayerful and Practical

Perhaps this is the most revealing characteristic of good city facilitators. They have spiritual balance and common sense. They listen and commune with God, knowing this is His city. They are practical and not distracted by impostors dressed up like apostles.

Risk-Taking, Creativity, and Perseverance

City facilitators are required to continue thinking about possibilities when the money runs dry or others fail to help. They learn to live and minister on a shoestring. They learn to put things together with few resources or little assistance. They act like glue in a city and pursue their goals, whether funded or not. People often wonder if these facilitators are still there when little is heard from them or about them. Nevertheless they are found in obscure places of the city, bringing people together. Their career location and job description may change, but their role stays the same.

Ability to Listen, Learn, and Be an Incessant Student

Effective city facilitators continually learn. The city is intellectual. It requires full attention at all times. Those who excel at facilitation listen a great deal, learn even more, and believe they are learning every day. The city teaches them each day and provides bountiful lessons and wisdom.

A Passionate Spirituality that Knows How to Live in the City

Perhaps this is the most telling point for most city facilitators. Can he or she live out a deep spirituality in sinful places? The city throws everything at a person. The urban environment, where people congregate in great numbers, increases temptations to default from faithfulness. The city makes room for people to be anonymous and evade accountability. The leader who develops a deep spirituality within the city must learn to take pleasure in simple things such as watching a little child at play, or observing a blade of grass pushing through concrete. These simple things send messages that God is in control. The city facilitator looks for God in faces and places.

I have been intrigued with the ministry of Jonathan and Thelma Nambu of Manila. They founded Samaritana, a ministry to women involved in prostitution. When Jonathan began his doctoral studies at

Bakke Graduate University, he chose to specialize in spiritual formation. Watching Jonathan and Thelma is a study in contrasts. Serving
young and old women at the bottom of urban society, Jonathan and
Thelma recognize the need to go deeper in the Spirit of God. The
godly facilitator hears God speaking when others hear thunder! The
urban facilitator is a servant in communion.

Reads the Bible with Urban Glasses

Those of us who grew up in the country learned to read the Bible with
a set of rural glasses. Since the early days of the United States, Americans have read the Bible with rural eyes. In contrast, many who
migrate to the city with a sense of calling now read Scripture with
urban glasses. They see urban settings and recognize the call of Christ
in the center of the city.

These 12 characteristics reflect the perspectives we seek to model.
It is important to identify values and perceptions as we look for key
people in consultation leadership.

Transformational leadership is birthed by the Holy Spirit and
years of experience. Now in the next chapter we turn to the design of
a consultation.

REFLECTIONS

1. Discuss with a friend what you learned from the three stories of
   John Hayes, Bob Lupton, and Tim Svoboda in this chapter.
2. How do you respond when attending a meeting with a guest who
   cuts across sectarian lines? Discuss your response with a friend.
3. What part of the Barnabas spirit appeals to you and what part
   doesn't? Why and why not?
4. Which of the characteristics of a city facilitator do you think is
   most important and which is least important? Why?

Chapter 11

How Do You Consult Your City?

Walk into any bookstore in the United States and one of the largest sections will be the how-to books. We seem to thrive on any and all information that helps us accomplish goals we set for ourselves. So now we get to the how-to of consultations. Designing a consultation for your city is not an easy task but it is a doable one if you know what is involved. We hope to help you with some of the praxis to design your own city consultation. This how-to utilizes a "step one, step two" approach. I will provide a lot of material that we have compiled for hundreds of consultations from which you can gain insights on how to prepare for a consultation in your city. For specifics, see appendix 1.

WHAT HAPPENS IN A CONSULTATION?

The consultation in Manila in 2000 was billed as the Pacific Rim Think Tank. Catholics and Protestants came together to work on issues of poverty, education, and a crumbling environment in this sprawling megacity. Corrie DeBoer, mentioned in the previous chapter, is a professor and networker in the Philippines who had been working day and night to facilitate a unique urban consultation. We were amazed that she was able to plan a spectacular three-day-long consultation on the heels of completing two doctoral dissertations! Experienced ministry practitioners from around the world converged on Manila for this experience.

215

Dialogue opened around educational initiatives and ministry cooperation in the city. Midday tours through Manila exposed participants to the streets of intense need and also to rich signs of hope. The participants visited ministries brokering small loans for microenterprise in the most extreme poverty-stricken communities. We saw dynamic Christian community living and working within the infamous Smokey Mountain dump site, one of the largest in the world. Benigno Beltran, a brilliant Roman Catholic priest, committed his life to building this community after serving in Rome. His journey from Rome to Smokey Mountain was an exercise in downward mobility and, in his words, "giving up the fine perfumes and wine of Rome and coming home." Father Beltran talks about the stark contrasts of these two worlds. He recognized home for him would be serving with the poorest of the poor.

The consultation participants stood in amazement as this Catholic priest walked the streets of this little community wearing his flowing white robes, surrounded by children, while sprinkling holy water over the new garbage trucks. The whole community came out to see this marvelous expression of hope and joy. This garbage dump community had developed to such an extent that they were now able to challenge the powers of corruption by building a garbage system of their own. Father Benigno and his congregation had recruited a large Christian following all over the city to stop using the corrupt city garbage system in favor of their new Smokey Mountain garbage service.

We have learned from our own successes and failures that consultations cannot be downloaded into a city but must be networked into the fabric of the community. Ray often says, quoting Karl Barth, "The gift of the outsider is the power to convene." The best consultations come as a result of a long-term networking effort by trusted facilitators and the input of an outsider. The outsider brings a listening ear, a desire to learn from the city, and his or her power to convene the leadership of a city—social, political, and religious. This has been the formula for effective consultations held by Ray all over the world.

CONSULTATION COMPONENTS

Following the relational approach to entering a city, the consultation is a live, surround-sound environment where participants hear different rhythms and beats from each unique neighborhood. Glenn Smith of Montreal, Canada, notes the consultation is designed with an adult learning approach (andragogy)[1] which demands hands-on participation, not a stilted learning by rote. One must remember that andragogy works best when it is preceded by pedagogy in the adult's life. Otherwise it can be quite disconcerting when a group of adults sit around and share from their own ignorance on a subject.

After consulting in over 250 urban consultations, we have discovered two key components central to people engaging their city and stimulating ongoing collaboration. First is the "who," the ones who become stakeholders, participants, and blessers. Second is the "what," the things that need to be accomplished—building a network, city research, invitations, and delivery. Let's begin with the "who."

THE "WHO" OF THE CONSULTATION

Stakeholders

Stakeholders really are invested in the success of the city and come with a kingdom vision for the whole church, the whole gospel, and the whole city. Every community has those who care deeply about their city and have usually networked a significant portion of the church in the city. It doesn't take long to identify these folks, as others will usually point them out to you.

In Seattle for instance, Cal Uomoto is known for his work with immigrant churches. Cal directs the Seattle World Relief office, whose primary ministry is settling new refugees as they enter the Seattle metropolitan area. World Relief not only settles refugees, but Cal and his capable team also are instrumental in caring for pastors of the immigrant churches and bringing them together from time to time to help them with their challenges. Ray and I have dubbed Cal the "apostle to the immigrant church."

To hold a consultation in Seattle without utilizing Cal's vast network would mean missing many of the most important stories of God at work. The entire immigrant church, which numbers in the tens of thousands, would be outside the mainstream church purview without Cal's input. Finding stakeholders means finding the people who have demonstrated they care and have an active stake in the ministry of their city.

Consultations in major world-class cities include representatives from denominations, churches, theological schools, mission organizations, and in some cases, business and civic leaders. In every city, you can identify stakeholders by asking pastors, mission leaders, and educators for the names of people who connect the whole church and who care about the city. It is vital to find the most comprehensive expression of the church in a city. All too often people want a citywide consultation, but at the conclusion of the experience they realize they were not inclusive but rather exclusive. Consultation planners often find they did not initially cast the net widely, but simply had invited their friends. The biggest surprises in effective consultations come when participants discover something wonderful God is doing in their city about which they had no prior knowledge. God's best surprises usually come out of unexpected places, much like the Good Samaritan, who was not in the normal social circles of the devout Hebrews.

Stakeholders may be businesspeople, educators, theologians, pastors, or missionaries. We often identify stakeholders as those with a Barnabas spirit of friendship and encouragement, as we discussed in the previous chapter. You can be a stakeholder in your city by building relationships across sectarian lines, discovering the ministries who are providing vital services, and networking people together. Anyone with a heart to serve can be helpful to a citywide movement of transformation.

Key Facilitator

It's popular now to highlight the ministry of the apostle Barnabas. Perhaps it is a knee-jerk reaction to an overemphasis on the apostle Paul throughout Christendom's centuries, or maybe it is a fascination with the ever-increasing networking phenomenon. The scriptural narrative gives honorable mention to Barnabas, which provides a glimpse into a facilitative leadership style. Barnabas was adept at calling many diverse personalities and groups to a common table and then applauding as gifted people moved to center stage. Barnabas seemed to have that wonderful quality of identifying gifted leaders and helping them move into their field of expertise. (See chapter 10 for more information on Barnabas.)

In 2003 we surveyed 12 city facilitators, asking them to unpack what a good facilitator profile looks like. The veterans we surveyed agreed that a good facilitator easily crosses sectarian lines (tough for most Christians), relates meaningfully with key leaders throughout the city, is able to celebrate what others are doing, and personally remains in the background (it takes a tough skin and good ego to do this). He or she is aware and connected to multiple city ministries, networks widely, dreams for the welfare of the city, takes risks, listens, learns, lives in the city with a sustainable spirituality, and reads the Bible with urban glasses.

Glenn Smith of Montreal, Canada, facilitates urban ministry and is known as a catalytic person others can turn to for help. His long-term commitment to Montreal is legendary. Glenn leads Christian Direction, a ministry making dramatic impact in that French-speaking city. One leader said that when he is in a crisis, he always expects a phone call from Glenn. Glenn sees all of Montreal as his parish.

It doesn't take long after reading the facilitator's characteristics to realize these folks don't just naturally pop up but are often produced by good mentoring and godly vision. Effective facilitators within a city clearly are signs of God's grace, and cities are blessed when these folks become evident within their fabric.

To be recognized as a city facilitator is a privilege and an honor. To be an effective city facilitator means you have the special gift of being willing to spotlight others rather than yourself. Having the strength of character, leadership, and an ego that doesn't need to be constantly stroked is the fertile personal ground for the development of a good city facilitator.

Envisioning Team

An Envisioning Team is not just thrown together willy-nilly. They do not really become a team until they move effectively toward a common goal. Jon Katzenbach and Douglas Smith, in their award-winning book *The Wisdom of Teams*, differentiated between pseudo-teams, working groups, and real teams.

Effective teams are small in size. They have complementary skills, a compelling mission, well-defined individual and group goals, and a common approach, and team members hold each other mutually accountable.[2] A team capable of networking widely in the city and providing the necessary resources to do good research is vital. This team should represent diverse ministries, churches, mission organizations, educational institutions, and ethnic groups and should have whole church connections. The team should include Roman Catholic, orthodox, mainline, evangelical, and Pentecostal representatives, as well as people from ministries working with homelessness, poverty, refugees, youth at risk, and other social issues.

Once selected, the team's responsibility is to conduct urban research, survey pastors and ministry leaders, provide survey results, find and deliver ministry models from the city, and help others read those models. In some cases it also helpful for the team to provide case-study booklets built from their research.

Seasoned consultation facilitators say that great teams consist of people with proven relational equity throughout the city; skilled community mobilizers; and people committed to learning, networking, and fund-raising. Identifying these folks is to simply ask the question,

"Who knows everybody, and who can we trust?" If you ask this question, invariably people will identify the gifted facilitators in their city. In Manila, Corrie De Boer is the person with relational capital. In Seattle, Doug Engberg carries vast social capital. In Mumbai, Viju Abraham has built his social equity since the '70s. There are Corries, Dougs, and Vijus in every world-class city in the world.

It is important also to have team members who can analyze socioeconomic and political realities in a city. Team members need to be willing to make a commitment to oversee the implementation of the consultation. Teams are not well served if there is naïveté about social, class, and religious issues. People who simply want to "pray everything away," will not be helpful in this role. Prayer is vital, but you also need other gifts expressed relationally to move a city forward.

Neutral conveners serve a wonderful purpose where competition is rampant. Few cities escape a competitive environment, and the best team members are those who can move in and out of sectarian groups with ease. If a team member exhibits a contested political, sectarian, or doctrinal view, he or she will not usually be helpful in a key facilitative role. A citywide geographic representation is important so areas of the city are not overlooked and whole people groups ignored.

Finally, every group needs a few key administrators to get the work done. In my own experience in Seattle we had two such people: Cal Uomoto, the key World Relief director and a consummate networker, mentioned earlier, worked selflessly to connect people and to support the immigrant churches and people of the Pacific Northwest. Not only did Cal serve all of us in the city but he loaned us some of his best staff to assist the Serve Seattle effort as we sought to bring the church together for the good of the city. Kelly Pearson was another person Cal brought to us, and she turned out to be a gifted administrator and networker. Her selfless and tireless work became the backbone of the entire group. Kelly represents the kind of people who build a Christian community within a city. Her work is filled with grace, and she is passionate about the church and the city.

Blessers

When planning a consultation, the planning team would normally enlist the permission of blessers, who come from the ranks of well-known pastors, ministry leaders, mission leaders, business leaders, and in some environments, bishops. Churches, denominations, and ministry and mission organizations are encouraged to choose their best models of ministry or a sign of hope to demonstrate God at work in their city. Blessers are normally found within these organizations. Blessers do not often make the time to be deeply involved, but they do open the door for other mission-minded workers. In Seattle several pastors of large churches and organizations served as blessers and appointed people from their ministry to serve on the Envisioning Team. Blessers are asked to highlight and showcase the signs of hope from their spheres of influence.

A significant way to engage blessers is to ask the question, "If you had to prove God is alive in your city, to what would you point?" Most leaders can point to a particular ministry in their domain that reveals God's hand at work. After engaging a particular ministry leader in this discovery process, it is important to have them attend the consultation to bless and support it.

Blessers are identified in a variety of ways. They may run large ministries within the city and have unusually strong networks. Jim Gwinn in Seattle is an example. Jim was president of Crista Ministries for more than 20 years and built extensive relationships. The gigantic ministry he led is the Christian communication hub for the Seattle metro area. Not only did Crista have three powerful radio stations serving the church with Bible teaching and Christian music, they also had the largest Christian schools and the most services for senior adults in Seattle. Jim exhibited a passion to serve the church. I remember well my visit to Crista to meet with Jim Gwinn when I began to network the city of Seattle. This was not my first visit to Crista, and I had known Jim for quite some time. I knew he needed to be one of my first stops when I was looking for blessers. Another blesser within the Seattle Parish is Cal Uomoto. His link to the immigrant church can bring ethnic leaders to a meeting or help open doors to ethnic relationships. Another blesser in our city is Sister Joyce Cox. Sister Joyce serves as the Roman Catholic archdiocese ecumenical director. Sister Joyce is an encouragement to many groups seeking to bring about unity in the city.

Corrie DeBoer facilitated the consultation in Manila in 2000 and was able to bring many leaders to the consultation to share short words of encouragement or to pray. Roman Catholic, Pentecostal, and mainline church leaders were involved. We have learned that having bishops and other Christian leaders in attendance gives many individuals the permission to participate. The example Billy Graham set throughout his ministry of involving civic and religious leaders of every Christian stream has been exemplary. Each time a Catholic bishop sat on a stage with Billy Graham, Catholic laypeople realized it was okay for them to participate. When boundaries are crossed, people often show reluctance to get involved until they see a recognized leader participating.

Corrie sat down with some friends several years later and discussed the value of the consultation in Manila. She wrote:

> Recently, a group of friends gathered around my dining room table in Metro Manila. We all were a part of the Signs of Hope city consultation in 1998 with Dr. Ray Bakke. Out of that consultation came a variety of citywide seminars and ecumenical retreats on which we all agreed because of the consultation. The National Coalition for Urban Transformation (NCUT), a Catholic and Protestant coalition, was strengthened and became a force of influence in the city. I could see it impact lives and ministries. I was pleasantly delighted to hear their story of how God had used the consultations to transform their lives, ministries, and communities.
>
> Peter Bautista, a Catholic lay leader and president of a coalition of homeowners associations, recalled how he captured the "transforming cities" paradigm. He came to see the real importance of transforming his subdivision.

Peter went to work in the areas of zoning, traffic, poverty alleviation, land rights, and waste management. He organized the neighboring presidents of various subdivisions and shared with them his vision of transforming their zone. Today Peter is happy to see that his area in Libis has zoning rules and traffic jams are a thing of the past; traffic now flows well. Garbage-strewn streets are gone, a waste recycling system is in place, and the poor people in the vicinity soon will receive land titles and own their property.

Art Medina, an evangelical Protestant and businessman, got involved in NCUT's Waste Recycling Environmental Management project. Through his involvement, along with Elsa Unson, a Catholic lay leader, and Raineer Chu, a Protestant lawyer, NCUT played a key role in maintaining the citywide environmental coalition. Other players include the Metro Manila Development Authority, the Quezon city government and the Department of Natural Resources. NCUT provides leadership in implementing the projects. It adopted district 3 as its pilot area and cast the vision of the project to various churches.

NCUT also gave birth to Punlad Buhay Cooperative. Art is leading this project. Today the cooperative has 80 members. Using Bayanihan Banking as its approach, Punlad Buhay currently works in four local churches, training them how to save and run a cooperative. [The Bayanihan Banking program aims to empower the poor by enabling them to save and gain access to credit.]

As we continued our discussion around the table, Dr. David Lim, a Protestant theologian and professor, said that NCUT's Political Advocacy project was strengthened during the coalition members' retreat. David met Nanding Pacheco, a Catholic political leader, during the retreat. Nanding founded Kapatiran, a political movement advocating for national transformation. David was elected vice chairperson of the movement. By December 2007 the movement envisions to have four million members, using the seven-for-seven strategy (every member recruits seven new members).

As we shared before, Father Ben Beltran, a Catholic priest, political activist, and theologian, known for his work with the poor in Smokey Mountain, has said that NCUT has inspired him, as he was exposed to and networked with Protestant groups.

Protestants have seen how he transforms communities and have helped him in various ways, providing him funds, computers, human expertise, and other resources. He in turn helps Protestant churches in the inner city by sharing his knowledge, experience, and expertise. He is now engaged in e-learning, providing opportunities for out-of-school youth to get back to school. The e-trading network attempts to connect rural and urban communities to trade with each other. He is also building an e-church in Smokey Mountain, formerly a garbage dump community, one that would be environmentally sound.

Earning my doctor of ministry degree through Eastern Seminary (now Palmer Seminary in Pennsylvania) as a recipient of the Raymond J. Bakke scholarship through the Mustard Seed Foundation and being mentored by Dr. Bakke gave me a desire to help bring Asia and the West more closely together. I have been facilitating the Urban Leadership Development project of NCUT. In partnership with Dr. Bakke, this project contributed to the birth of a doctor of ministry program in transformational leadership in a joint Asian-Western degree program with Bakke Graduate University in partnership with Asian Theological Seminary. ATS currently has four doctor of ministry students enrolled. It also graduated three leaders with significant ministries, one of whom is Dr. Jim Hayford, who pastors a 6,000-member church on the east side of Seattle. His project influenced the Philippine Foursquare churches to successfully plant over 60 churches among the poor in the Philippines. The subject of his dissertation was to train the Philippine Foursquare leaders in a transformational development paradigm.

Joetique Lamigo is a quiet, sincere, and thoughtful person who has influenced many of the coalition's projects. He serves as the Asian director of the Christian Reformed World Relief Committee, and as a consultant for organizations in management development. He carefully listened to us and aptly pointed out the role of the city-wide consultations introduced by Dr. Bakke as a catalyst in nurturing champions in urban transformation. He believes that the strength of these consultations has been in focusing on equipping key strategic leaders, like the NCUT core and its members, in transformational development.

It is true: city consultations done correctly can change a city and have an ongoing effect many years after the initial consultation is complete.

THE "WHAT" OF A CONSULTATION

Working together to provide a consultation spirit and a consultation in a city is not as simple as marketing an event from a remote site through a direct mail or e-mail blitz. Consultations by their very nature are networking experiences, where relationships are utilized over a significant period of time to get the right people in the right place at the right time. Many months and sometimes years of contact and preparation time is necessary to make this experience meaningful. People-to-people contacts are effectively leveraged to insure that appropriate models are highlighted and that key participants from every sector of the city are involved. In some cases, large cities may need to think about doing consultations in sections of the city. For instance, Los Angeles is an expansive city, and the LA suburbs find it hard to distinguish themselves from Los Angeles proper. Sprawling megacities present unique networking and facilitation issues.

From our experience and research we have found that the following steps are essential as you prepare to be used by God in your city.

Attend a Consultation in Another City

Seeing what takes place in other locations is the best way to catch a vision for your own city. You can often see personalities and gifts at work that will remind you of people in your city. You also will see signs of hope to inspire you and others to be creative. I remember being involved in the Manila consultation and realizing the ministry site visits were so thrilling and made such an impact. As I walked away I could see the value of visiting vibrant ministries on the streets of Seattle. A year later I was leading city ministry tours in my own city.

Meet with a Seasoned Consultant to Determine Timing and Appropriate City Venue

I seem to learn the hard way. Sometimes I think the hard way is the only way to learn! We have been involved in consultations that did not have the intended impact. Often people are inspired by consultations or the idea of having Ray or some other urban expert come to their city, so in their zeal they rush toward a consultation without the appropriate template or environment. The spirit of a consultation is violated if the hard groundwork has not been accomplished. Consultations require relational equity. To build equity often takes years of connecting and a serious exegesis of the city. We recommend that people think in two- to three-year time frames as they plan for a consultation.

Identify and Gather an Envisioning Team

Holding a consultation without a good team would be like Nehemiah attempting to build the walls of Jerusalem without any workers. Although many of us think we are the key person in our city, it is naive to believe a consultation can happen without a team. It is also vital to get the team on the same page. Our research indicates that training is needed for those responsible for planning the consultation. A learning laboratory is crucial as the team begins the planning and networking processes leading up to the consultation. Issues of funding, speakers, spotlighting certain ministries, inviting government leaders, costs, whole church involvement, and other sectors of the city being connected need to be addressed.

One consultation with real difficulty from the beginning had a fundamental flaw in the vision and the process. The conveners attempted to "buy their way" into the city. Although they spoke of their work as indigenous, they actually did not do the hard work of networking their city. When I arrived in the city a few days prior to the consultation, I found that most of the local leaders I spoke with were totally unaware that a consultation was about to take place. As the consultation proceeded we found that the presenters were "hired" to make presentations but were not involved in any part outside their solitary presentation. The conveners wanted to build a reputation as an urban network, but they did not want to work within the city or wait for the networking piece to take place. We found they resisted some of the indigenous leadership because it did not come through their network but through the efforts of another networker.

This experience highlighted the need to spend time developing a committed team in the city, a team that shares common values and purpose. We have learned that pulling a team together and keeping them focused is difficult and takes much time and great effort.

Another consultation effort began with great promise but fell through for two reasons: (1) the leader didn't have time to commit to facilitating team planning and networking, and (2) the leader was unwilling to give up his place of leadership so another could step in.

This team started correctly by allowing us to train them. In fact, I spent a week with a prospective Envisioning Team, exploring vision, values, goals, objectives, ministry sites, and networking within the city. The team was energized and ready to roll.

However, as the date for consultation drew closer, I began to hear from a variety of team members that the key facilitator was not calling the team together and instead planned to pay people to take on a variety of consultation tasks. Although we do not think all the work of a consultation needs to be accomplished through volunteers, it should be initiated by those who are committed to the understanding of the vision, values, and goals.

The conveners attempted to "buy their way" into the city.

Another Envisioning Team that had a shaky start was propelled by setting a consultation date and began moving forward but soon realized they were fragmented in their vision, values, and comprehensive understanding of the consultation. Their problems seemed insurmountable. Any member of the team could have planned a seminar, site visits within the city, and lectures, but to work together was another matter. It became clear to the team that all the members had different visions and were pulling different ways. The team persevered, however, and actually expanded their leadership capacity by facing their problems head-on and addressing them issue-by-issue. Although that particular consultation was not the best expression of a whole city, whole church, and whole gospel, it did build mettle into the team and will undoubtedly bear fruit as they consider how to move forward.

Some of the issues that need to be addressed by the Envisioning Team are:

- Do we share the same values?
- Are we including people from a variety of sectors in the city?
- Do we understand the global issues facing our city?
- Do we have access to appropriate leaders in our city?
- Is our team growing and developing?
- Are we networking throughout the various sectors of the city?
- Do we understand our goals and objectives?
- Do we have a clear consultation development path?
- Are we building a strong team and the appropriate infrastructure for an effective consultation?
- Do we have a neutral location (think about the most marginalized and access)?
- Have we done adequate research to identify good models for site visits?
- Do we have adequate funding to support the effort?
- Have we done a good job of mapping the city?
- Do we have follow-up plans in place?
- Do we have an ongoing relationship with a consultant?
- Do we have adequate transportation, accommodations, and registration capacity?

Mapping and Researching Your City

Often Christian leaders lose touch with the present reality of their own city by using old demographics and old paradigms of ministry while they seek to address contemporary need. Built into the consultation is the hope of fresh discovery. One of the key questions critical to a consultation is, "What is God doing today?" As a city prepares for a major consultation, part of its task is to scope out what God is currently doing in the city. The team responsible for the consultation seeks to build relationships across the sectarian boundaries of the church to encourage self-discovery, unearthing signs of hope from within the church and city. Completing careful research within the city and the church, and in a sense by being the urban paparazzi and finding the celebrative stories in the city, enhances this learning curve.

In Manila one of the rich discoveries was when the Protestants and the Roman Catholics found each other. The Protestants were startled to find the Catholics working in garbage dumps and developing strong family ministries. The Catholics were impressed with the extent to which the Protestants had moved into social mission with microenterprise ventures and planting churches among the urban poor.

A consultation seeks to strengthen the church in the city as it develops a missiological approach to its city. One of the objectives is to help the church research communities traditionally outside the reach of the gospel. Often whole ethnic groups, communities, and special classes of people have been outside the peripheral view of the church. One question to ask is, "Who is not yet with us?" Follow that up by asking, "How do we serve these groups outside our purview?" The consultation seeks to highlight the needs of immigrants, youth at risk, the poor, the sick, the unemployed (or underemployed), the institutionalized, those lost in gated communities, and the aged. This has often been described as caring for the last, least, and lost.

Recently we discussed an upcoming consultation with a city's Envisioning Team and they appeared to be startled to realize their city would produce signs of hope beyond their sphere of influence during the consultation development. It had not occurred to them that they didn't know *all* God was doing in their city.

Networking congregations, ministries, seminaries, civic leaders, and businesses together is the task of the Envisioning Team. This is a whole team effort. We keep reminding facilitators that our global circle of influence is only relationally six degrees away. As Duncan Watts puts it, we "live in a connected age."[3]

Selecting Site Visits and Ministry Models in Your City
As the Envisioning Team explores various sectors of the church and the city, listening skills must be at an all-time high. The team will hear stories with the power to change lives. Four years ago, Ray participated in a consultation in Bangalore, India, and the theme of the consultation was "diver-sity." The double entendre of this theme set the stage for exegeting a complex city in a complex culture. The latest and best technology was contrasted with a culture struggling to find its way even as it embraces and reacts to new global realities. The burgeoning middle class of India is now larger than the entire population of the United States. Infosys Technologies Limited, led by Nandan Nilekani (CEO), has been described by Indian leaders as the newest Taj Mahal and is centered in Bangalore.

Contrasts abound in this beautiful city. First, we drove through the crowded streets, avoiding cows, trucks, automobiles, poor beggars by the side of the road, and whole families on small motorbikes, and then we were suddenly whisked behind tall gates into the high-tech world of Infosys. In one brief moment the noise and smells of the streets subsided as we casually strolled through a magnificent industrial complex filled with the new, young, urbane middle class.

Atul Aghamkar, professor of urban mission at the South Asia Institute of Advanced Christian Studies (SAIACS), led this creative Bangalore consultation team and did not miss the technological advances in India that intersect with ancient religious practices, poverty, and Christianity.

We could walk away from this complexity if we were not startled to find a life-changing story in the midst of this diverse city. One cab driver with a reputation as a tough guy explained how one day he could not continue to ignore the poor, diseased people sitting by the side of the street. He had to do something about the uncared-for, dying folks he observed every day. One day he was so troubled by the plight of the poor that he stopped and picked up a dying man and took him home to bathe and feed him. Now, several years later, he has over 40 poor and dying folks living with him! His goal is that each one would understand God's love for them and be able to die with dignity. This was a story just waiting to be told.

Ministry models that tell a variety of stories are selected. Perhaps it is a ministry serving troubled youth, a church planting among the poor, a microenterprise business and Bible study, or an educational model serving the poor. Perhaps the model is an advocate for the poor confronting the halls of power in the city, or an advocate confronting the wealthy for their abuse of the poor. Sometimes it is a business person giving most of his or her income to alleviate poverty.

One story worth telling is about Jim Hayford, mentioned by Corrie DeBoer, pastor of a church on the east side of Seattle. When Jim entered our partnered doctoral program with Asian Theological Seminary, he began to dream of a way to transform church planting for the Foursquare denomination in the Philippines. He was concerned that the church-planting efforts seemed to target the middle-class Filipino but not the poor. He developed a model of church planting with the poor in metro Manila using community development and education as the starting point. At last count the denomination had targeted over 400 locations for these churches in metro Manila. These real stories become grist for case studies in a city consultation.

Who Needs to Attend Consultations?

The consultation is not designed to be a large event; rather it is designed to be an interactive, life-changing event. Participants are chosen around strategic network capacity. The social capital of a city grows when people in crucial positions operate with a greater understanding of the city and the church.

People within a denomination, a mission organization, a congregation, specialized ministries, a network, a seminary, or a university, or people who have networking gifts, should be included. Malcolm Gladwell in his book *Tipping Point*, writes that there are few people who function in a catalytic, movement capacity. These unique people are the folks who promote ideas that others readily adopt. Thus it is vital to have as many of these "good news" bearers in attendance so the news travels through natural urban networks.

The consultation should also seek to engage people from specialized ministries dealing with youth at risk, prostitution, homelessness, and disabilities. It seeks to bring together pastors and ministry leaders—helping them ask questions about their greatest ministry challenges—and seeks dialogue around constructive development.

Christians in the marketplace must find their voice and their service validated in their vocational parish. Those working within law enforcement, education, sports, entertainment, media, health care, government, food services, arts, business, or transportation need to be affirmed and find networks within the church and city. Networks that strengthen this lay witness should be recognized and highlighted.

A consultation also seeks to draw those with financial and social capacity toward holistic action in their city. Many well-meaning people with wealth or wisdom do not know how to spend their resources for effective change. Without a consultative process, they are often captivated by the best-marketed story in their city. A consultation seeks to open a window for these individuals, foundations, and corporations so they can build social capital in their communities.

The City Environment

The environment of your city impacts the timing for a consultation. When we surveyed several experienced consultation facilitators, they noted that when a city has an urgent need to address issues, the consultation is most effective. They also noted that if the stakeholders in the city are committed to the long view and persistent in seeing transformation in their city, the consultation can be a benefit. In addition, having a manageable-sized city was a benefit. Finally, the importance of a central and neutral location for the consultation is key. If consultations are held in locations perceived as dominated by a sectarian group within the city or a place that has negative connotations, this can be detrimental.

The Consultation Content

Once the Envisioning Team completes its research and the models of ministry are selected and participants invited, the next step is to detail the entire consultation. Whether it be one, two, or three days, it is important to have the details worked out and placed in every participant's hands. See appendix 1 for more specifics.

Time Factors

Appropriate time must be given for each presentation and for ministry site visits. The site visits and the speakers always take longer than expected. We have found that leaving plenty of "blank space" is helpful, and we have had many laughs over consultations with too much information where we end up feeling as if we are "drinking from a fire hose." Too many presentations and too much of everything can overload the participants. An effective consultation ends with participants knowing they were able to be involved and have full participation without feeling too overwhelmed.

We have also found that presentations and group discussions in the morning are good, with working lunches always an option. Remember to leave space for people to ask questions, dialogue with others, and work on common issues. Andragogy (adult learning as explained above) demands we talk face-to-face with others, not just download what experts have to say. The afternoons, when people are easily distracted or sleepy, are good times to visit ministry sites and see the signs of hope in the city. Evenings work best for city walking and group dinners together. If the city has unique public venues, the evening is the time to involve everyone. The Manila consultation provided wonderful Filipino cultural dinners and experiences during the evenings.

When a consultation is held over a weekend, it is always important to visit several churches and allow participants to see diversity in worship expression. In Mumbai, India, we began our morning at a Roman Catholic church packed with worshipers; just down the street we visited a North India mainline church, also packed with worshipers. Many of us began to recognize that the church in India was alive. Then we drove across the city to the largest slum in the world and visited a little home church filled with children and a Methodist church filled with new converts. We ended the morning by visiting one of the largest evangelical churches in the city.

Many Christians have not ventured outside of their own congregational environments. We suggest that the team should identify at least three significant expressions of Christian worship and determine how to get participants inside these worshiping communities.

Facilitation of the Consultation

The actual facilitation of the consultation takes a gifted public facilitator. The person chosen for this role needs to keep everyone on schedule, make introductions, and usher the whole process forward. At times he or she must intervene when the program is running too long. When difficulties develop during the consultation, the facilitator makes appropriate adjustments. It is wise to have a person assigned as a special assistant to the facilitator during the consultation. The facilitator needs to insure that breakout discussion groups have enough time to do their projects or to respond to issues that surface during the day.

Creating Listening Teams

Consultations, by their very nature, demand listening. One of my preaching professors told our class, "Preaching well means listening to God, yourself, and others." Consultations have the same rule. The consultation is all about listening. We have found that the formation of a listening team is vital to the success of the process. At the end of the consultation, the listening team reports what they have heard. At that point it is important for the facilitator to then break the group into small segments and decide what next steps should be taken or which points of action need follow up. A listening team can be made up of a pastor, educator, men, women, and a variety of ministry leaders.

Important Incidentals

Through the school of hard knocks we have learned that the little things left unattended can leave participants confused and frustrated. Of course depending on your context, different expectations will be in place. We discovered that we needed a point person to lead a team to preregister the participants. Preregistration is vital so you know how many participants will attend, especially when it comes to seating and meals. Registration at the door is also vital so that everyone pays the appropriate price. Without a clear door-registration process, people often become confused, end up frustrated, and lose the benefit of the consultation. We know from experience!

Finally, meals served during the consultation must be easily accessed and allow participants to continue their conversations.

RECOMMENDATIONS FROM THE FIELD

When I surveyed experienced city facilitators about key ingredients for developing a consultation they came back with these recommendations:

- Recognize that long-term community involvement is the goal.
- Anticipate stress around planning, implementing, and funding.

- Expect the challenge of too many opportunities after the consultation.
- Develop enough funding to do it well.
- Prepare for a paradigm shift in theology and practice.
- Develop sufficient volunteers from many sectors.
- Develop a committed facilitation team.
- Seek spiritual people for the facilitation team.
- Develop an ongoing prayer effort.
- Plan one to two years in advance.
- Contextualize with styles of learning in mind.
- Seek a well-positioned group to facilitate the consultation.
- Be ready for hard work.
- Plan follow-up meetings with action in mind.
- Conduct one consultation as a learning experience, then repeat it.
- Obtain solid commitments from senior leadership in the city.
- Make sure you have enough resources to pull it off.
- Develop three to four levels of sponsors who want to connect with the church.
- Provide a good mix of international resource speakers and participants.
- Document the consultation.
- Incorporate music and devotionals.

REFLECTIONS

1. Who are the stakeholders in your city?
2. Could you identify a person in your city that could function as a key facilitator?
3. If you wanted to begin the process of consultation in your city, what could you begin to do?

Chapter 12

Cities and Consultations: It's Never the Same, It's Always the Same

It has been my experience that consultations are never the same, but always the same. Sounds like a conundrum! Over the years that I have worked with city consultations, all of them have the same dynamic framework, but the people who participate bring a different flavor, so every consultation is unique. In considering consultations, some important questions must be addressed. First, why do senior pastors, denominational leaders, or parachurch ministries have a difficult time participating in a consultation? Why is it important for people in a city to learn to communicate with each other? What makes up a good consultation? Let's begin with the first question.

GENERALS MOVE WITH GENERALS

Throughout history, military rank and protocol have been the dominant leadership motifs for most cultures. Military roots may be tribal. Tribal chiefs have a place of honor in the community and usually wield it with gusto! Chiefs often expect special treatment. They are inclined not to waste time with trivial matters. Jesus taught about masters and servants, and His teaching must be seen through a lens of the culture of His time in human history. When Jesus encountered the centurion, the man told Him, "For I myself am a man under authority, with soldiers under me. I tell this one, 'Go,' and he goes; and that one,

'Come,' and he comes. I say to my servant, 'Do this,' and he does it" (Matthew 8:9 NIV). The message of the centurion was clear: "I know rank and power when I see it." We cannot ignore power and rank, for they are part of the human mores and institutionalism that surround and impact all human activity.

The spirit we encourage in consultations is one of listening to and learning from cities. The heart we embrace is to the least, last, and lost. However, we acknowledge that we live in a world of rank and status. We also recognize that engaging people at various levels of leadership requires the wisdom to speak to and connect them at levels of common interest. Using a familiar military metaphor, we might say, "Generals want to meet with generals because they share common interests, issues, and strategies." Similarly leaders within a city want to be engaged at their level of interest and need.

Consultations are strategic, invitational events. Bishops and other church leaders invite their key people. Gatekeepers within each city are the hoped-for attendees. One must be realistic when setting up a consultation. Some pastors will never participate. Whether it is because of insecurity, lack of understanding, intense personal or family pain, theological boundaries, or feelings of self-importance, many pastors simply feel no obligation to attend something outside of their perceived span of control. The people who may attend a consultation want to know that it is worth their time and will add and not subtract from their lives. The hard reality of life is that people like to be involved where they can meet with others they consider to be colleagues. They want to associate with people they know will add to their lives rather than deplete their energy and life margins.

If congregational, ministry, or denominational leaders attend an event of any kind in their city, they want to be actively involved in some significant way so they can justify time spent away from their primary ministry focus. As the saying goes, "Unless other generals are coming, I'll send my deputy!" Leaders will usually attend events if they are small enough or significant enough to have an executive level feel and guarantee to address the issues or problems they know they need to solve.

Getting leaders (blessers) involved requires extensive effort and meaningful personal contact well in advance of the actual consultation. Calendars are full for most leaders. To attend any meeting, they need advance preparation. We have found that asking a leader to share a short word on a selected topic or to give an invocation or benediction is a good way to involve them. Some busy leaders also enjoy being involved in a panel discussion around a preselected topic.

Our experience demonstrates that public officials are eager to be involved if they can share some personal observation and if they already know another public servant who will be attending. In 2006 the Los Angeles, California, Signs of Hope Envisioning Team (our name for the planning team) was able to assemble a group of public leaders to serve on a panel during the consultation. Each one of these leaders was asked to tell the consultation participants what they do, what major issues confront the city of Los Angeles, and what they see as the greatest sign of hope in Los Angeles. It became

> **"Unless other generals are coming, I'll send my deputy!"**

apparent during the consultation that these public leaders were quite familiar with the church in the city and eager to engage it. Janice Hahn, a City of Los Angeles councilwoman, served on an erudite panel and was well aware of the church and its service in the community. The Hahn family has been involved politically in Los Angeles for many years, so she was eager to be involved. She also knew the language of the church for she kept referencing "her Holy Spirit."

Likewise, in my own city of Seattle, it was not difficult to get the mayor of our city involved when we told his office that many pastors and ministry leaders would be in attendance. Each time we asked the mayor's office if the mayor would attend our consultation, he or she did attend and gave his or her vision for the city and some of the signs of hope from city hall. Every public official knows that public contact with significant groups of people is a way to gain social capital for the city.

PROPHET, PRIEST, AND KING, REVISITED

Determining the role of a leader (blesser) is important. Civic leaders do not usually attend the entire consultation but often make cameo appearances. When planning a consultation, expectations for meaningful involvement for each type of participant must be kept in mind. A helpful metaphor I've found as I attempt to understand roles and expectations for consultations is the biblical example of *prophet, priest,* and *king.* Jesus fulfilled each of these roles in His ministry, offices frequently highlighted in the Old Testament.

One way to think of public officials and senior leaders of large Christian ministries or congregations is in the role of a *king.* They administrate grand plans and mobilize large groups of people. However, they are often controlled and constrained by their own domain and responsibilities. It is difficult for leaders of large constituencies to have "hang time" outside their primary responsibilities. Often these public leaders (kings) are seen as stuffy or proud when they don't spend quality time with others in ministry. The reality is that their world and responsibilities are clearly defined by the expectations of their immediate constituency, whether it be congregational boards, donors, or staff.

Consultation facilitators can help the key leaders within a city to fully engage in a consultation by asking them to be full participants— serving on a panel, leading breakout groups, or leading prayer groups. One way to involve pastors of large churches is to set up a small group of large church pastors who collaborate and interact throughout the consultation and during the site visits. Bring them together prior to the consultation to hear the vision, give input, and bless the effort. Their interaction prior to the consultation and during the consultation can be life-changing and city-changing! In January 2006 the Signs of

Hope LA Envisioning Team asked Dr. Jack Hayford, president of a prominent Foursquare church, to lead a morning devotional. His inspirational devotion was an encouragement to all the participants. Pastor Hayford was born in Los Angeles and has spent the majority of his life ministering in that great city. To hear his heart and love for Los Angeles was a moving experience.

Prophets, on the other hand, come in a variety of packages. I think those of us who identify with this calling have a variety of opinions (prophets without opinions would be an oxymoron) about what a prophet is or does. Yet we all see ourselves as "outside the camp."

When the true prophets of Old Testament Scripture shattered the status quo of their culture, they were either heeded or rejected based on the powers in place. The kings, who set themselves to pursue their personal agenda at the expense of God's revealed will, resented the prophets who spoke for Him. Jeremiah's prophetic calling led to a life of sorrow as he happened to pull the assignment of prophesying during a hard-hearted power season in Jerusalem. Still, Jeremiah persevered throughout his lifetime, consistently speaking the truth to those who would not turn from their crooked paths. Elijah made an art form out of being on the wrong side of the tracks of power. The palaces of Jerusalem were not a happy place for him. He had a following but he didn't manage a government. Elijah's constituency did not determine his actions, yet His mission was not to lead large groups or organizations but to speak the word of the Lord.

Prophets (at least for this analogy) more often than not find themselves outside of the organization or on the outside of the current administrative systems. Those who spend time in the world of creative strategic change and speak with authority based on insight and wisdom often speak with prophetic clarity. However, they often are not welcome when an organization seeks to develop its structures.

Prophets usually have a keen interest in any movement of change or leadership shift and transformation within the city. They often have significant insights to offer and they are not typically constrained by managing large organizations. The prophetic imagination can be seen around the edges of most current movements. Engaging prophetic types as consultation participants means giving them meaningful ways to interact with each other and to speak to the city as God gives them insight. Enlist these prophetic gifts to serve the whole church and the whole city. Without the prophetic types in the consultation, it will be organized but dull!

Finally, *priests* are symbolic of those who consistently do the work of prayer, healing, good deeds, counseling, and renewal. These folks do people-to-people work every day. However, this priestly function has many constraints that can impede involvement. A person focused on ministry productivity is usually focused on *doing* the work, not simply *talking* about the work to be done. People called to the priestly ministry do not usually want to spend hours discussing a city's needs; they want to get their hands dirty actually doing something about real needs. People motivated by service are often critical of those who want to spend too much time engaging creative ideas. People committed to action will often say, "When are we going to quit talking about this and do something?"

An effective consultation is designed to meet these three levels of leadership and perspective. Public officials and many pastors (kings) will be involved for short periods of time, and this will usually mean that they need to give some public input for making this commitment. Writers, networkers, and professors (prophets) will be willing to spend more time in conversation and transformational idea formation. Ministry implementers (priests) will seek action steps at the conclusion of each consultation, and if those are not met, will lose interest.

CITY COMMUNICATIONS

The social and spiritual needs of cities can be overwhelming for those seeking to bring meaning and healing to the neighborhood. In many cases cities have not developed adequate communication and social linkage between various sectors—religious, private, and government.

Existing leaders rarely have space or opportunity to do serious reflection around their own neighborhoods, schools, and businesses. A question typically not addressed in a cooperative spirit across multiple sectors might be: "How do *we* care for our city?" H. P. Spees, former executive director of One by One Leadership in Fresno, California, reminded a city consultation recently that "Cities cannot be whole unless they have effective communication channels and relational links between the various community sectors."[1]

From our work we have learned that leaders within cities are increasingly aware that whole community reflection is vital for community health. They know that isolated leaders, communities, and initiatives ultimately breed a myopic view of life rather than integration. Communities cut off from other communities, families cut off from other families, and individuals isolated and alone develop a psychosis of the worst kind. Creative models and mentors can break cycles and archaic systems. Urban leaders also are aware that significant social connections, spanning all the systems in a city bring social capital or capacity to a community. When people within the educational system build bridges to people from the religious community, city government, and education, they develop social spans. If these social bridges are maintained, they bring health and vitality to the whole city. This communication span builds a community rather than simply allowing a large city with isolated sectors to exist.

City Communication Span

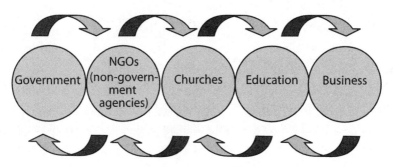

Consultations Help Build the Communication Span

A consultation approach to a city has the purpose to connect people from multiple sectors within any city. Whether the consultation is a typical three-day experience or a two- or one-day event, its design is to open the doors of conversation. We have often described this work as "keeping the conversation going." When the Signs of Hope LA team brought government leaders into the consultation in Los Angeles, they opened conversation in a new way. It was not a confrontation but a listening post, where church leaders and ministry leaders asked public officials to share their knowledge, concerns, and signs of hope. Listening to those from other sectors is contagious! When we ask people about their world, a new bridge begins to form.

CONSULTATION DESIGNS

> There's no way you can know enough to enter a city. The only way is to come to learn. When you approach people and allow them to teach you, you will learn an incredible amount.
> —Ray Bakke

Consultations are helpful if they are designed to fit the community and the context, and have an indigenous DNA. The design of a consultation is vital to meet the needs of a community. If we really want to listen and learn and not just spin another event, we must be patient and seek to design around reality and not hype. This is perhaps the toughest assignment for any of us.

Most leaders have been schooled in the art of hype and find it hard to wait for substance. Often resources and funding seem to follow great events rather than reality. In the consultation in Los Angeles in 2006, the Envisioning Team paid a price to resist hype and cling to a vision of reality. To their credit they wanted authenticity and were willing to pay the price. Brad Fieldhouse, Arthur Gray, Eric Leocadio,

Cheryl Elson, Mary Glenn, and Michael Mata made up the original Envisioning Team, which took the consultation spirit seriously. The journey was tough but they persevered. At one point it seemed the consultation effort would crash, but God provided a good coach in the Los Angeles area who helped the team gel and move into high performance. Kathy Dudley, who served for many years in Dallas, Texas, where she founded the Dallas Leadership Foundation, became their coach. She lived and studied in the Los Angeles area at the time of Signs of Hope LA. While she didn't plan on much involvement, the team recognized they needed serious coaching and asked her to help, so she stepped in and made a huge difference with her coaching skills.

When designing consultations, we need to ask: What is the present environment of the city? What meaningful relationships exist that can help bridge city sectors? Are trusted networkers available? Do churches and ministries want to come together, or will they come together if asked? Should we do a one-day, two-day, or three-day consultation?"

These questions need to be asked of people throughout the city who know the area and its present climate. Once the climate of the city is known, the Envisioning Team can move to a consultation design phase. Consultation probes are the most strategic preconsultation activities in which your team will invest. These probes take time and energy. A primary difficulty in developing an effective consultation is finding people with the time, gifting, and energy to do the necessary probing. Most organizations do not think they can afford the time and effort to exegete the environment of the city at a significant level. However, once a good probe is complete, a consultation can be designed to meet the current profile of the city.

In our work with consultations, we have discovered several effective city consultation designs. Remember that these designs are simply templates, because each city is unique, but also keep in mind that each city has similarities common to all.

A THREE-DAY DESIGN: OPTIMAL FOR LEADERS IN ANY CITY

First Day: The Big Question

The consultation construct is designed to be contractual, between the participants, the Envisioning Team, and the consultant. When participants arrive at the consultation, they will find that the Envisioning Team has already gathered good research and asked many questions. The city has been surveyed, the ministry models have been identified, and a wealth of information is ready to be shared. However, this is really the starting point for the consultation, not the ending point.

The big question for the entire consultation is: What do you need to receive from this consultation to make it worth your time? The consultant or Envisioning Team will begin the consultation by asking participants to identify what they need from this experience to make it worth their while. Participants' responses may cause the Envisioning Team some angst, as they have spent many hours in preparation and often feel as if asking participants this question is akin to "starting over." However, by asking participants what they need, the consultant opens up the door for an authentic consultation process, not just an information download. Participants will be separated into small groups, where they will unpack the burning issues confronting them, list current signs of hope they engage, and identify the best thing about their city and the toughest issue confronting their community.

The small groups will feed back this information to the consultant, and from that point on, perhaps hanging on the wall or in a PowerPoint presentation visible to all, the most significant issues listed will frame the entire consultation. This highlighted list becomes the contractual agreement with the participants. From that point on, this list becomes the "true north" for everyone involved. Identified issues may be too involved and complex to even be adequately addressed, but they must at least be mentioned and given some attention so participants know they will either be addressed during the consultation or through an ongoing response to follow. At the end of each consultation the Envisioning Team and consultant must take time to unpack what was learned and what was missed. Although listening is a key component all along the planning process, listening moves into high gear after the consultation begins. Now, the Envisioning Team and the consultant hear input from a larger group and have to incorporate this new knowledge as they seek to bring ongoing oxygen to their city.

When the issues for the consultation are initially introduced, this is an appropriate time to turn to the educators who are participating and ask them to begin to think about designing educational initiatives to address the challenges that have surfaced. These issues are "real-time" struggles that demand an educational response. The Envisioning Team also should be encouraged that the hard work they have done in preparation is now being complemented and affirmed by the participants in the room.

Present at least two case studies so the participants have a living narrative with which to connect. After the case studies, participants should break into small groups to discuss what they are observing. Then bring the groups together to share their feedback with the whole group. Since we live in a fast-paced world, it is important that the first session be fast-paced. We have found that the best delivery system for case studies is a video presentation. For instance, in Bangalore, India, the team presented their production of "Bangalore, the Diver-sity," with visuals playing off an ancient Indian city with ancient customs and street scenes contrasted against a high-tech explosion. The video was first-class, and it offered an explosive first-time encounter for all participants.

Second Day: Visiting Model Sites

Devote the second day to visiting model sites. As participants prepare for the site visits, instruct them how to use a Model Analysis Guide Process, the following ten-question review, to help them dig deeply into the inner workings of each ministry. The analysis questions are:

1. What is unique about the context of this model?
2. What is the history, the big idea, the vision, and the origin of this model?
3. What is the actual program delivered? Where and how is it delivered?
4. How is this model organized? What kind of structures? When did they organize?
5. Who is the primary audience? Who do you actually reach?
6. What are the costs associated with this model? How do you pay for it?
7. What is the theological rationale for the model?
8. How does this model equip others so that it is sustainable?
9. Bicycle or airplane? What are the strengths and what are the limits?
10. What is the transferable principle?

At the end of the second day, the group usually returns for debriefing, and the entire group responds to what they observed that day. If necessary, the debriefing also can be performed the following morning.

In Manila, it was interesting to watch the participants wrestle with a Catholic ministry working in the garbage dumps. Benigno Beltran, a Roman Catholic priest, moved into the garbage dump near Manila and began to organize a Christian community. To date, this vibrant community has a school, a recycling business, a garbage business, and a church. When we look at this model in light of our ten questions, what do we learn about this and how does it impact our city and give us insight for our own work in the city? I often have our doctoral students at Bakke Graduate University ask these three questions throughout the day as we observe urban ministry models:

1. What is your biggest "A-ha"?
2. What is your biggest question?
3. What can you apply to your own life and ministry?

In Amsterdam, two African pastors seek to lead African immigrants in Western Europe. As immigrants continue to move north from Africa to Europe, they bring Christian life and hope, but at the same time they face ugly racism, exclusion, distrust, and social intolerance. With this in mind, Eric Amonoo-Neizer from Ghana and Moses Alagbe from Nigeria have pioneered an Afro-European network, Gifts from Africa to Europe (GATE), for African pastors living and ministering in Europe. This network seeks to educate and encourage African leaders theologically and economically. They also recognize the spiritual need of Western Europe and have determined that their presence there is hope for the gospel in Europe. When we look at their model of ministry, is it a bicycle or an airplane? We can ask the question, "What is the transferable principle?"

Third Day

First Small-Group Session: The day often begins with the question, What did you observe from your site visits? If this was done the afternoon or evening of the second day, it would still be good to review at this point to set the tone for the concluding work. Educators present are reminded that the city as a *learning lab* is the best way to educate; emphasize that urban cannot be fully taught in a sterile classroom.

Second Small-Group Session: As the consultation moves into the wrap-up phase, it is important to break participants into small groups again and have them begin to ask, "Given what we know and what we have observed, what needs to be done in our city?" The groups should have 45 minutes to an hour to work on this and then report back to the consultation. For example: What needs to be done to address poverty, homelessness, illiteracy, or health issues? Have the groups write their responses for everyone to see.

Third Small-Group Session: Next the participants are asked to design a program to address the identified issues. Again, this group should be allowed to work for at least an hour on the program design. If the participants are really narrowing in on a key issue and good design, this is a good time to provide extra space for them to work. Monitor each group to check on its progress.

Fourth Small-Group Session: In the final session, it is vital that the groups identify major barriers to completing the mission and address the identified issues. At this point in the consultation, the real issues of a city surface. We have noted that often the barriers to urban mission progress are within the church, where hierarchy, competition, or open conflicts create an environment preventing partnerships and effective action for the church. Ray addressed this in chapter 7.

ONE-DAY MODELS

City Ministry Summit

The city ministry summit is a one-day consultation we have used multiple times to build mutual awareness and a sense of Christian community within the greater metropolitan community. The city ministry summit develops its own theme about listening to the city, hearing from ministries and congregations, building relationships, and addressing issues of common interest. The ministry summit is designed to celebrate the current signs of hope in a city and address the most pressing issues facing the city and the church. The issues often addressed are homelessness, racism, youth at risk, education, poverty, and unity of the body of Christ in the city.

If the ministry summit becomes an annual event in a city, it can promote a sense of Christian community. A key foundational purpose of the summit is, "knowing as we are known."

The design of the summit brings congregational mission leaders and ministry leaders together within a city to hear from one another, pray for one another, and discuss and address issues and needs within the city. The hope is that many ministries and congregations will find ways to partner together as they begin to understand the "other" ministries and their heartbeat. Presentations are helpful in this setting because they provide "talking points" for the summit participants. The presentations have to be limited in number so ample time can be given for discussion and partnering strategies. Balance between presentation and interaction is vital. Each participant needs to know that they will be involved and that their work and input matters.

The city ministry summit idea was birthed in a Serve Seattle pastors meeting. The city summit became a semiannual consultation in the city.

New Pastors Orientation

A new pastors orientation seemingly has its roots in the ministry of Sam Shoemaker in Pittsburgh, Pennsylvania. He took every new pastor to a hill overlooking the city and exclaimed, "Behold your city!" When a new pastor enters a city, it takes awhile to get acquainted with the new environment, and as everyone knows, churches and cities can be tough places to break into.

We have found that a new pastors orientation is a wonderful way to introduce new spiritual leaders to civic leaders, multiple ministries, and existing congregations. It often takes new pastors several years to exegete their city, unless they are welcomed and guided by others. When an Envisioning Team or network exists in the city, and is connecting churches and ministries, they can do a great service to the kingdom of God by welcoming new pastors.

City Tour

A city tour exposes congregational members, lay leaders, and pastors to the city at large. The focus of the city tour is to give a theological overview of God's heart for the city, a missiology of the city, a historical perspective of the city, some current demographics of the city, and a tour of four or five key ministries serving in the city that are often overlooked. We have found this kind of day-long exercise for churches expands and energizes their urban mission and helps them identify needs within their own parish as well.

A typical city tour plan begins in the morning with a theology of the city, a missiology of the city, the history of the city, and a prayer preparation for "Seeing what God sees" in the city. The morning session usually lasts one to two hours, and then the tour group hops on a bus to visit different ministry sites. During the drive to the ministry site, the guide can point out interesting things that people would not normally notice. Who stands at the bus stop? What languages are written on the stores in various neighborhoods? Can you observe the different class and cultural levels in your own city?

A key aspect of visiting a ministry site is to identify how the ministry was born. What vision inspired this work? Who were the founders and are they still involved? How do the workers spiritually sustain themselves for their work? The ten questions asked above are good to use during these visits.

After visiting the ministries, and sometimes between visits, the consultant always makes sure there is time for a prayer walk. During a prayer walk in the city, participants walk in a very busy area of the city where people can be seen, preferably in a public place. The purpose is not to "show pray" but to pray with your eyes open, observing people and places. What does God see in this city? What breaks God's heart? What gives God joy? What can God use here and what would God like to clean up? It has always been interesting to watch the impact this has as people begin to see the city through new eyes while prayer walking.

The city tour ends when people return to the place they started from and begin to share with each other what they saw, what touched their hearts, and what they want to do about it. We have seen ministries and people become seriously involved in urban ministry just by spending one day on a city tour.

Summary of a City Tour

- *Morning:* Unpacking theology, missiology, and history of the city. The exegeting city process.

- *Midmorning:* Site visits to four or five ministries, listening to their stories—homelessness, youth at risk, immigrant resettlement, community development, drug rehabilitation, to name a few.
- *Afternoon:* Prayer walk in a public place. Learn to pray without making a scene! Carefully complete an exegesis of people and places.
- *Evening:* Small groups respond to what they observed and what they sense God is speaking to them personally and corporately. Groups report back so everyone can hear what God is speaking to the church.

Think Tank

The think tank is usually built around a particular issue that needs to be addressed. The participants are selected for their demonstrated interest in the topic and for an area of expertise they bring to the topic. Often professors, authors, pastors, and mission leaders are involved in these sessions.

The think-tank preparation usually involves asking several people to prepare papers on a given subject. Books and articles may also be selected to be read by all participants in advance. The day of the think tank, the facilitator opens the session with personal introductions and an introduction to the topic of the day. Then papers are presented and small discussion groups formed. After the discussions each group is asked to report a response to the general session. Everything is recorded and ready for distribution to the participants at the end of the day. Finally, at the conclusion of each think-tank consultation, the facilitator should ask the group for their agreed-upon "next steps."

Denominational Consultation

The denominational consultation brings the urban leadership of one specific group together to assess its urban ministry, both nationally and internationally, with a view to strengthen it in existing cities, expand it to new cities, and train more effectively for it in all cities.

The consultation introduces the values of the whole church, whole gospel, and whole city to denominations, encouraging them to partner with, rather than compete with each other.

A typical format for the denominational consultation would be to hear the participants' primary issues in urban settings. What are their struggles, their joys, their strengths, their limits? The second part of the day would expose the group to ministry models doing the "heavy lifting" service in the city. The purpose would be to demonstrate that the church can move beyond planting and "shoring up the congregation," to renewal, engagement, and transformation.

Academic Seminar

The urban intensive lectureship or continuing education seminar event usually is one week in length and participants gain academic credit for their enrollment and participation. This seminar includes reading assignments, journaling, projects, or papers. This seminar can be taken for credit from Bakke Graduate University or in partnership with other schools at several educational levels.

As Bakke Graduate University expands its global reach, partnerships with other school are available, as well as a global mentoring system. Presently three international seminaries and numerous international faculty network to make the master of theological studies and the doctor of ministry programs a unique study experience for those interested in transformational leadership for the global urban world.

REFLECTIONS

1. Find a group within your community and pick a ministry in your city (or more than one) and ask the 10 questions under the heading "Second Day: Visiting Model Sites."
2. What specific things did you learn from this exercise?
3. What can you, your group, or your community of faith do about what you learned?

Chapter 13

What We've Learned from Consultations

Over years of holding consultations in world-class cities all around the globe, Ray and I have gathered some assumptions and objectives and can reveal some outcomes for your consideration. The following information is best understood as a summary of these three areas—24 assumptions, 11 objectives, and 9 potential outcomes from a consultation. Finally, we end by reviewing the five things we learned from holding hundreds of consultations in world-class cities all over the globe. These are presented in a brief overview format. Both Ray and I teach graduate courses that explore and significantly expand these ideas.

CONSULTATION ASSUMPTIONS

The urban world is out of control! To visit Mumbai, New Delhi, Los Angeles, New York, London, Mexico City, Lagos, and other great world-class cities is to hear and smell the sounds and scents of motion without limits. These cities and others are awake 24/7, and no one knows quite what to do about it. When the church steps into this turbulence, it takes on the powers of Satan with the power of Jesus Christ. Cities are made up of masses of people on which Jesus has compassion, and His body demonstrates that compassion within cities today.

As we continue to visit the urban world, we connect with 24 assumptions that drive the city consultation process. When you look at a consultation in your city, you can count on these realities.

1. The phenomenon of mass migrations to cities is a global reality. Visiting Los Angeles in January of 2006, we realized again that wherever jobs can be found, people will go. A Mexican pastor told us, "If you create paying jobs, even low-paying jobs, our people will come and they will work hard and be happy to have a job."

2. The city, by definition, includes the metropolis. Gone are the days when cities have fixed boundaries and walls. Cities now are sprawling places where it is impossible to distinguish where one begins and another ends. Suburban and urban collide and intersect in multiple ways. In Phoenix one ministry leader noted that if they did a study of the immigrant population in the daytime, they would find it is larger in the gated communities during the day than the white population. People trade places at day and night.

3. The lost and the poor are most often the same people. Those who know they are lost are usually the poor. Recently we did a survey of a fairly wealthy Seattle suburb. We found that most of the people near the shopping malls and Starbucks coffee shops attended church and identified themselves as Christians. Then some of our team went to the bus stop and interviewed people waiting for the bus, and none of them claimed to be Christians or admitted they attended church. In Jesus's ministry He cared for the poor and proclaimed that they should be the recipients of the good news.

4. To engage a city successfully we need to stand at the crossroads of the powerless and the powerful. When we work for justice, it means that the powerful (those with resources) must be engaged to change systems, laws, and attitudes in ways that benefit the poor.

5. The answers to the city's needs are found in the city and do not need to be imported from the outside. The lesson from community after community is: the city has resources, but they need to be reallocated for transformation. The theory of "appreciative inquiry" tells us that we need to identify what is working and what assets are already available, and then help the people of the city unlock those resources.

6. Consultations are learning events where people come together and discover how to exegete their community within community. The consultation is not a download of information by an expert from "out there." It is a learning feast for people within their own community. When people begin to tell their stories to one another, the light begins to shine. In our doctoral courses at Bakke Graduate University, we have a tradition we use to recognize the community that has been built among us during a week and a half of working, talking, and listening with and to each other. We invite Nancy Murphy, one of our professors, to come in for an afternoon and teach us how to listen and to not interrupt our friends as we sit in a talking circle. After a week and a half of observing each other, people have pretty well sized each other up. Nancy has each person hold a "talking rock" while they talk. They are encouraged to talk about whatever they want to share at that moment while others listen. As the rock passes from person to person, we see God's work in them and God's work in all of us. Our appreciation grows as we hear others' stories. We enter into a fuller expression of community. This is not a time for experts; it is a time for us. Consultations give people within the city a "talking circle."

7. At least 90 percent of all city people come to Christ through relationships. We need to build relationships in the city. The city is a web of relationships, not simply transactions. Years ago, James Engels produced the Engels Scale, which demonstrates that people come to Christ through a series of exposures to relationships and to the gospel.[1] The consultation is designed to reveal relational bridges built over a long period of time.

8. Most of what we need to know for effective urban ministry is not yet being taught in our seminaries. The model of medical training for surgery is best referenced here. Training hospitals tie the medical student to real-life surgery while working next to an experienced surgeon. Seminaries, on the other hand, often offer courses taught not in the laboratory of ministry but in the classroom of information. The consultation seeks to break students and professors out of the classroom and into the field, where mentors and models can be experienced. We find that the learning curve goes up exponentially when this type of learning is employed. Consultation attendees are pleased and excited to have on-the-job learning experiences.

9. Denominations can be a gift to each other in every city. In the past we have seen denominations as fierce competitors everywhere their ministries intersect. Today denominations and other Christian groups actually bring gifts to each other and to the city as they provide multiple expressions of life.

10. If you penetrate the city, you will affect the countryside. Paul demonstrated this by his work in Ephesus, recorded in Acts 19. Cities influence regions, and rural areas are impacted by what happens in the city. Recently I visited the United Nations offices in Nairobi, Kenya, and found a poster that proclaimed: "Cities: Engines of Rural Development."

Sustainable development can only be achieved in both areas if they are considered holistically as part of the same, integrated system. The links between cities and the countryside depend on the infrastructure connecting them. Improve the infrastructure network and rural production increases, giving people in the countryside better access to markets, information, and jobs. Cities are magnets for rural trade. Cities are the gateway to national and international markets, and they benefit from rural demand for their output.

11. The church is the only credible institution in some hurting cities. John Dilulio, the former head of the White House Office of Faith-Based and Community Initiatives, and others pointed to the work of the church as the only agent of grace and change in many cities where other institutions fail to care for the poor and needy.[2] Many African American churches have been the best hope for social stability in the most difficult inner-city neighborhoods of America. Cultures that consign the sick and dying to their karma have often found the church as the best hope for love and mercy.

12. Some urban environments are so dangerous that only women can have effective ministry there. Men threaten emasculated males, while a woman's vulnerability is her power. Mother Teresa of Kolkata (Calcutta) is the model.

13. We do not start with the needs of the city but rather with the signs of hope. Starting with needs may lead to a victim mentality. Needs are overwhelming in any major city, and we are tempted to throw up our hands in despair when we visit the teeming masses living in squalor and poverty. Discovering the signs of hope in a city will increase our faith that Jesus Christ is continually raising up His people to penetrate darkness with His grace and resurrection power. Recently in Mumbai, the largest city in India, we walked away from the Youth with a Mission and Teen Challenge ministry working with the children of prostitutes and knew that the Holy Spirit was at work in this desperate place. Thousands of prostitutes and their abusers on the streets could not dim the light of the gospel shining through these missions. At the Teen Challenge center, we watched the children of prostitutes, with faces turned and hands raised to heaven as they prayed for one another and gave God praise for all of His grace and goodness. We are never the same after such encounters.

14. The major barriers to effective city ministry are not in the city but in the churches and their structures. The old song "We Are One in the Spirit, We Are One in the Lord" tells a message that compels the world to take notice of the gospel. Lesslie Newbigin, a former bishop and missionary to India, said, "The hermeneutic of the gospel is the Christian community." Recently Jim Henderson of Off the Map[3] interviewed two "lost people" and asked them what they thought of Christians. One of them said, "It would help if you did more of that thing you do after a hurricane hits." We could say that creation groans for the manifestation of the children of God.

15. The Bible contains a clear urban theology, but most of us were taught to read Scripture with rural eyes. Cities are mentioned 1,250 times in Scripture, and the book of Revelation reminds us that the New Jerusalem is coming—a city out of heaven. We have an urban future! I would certainly endorse Ray's book *A Theology as Big as the City* as a great read to help find another paradigm for reading the text of Scripture with urban eyes.

16. The basic functions of the church are the same everywhere, but the forms must be adapted to the context. Although the church baptizes, administers the Lord's table, preaches the gospel, teaches Scripture, prays for the sick, serves the poor, and loves the lost, it always seeks to carry out mission and ministry in its own specific context. The Russian Orthodox missionaries did not try to import little lambs as object lessons of God's great eternal sacrifice when they first arrived in Alaska. These seasoned missionaries, armed with an Eastern Orthodox understanding of the Holy Spirit, looked for the sacrificial stories in the Alaskan culture and used the sacrifice of the whale to convey God's redemption story.[4]

17. The basic roles of the outsider include catalyst, interpreter, encourager, fellow learner, permission giver, and resource broker. We believe in the indigenous approach to ministry, that all of the resources necessary for transformation already exist within each community. However, often it takes the gift of the outsider to let the light shine through on those resources. The outsider often can see what others take for granted. There is some truth to "you can't see the forest for the trees." The outsider references other contexts and cultures as case studies for transformed living.

18. Urban ministry requires specialization for this generation. These specializations include cradle-to-grave ministry with at-risk populations, community organization and church-based community development, ethnic and linguistic ministries, round-the-clock churches working in many languages and cultures with pastoral teams, lay marketplace ministries in complex urban environments, new models of funding, and collaborative partnerships.

19. A theological divide needs to be bridged to those who care only about people and not places. The common mistake of the church has been to value people and not places. However, Scripture clearly values places as well. Jerusalem was considered "the joy of the whole earth" (Psalm 48:2 NIV).

20. Never play defense, but invite the whole church and see who shows up. Do not let differences rule the day. Focus on our commonality. Billy Graham was the master of "running up the flag and seeing who would salute." He told Ray once that he made a vow to not speak evil of others but to invite everyone to be with him as he proclaimed the gospel. His crusades were evidence that a whole city would turn out to hear the good news!

21. Environments are not neutral. Find the best environment to make everyone comfortable. In our January 2006 Los Angeles consultation, we had difficulty finding the right venue. Some of the team felt that one of the prime locations for hosting the consultation would be offensive to some of the ethnic churches. Those of us from outside LA did not know the history and we would have stumbled on this. However, the LA folks knew the territory and were able to guide us around the location issue. When we want to bring people together we want to find a location that speaks of grace and safety.

22. Get leaders to commit to showing up for the consultation and others will follow. People follow leaders. Or as Ray often reminds us, "Leaders have followers."

23. Consultations should be financed locally for local ownership. Whenever the church comes together within the city, it has to wrestle with finances. The Western church has damaged much of the other two-thirds of the world by introducing "funds from the West." This outside funding principle has produced the well-known expression, "rice Christians," those who join the church or mission for funding and resources. If a consultation designed to be a local conversation is funded from the outside, it ceases to be indigenous.

24. Those who become consultation facilitators join a global network seeking to bring about transformation in the cities of the world. We have watched a phenomenon take place over and over as people have volunteered to facilitate consultations in their city. Major cities of the world have a common language, common joys, and common sorrows. Those who dig deeply and listen closely are grafted into a cloud of witnesses serving in cities around the world.

Consultation Benefit

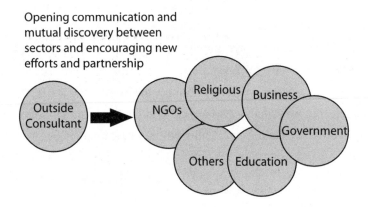

Opening communication and mutual discovery between sectors and encouraging new efforts and partnership

Outside Consultant

NGOs

Religious

Business

Government

Others

Education

OBJECTIVES OF THE CONSULTATION

The objectives of the consultation have been pounded out over many years as we traveled from world-class city to world-class city. Our objectives are based on a values-change outcome for urban leaders, which builds momentum for transformation.

1. To Develop a Theological Framework for Mission in, from, and to the City

A city consultation seeks to help Christian leaders develop a theological framework for mission in, from, and to a city. We are keen on helping people understand how much God loves cities. We often remind people (as we have written previously) that cities are mentioned 1,250 times in Scripture. If the narratives around the great cities in Scripture were ripped out of the text, the stories we read would be quite limited. Think of a Bible without the story of Babel, Nineveh, Babylon, Jerusalem, Rome, Corinth, Ephesus, or Philippi. What would the Bible be like without the salty story of the two sinful cities of Sodom and Gomorrah?

Many have noted that although the Bible starts in a garden, it ends in a city! In the book of Revelation, we see the New Jerusalem, a glorious city with streets of gold coming down out of heaven. The author of Revelation pens these urban words.

> Then I saw a new heaven and a new earth; for the first heaven and the first earth had passed away, and the sea was no more. And I saw the holy city, New Jerusalem, coming down out of heaven from God, prepared as a bride adorned for her husband; and I heard a loud voice from the throne saying, "Behold, the dwelling of God is with men. He will dwell with them, and they shall be his people, and God himself will be with them; he will wipe away every tear from their eyes, and death shall be no more, neither shall there be mourning nor crying nor pain any more, for the former things have passed away."
>
> —Revelation 21:1–4

The Bible paints a picture of God as an architect and city builder utilizing urban renderings, designing the City of God. As we read the text we discover that God is willing to use rural places, motifs, and even dry, endless deserts to get us to His city!

The consultation also seeks to demonstrate that the good news of Jesus Christ is about the whole gospel and not simply a verbal, written, or media proclamation. Although camps have been formed within the church separating proclamation and social justice, we declare they are inseparably connected. John Stott's work at Lausanne made it clear that the church needs to have two wings rather than one. The words of Isaiah sound out the merits of caring about justice:

Is not this the fast that I choose:
>to loose the bonds of wickedness,
>to undo the thongs of the yoke,
to let the oppressed go free,
>and to break every yoke?
Is it not to share your bread with the hungry,
>and bring the homeless poor into your house;
when you see the naked, to cover him,
>and not to hide yourself from your own flesh?
Then shall your light break forth like the dawn,
>and your healing shall spring up speedily;
your righteousness shall go before you,
>the glory of the Lord shall be your rear guard.
Then you shall call, and the Lord will answer;
>you shall cry, and he will say, Here I am.
If you take away from the midst of you the yoke,
>the pointing of the finger, and speaking wickedness,
if you pour yourself out for the hungry
>and satisfy the desire of the afflicted,
then shall your light rise in the darkness
>and your gloom be as the noonday.
And the Lord will guide you continually,
>and satisfy your desire with good things,
>and make your bones strong;
and you shall be like a watered garden,
>like a spring of water,
>whose waters fail not.
And your ancient ruins shall be rebuilt;
>you shall raise up the foundations of many generations;
you shall be called the repairer of the breach,
>the restorer of streets to dwell in.
—Isaiah 58:6–12

2. To Develop New Research in the City

Often Christian leaders lose touch with the present reality of their city, using old demographics and old paradigms of ministry while seeking to address contemporary needs. Built into the consultation is the hope of fresh discovery. One of the key questions critical to a consultation is, "What is God doing today?" As a city prepares for a major consultation, part of its task is to scope out what God is currently doing in the city. The Envisioning Team responsible for the consultation seeks to build relationships across sectarian boundaries of the church to encourage a self-discovery, unearthing signs of hope from within the church and the city. The consultation team is encouraged to contact bishops and mission leaders within cities, asking them to provide the best practices from their area of the church and to present them as a witness to God's working in their city. This approach helps the church see other elements of the church involved in key mission and gives witness to the power of the Holy Spirit at work.

3. To Define the Missiological Significance of the City

The consultation seeks to strengthen the church in the city as it develops a missiological attitude and approach to its city. One of the objectives is to help the church research people groups and communities traditionally outside the reach of the gospel. Often whole ethnic groups, communities, and special classes of people have been outside the peripheral view of the church. One question to ask: "Who is not yet with us?" Follow that up by asking, "How do we serve these groups outside our purview?"

The consultation seeks to highlight the needs of immigrants, youth at risk, the poor, the sick, the unemployed (or underemployed), the institutionalized, those lost in gated communities, and the aged. This has often been described as caring for the least, last, and lost.

Often the consultation helps a city understand its own ethnic roots and migration streams. Ray has described Chicago as a child owing its heritage to other parts of the world. "We think of Mississippi as a father to Chicago because a million and a half black people from Mississippi moved there. Poland is her mother because 840,000 Poles immigrated to Chicago, 100,000 more Poles than San Francisco has people. Our cities comprise all kinds of cultures. How are we going to live together and work together?"

4. To Encounter and Celebrate Creative, Historic, and Contemporary Strategies and Models of City Ministry

A consultation seeks to highlight the city's history, recalling the work of God through prior generations. The consultations move people throughout a city to explore and discover the past and the present. This part of the consultation becomes a major piece of the puzzle for many in the urban center. Participants begin to realize that God's hand was at work in their city long before their own arrival. One large church with which we are acquainted is located at the center of the city in a large monolithic structure, a product of the '60s and '70s, a concrete-edifice architecture. Once a vibrant congregation with 10,000 members and a church that planted more than 26 congregations, birthed a college, helped launch a hospital, and shepherded mayors and governors, it now has a congregation of about 300. Although many would hasten its day of closure for something new and more contemporary, the consultation celebrates its rich history.

Understanding the historical work of the church is vital, but so are the unique ministries springing up in a city, often outside the normal consciousness of the visible church. By listening to the stories of the city, participants begin to discover works that are often under the radar screen yet having powerful effect. As risk takers and research-and-development (R&D) groups are discovered, learning takes place across sectarian lines within the church and the city.

5. To Build Respect and Cooperation Within the Christian Community

A consultation seeks to build a social climate within the church for cooperative attitudes and efforts. The heartbeat of this can be expressed as evangelical passion with an ecumenical spirit. The whole church is encouraged to recognize various gifts and expressions of Christ within the city. The consultation affirms the city as parish and denominations as families. The local church is seen as a sign and an agent for the kingdom of God in its local context.

The consultation also seeks to affirm grass-roots partnerships within the city, often across denominational lines, as congregations and ministries find they have much more in common at a local or regional level then they do with national or international affiliates. Although consultations affirm local partnerships, they also affirm the distinctive of each denomination and organization and seek to name them and celebrate them.

6. To Recognize and Affirm Specialized Ministries

The consultation also seeks to affirm specialized ministries springing up within a city. Ministries addressing youth at risk, prostitution, or homelessness are constantly being developed, and the consultation seeks to encourage the whole church within its city to recognize and strengthen these specialized ministries. The consultation recognizes the city as a complex place needing multiplied ministries and new paradigms in ministry to effectively bear witness to Jesus Christ. One effective means for highlighting specialized ministries is to create an updated directory of all ministries and to model new ways churches and parachurch ministries can effectively cooperate in the city.

7. To Encourage and Strengthen Pastors and Other Ministry Leaders

The consultation seeks to encourage pastors by conducting a survey, prior to the consultation, of the most frequently recognized challenges facing the pastor. Throughout the consultation these issues are addressed. The local consultation team and the consultants serve as listeners, encouragers, interpreters, and facilitators around these issues. The consultants will speak, but always in dialogue with the questions planners have surfaced in their survey.

The consultation seeks to encourage pastors in their leadership roles and to expose them to new networks of information and resources for ministering in their city. The consultation process hopes to broaden pastors' worldviews.

8. To Stimulate Lay Witness in All the Specialized Sectors in Marketplaces of the City

Recognizing the multiplicity and layered sectors of a city, the consultation seeks to strengthen the lay witness in each sector. It is not enough to simply encourage pastors or faith-based organizations. Christians in the marketplace must find their voice and their service validated in their vocational parish. Those working within law enforcement, education, sports, entertainment, media, health care, government, food services, arts, business, or transportation need to be affirmed and find networks within the church and city. Networks that strengthen this lay witness need to be recognized and highlighted.

Large cities have huge subsets in universities, military, foreign agencies, and so on, not to mention the night people, street people, and underworld. Laypeople need to learn how to articulate the gospel and face the ethical challenges in their vocations. Pastors will only be able to help them if they visit the workplaces of their people and affirm their ministries in those sectors of the city.

9. To Influence the Metro Region Relationally

City centers are gathering places for the entire region and offer services for the metropolis. Education, health care, government, and media hubs are found at the center of the city, and they touch the whole region. The city's multifaceted transportation linkage is now an interdependent system linking suburbia, urban, and sister cities together. The consultation seeks to raise awareness of this interconnectedness. The needs and resources of the region have direct correlation to one another. No longer can the suburbs say to the inner city, "I don't need you," or the inner city to the suburbs, "I don't need you."

10. To Challenge Those with Means to Invest in Social and Financial Enterprise for the City

The consultation seeks to draw those with financial and social capacity toward holistic action in their city. Many well-meaning people with wealth or wisdom are unaware of how to spend their resources for effective change. Without a consultative process, these people are often captivated by the best-marketed story in their city. The consultation seeks to open a window for individuals, foundations, and corporations to build social capital in their cities.

11. To Inform and Supplement Seminaries or Other Ministry Training Institutions

Often seminaries and other training institutions have not been exposed to the ongoing ministry in a city. The consultation seeks to open avenues of communication between churches, faith-based ministries, and educational institutions. The consultation seeks to strengthen educational initiatives that in turn will provide ministries with relevant educational resources.

A sample of consultation objectives would be:

1. Share new research
2. Create new relational networks
3. Orient new pastors
4. Commit to the unevangelized and marginalized
5. Develop new urban-suburban partnerships
6. Collaborate in highly specialized areas of ministry
7. Develop new public-private partnerships
8. Identify credible public leaders committed to transformation
9. Gain a shared understanding of God's work in the community
10. Lay groundwork for future transformation strategies
11. Provide a working model for other communities
12. Empower laity to think about ministry and mission in the public arena
13. Relate personal faith to community transformation

If you can take on some or all of these objectives, then a consultation may be possible in your city.

Consultation Outcomes

When it comes to outcomes, the expectations for one consultation may not be realistic for another. It is an exciting time for us as we begin to see our associates who have traveled with us through the years extending their networks all over the world. We rely on their input for the future as other networks are formed and expanded. When we work with consultations, we look to these associates for advice, input, and involvement. We have always had assumptions of what can and should happen in a consultation. However, after surveying these seasoned leaders, we have also included their input. Here is what they believe you can expect from a consultation in your city.

Five Key Areas of High Impact from a Consultation

1. Theological understanding of the city
2. Dialogue across sectarian lines with the church
3. Cooperation in the church
4. Discovery of what God has already been doing in the city
5. Understanding of the mission of the church in the city

Four Key Areas of Moderate Impact from a Consultation

1. Theological understanding of the gospel
2. Theological understanding of the church
3. The lasting relational impact in a city
4. Increased congregational understanding of the city

What We Learned from Our Research

Finally, from the feedback we've received and from the associate networks, ministries, articles, books, and DVDs bubbling up out of numerous consultations, we know the consultation adds value to cities. However, we want to add a caution: the objectives for consultations are not always met in every situation. Sometimes consultations will have limited success due to misconceptions about objectives, unreasonable expectations, or poor planning and development.

After examining many consultations and listening to our urban networks, we have concluded that well-planned consultations will find five common spin-offs for the church in the city:

1. Consultation participants will normally develop a new framework for thinking about the city. They will gain a historical, theological, and missiological grid for their ministry in, to, and from the city.

2. Participants will find new value in networking and cooperation with other Christian groups for the good of the city. The detrimental effect of competition for resources and recognition is recognized, and the value of partnering without fear is moved to the forefront.

3. A new openness to diverse groups working together is instilled. In the past most Christian groups were not used to living with dissonance. The consultation informs and highlights the value of working for the common good of the city with others with whom we may have minor disagreements.

4. Participants are surprised to find new partnerships and networks available during and as a result of the consultation.

5. Participants find lasting evidence that relationships and partnerships are ongoing after the consultation.

Effect of the Consultations

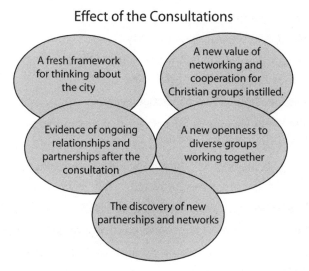

A fresh framework for thinking about the city

A new value of networking and cooperation for Christian groups instilled.

Evidence of ongoing relationships and partnerships after the consultation

A new openness to diverse groups working together

The discovery of new partnerships and networks

OTHER OUTCOMES

As we seek to faithfully love the church and cities throughout the world, we are pleased to find ongoing relationships with leaders God uses to change people and places. We constantly hear stories of lives and cities being changed by God's incredible power and love. As we hear these stories, we also hear that the consultation experience has been instrumental in providing fertile ground for God's work. These are some of the outcomes we have heard as a result of the consultation experience:

- Relationships are built.
- Awareness of the whole church increases.
- Pastors' support groups and prayer networks are begun or energized.
- The emergence of new focused-ministry partnerships.
- New training programs for pastors and missionaries emerge.
- Resource multiplication of articles, books, videos.
- Discouraged pastors report finding hope.
- Emerging leaders catch the vision and burden of an urban world.
- New pastors and directors get a much larger picture of their context.
- Theological schools add courses, personnel, and agendas in the city.
- Lay leaders find each other across denominational lines.
- Contagious inter-city links often develop.
- Overseas mission attendees change priorities, strategies, personnel, and training.
- Evangelistic, justice, peace, and social ministries find each other.
- Missiologists and evangelists sharpen their dialogue.
- Local congregations are empowered by lay leader participation.
- Local city public officials are often impacted.
- Historic denominations have roles clarified and stories affirmed.

- Financial donors become educated and change some
  funding priorities.
- Local congregations see they can link internationally
  or regionally.
- Awareness builds in the churches as a whole—city
  and suburban.
- Scholars find audiences for future research.
- New pastors can assess their personal and denominational
  gift in the mix and see other ministries as gifts and not threats.

OTHER COMMENTS ABOUT THE CONSULTATIONS FROM VETERAN CONSULTATION FACILITATORS

- Consultations seek to move people from problems to
  signs of hope.
- Consultations seek to facilitate Catholic-Protestant
  dialogue in the city.
- Consultations seek to create realistic expectations.
- Consultations seek to provide a contextual perspective.
- Consultations seek to provide participants adequate process time.
- Consultations seek to provide fresh stories of God at work.
- Consultations seek to open access to local and international
  networks.

Our hope is that this book will cause you to envision a consultation in your city, regardless of its size. Both Ray and I are hopeful that your city can find renewal, and that the people you minister to and with can discover the beauty of the city in God's plan, and evidence of God at work in your city, right now!

REFLECTIONS

1. Rate the 24 assumptions in an order that is meaningful to you. Why is your particular order meaningful?

2. Rate the 11 objectives in an order that is meaningful to you. Why is your particular order meaningful?

3. Which one of the outcomes appeals to you most? Why?

4. Of the five major things we have learned from providing consultations in cities across the world, which one surfaces as the most important for you? Why?

Urban Consultation Agenda

Concept: Bring together key people in the city to discover the signs of hope in the city, in a sense to cooperate with the Lord in the city.

The consultation is designed to bring people together, through a broad spectrum, to get a greater grasp.

"Whole church, whole gospel to transform the whole city."

Anticipates: 100–200 people in attendance

Three-Day Event

First Day

Evening: 7:00 p.m.– 9:45 p.m.

1. Start off with case studies / video (1 hour)
2. Singing (30 minutes)
3. Divide people in small groups (15 minutes)
    - What did they come looking for? (30 minutes)
    - What do they want to go home with?
4. Write responses on post-it board paper and maybe have three or four teams share (30 minutes). Their answers to these questions will serve as a "contract" for them.

Second Day

Morning: 9:00 a.m.–12:30 p.m.

Refreshments

1. Signs of hope for the city (60 to 90 minutes: 6 individuals, 10–15 minutes each)

    Government leaders, nonprofit leaders, business leaders: maybe three leaders share with everyone

2. Divide into small groups
    *   Share the signs of hope for the city
    *   Needs: what are the needs for the city
3. Lunch

Afternoon: 2:30 p.m.–5:30 p.m.

1. Visit sites: See ministry in action—homeless, orphans, street kids, government people, education, tutoring. Have about 15 available sites, each group will visit approximately three (duration: about five hours). Notice powerful vs. powerless.
2. Social event?

Third Day

1. Visit a few more sites
2. Talk about what we have seen, what we have heard
3. Ray Bakke speaks
4. In groups: what should be done about it?

    New network/new relationships

Endnotes

Chapter 8: Index to Seattle: My Journey to the City

1. Harvey Cox, *Fire from Heaven: The Rise of Pentecostal Spirituality and the Reshaping of Religion in the Twenty-First Century* (Boston: Addison-Wesley Publishing Company, 1996); and Philip Jenkins, *The Next Christendom: The Coming of Global Christianity* (Oxford: Oxford University Press, 2002).

2. David Brooks, *On Paradise Drive: How We Live Now (And Always Have) in the Future Tense* (New York: Simon & Schuster, 2004).

3. Dietrich Bonhoeffer, *Life Together: The Classic Exploration of Faith in Community* (San Francisco: HarperSanFrancisco, 1978), 15.

Chapter 9: Called to Seattle and Beyond

1. When we talk about city transformation, we don't necessarily mean people gathering for big unity events or huge prayer meetings. Much has been said in recent years about city transformation, and it seems that many expect God to swoop in and change everyone and everything. Of course, we hope this happens, but until it does or if it never happens as we hope, we know God has called His people to be transforming agents in cities. We want to be in the city working for justice, mercy, and peace. We long for God's glory to be revealed in every system, every neighborhood, and every individual. Isaiah 58 gives a picture of God's will for our cities.

Chapter 10: Barnabas: The Spirit and Nature of a City Facilitator

1. "Innovation Diffusion: Looking at the Process of Change," Lone Eagle Consulting, http://www.lone-eagles.com/innovation.htm.

2. I need to point out that this is one style or gifting in leadership, and not all situations demand the same gift. It is simply my point to highlight the gift of a Barnabas spirit. The apostolic gifting of Paul has been highlighted throughout much of the Western church, and I'm concerned that we have neglected the Barnabas gift.

3. We just received the sad news from Tim Svoboda that this wonderful young Indian leader was killed in an automobile accident January 6, 2006. Tim and Karol are now seeking God's wisdom in this time of sorrow.

4. Doug Engberg, "A Few Characteristics of a Networker," personal email, January 25, 2006.

Chapter 11: How Do You Consult Your City?

1. Andragogy makes the following assumptions about the design of learning:

    (1) Adults need to know why they need to learn something.
    (2) Adults need to learn experientially.
    (3) Adults approach learning as problem solving.
    (4) Adults learn best when the topic is of immediate value.

    (See M. Knowles, "Andragogy," http://tip.psychology.org/knowles.html.)

2. Jon R. Katzenbach and Douglas K. Smith, *The Wisdom of Teams: Creating the High-Performance Organization* (New York: Harper Collins, 2003); see also http://www.centeronline.org/knowledge/bookreview.cfm?ID=2482.

3. Duncan Watts, *Six Degrees: The Science of a Connected Age* (New York: W. W. Norton & Company, 2003).

Chapter 12: Cities and Consultations: It's Never the Same, It's Always the Same

1. H. P. Spees, "City as Parish," speech, Serve Seattle Ministry Summit III, Seattle Pacific University, May 7, 2003.

Chapter 13: What We've Learned from Consultations

1. James F. Engels, *What's Gone Wrong With The Harvest? A Communication Strategy for the Church and World Evangelization* (Grand Rapids: Zondervan, 1975).

2. Eli Lehrer, "The Real John Dilulio," pressroom commentary, Heritage Foundation, February 7, 2001, http://www.heritage.org/Press/Commentary/ED020701b.cfm.

3. Jim Henderson, Off the Map, http://www.off-the-map.org.

4. Michael Oleksa, *Orthodox Alaska: A Theology of Mission* (Crestwood, NY: St. Vladimir's Seminary Press, 1993).

New Hope® Publishers is a division of WMU®,
an international organization that challenges Christian believers
to understand and be radically involved in
God's mission. For more information about WMU,
go to www.wmu.com. More information
about New Hope books may be found at
www.newhopepublishers.com. New Hope books
may be purchased at your local bookstore.

Similar Books You May Enjoy

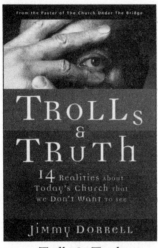

Trolls & Truth
14 Realities About Today's Church
That We Don't Want to See
By Jimmy Dorrell
ISBN 1-59669-010-0

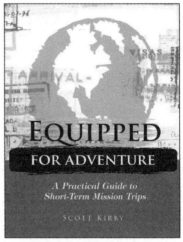

Equipped for Adventure
A Practical Guide to Short-Term Mission Trips
By Scott Kirby
ISBN 1-59669-011-9

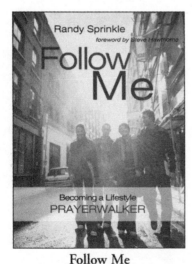

Follow Me
Becoming a Lifestyle Prayerwalker
By Randy Sprinkle
ISBN 1-56309-948-9

n e w
h o p e
PUBLISHERS

Available in bookstores
everywhere

For information about these books
or any New Hope products, visit
www.newhopepublishers.com.